Middle East Today

Series Editors

Fawaz A. Gerges, Department of International Relations, London School of Economics, London, UK

Nader Hashemi, Josef Korbel School of International Studies, Center for Middle East Studies, University of Denver, Denver, CO, USA

The Iranian Revolution of 1979, the Iran-Iraq War, the Gulf War, and the US invasion and occupation of Iraq have dramatically altered the geopolitical landscape of the contemporary Middle East. The Arab Spring uprisings have complicated this picture. This series puts forward a critical body of first-rate scholarship that reflects the current political and social realities of the region, focusing on original research about contentious politics and social movements; political institutions; the role played by non-governmental organizations such as Hamas, Hezbollah, and the Muslim Brotherhood; and the Israeli-Palestine conflict. Other themes of interest include Iran and Turkey as emerging pre-eminent powers in the region, the former an 'Islamic Republic' and the latter an emerging democracy currently governed by a party with Islamic roots; the Gulf monarchies, their petrol economies and regional ambitions; potential problems of nuclear proliferation in the region; and the challenges confronting the United States, Europe, and the United Nations in the greater Middle East. The focus of the series is on general topics such as social turmoil, war and revolution, international relations, occupation, radicalism, democracy, human rights, and Islam as a political force in the context of the modern Middle East.

Dalia Ghanem

Understanding the Persistence of Competitive Authoritarianism in Algeria

palgrave
macmillan

Dalia Ghanem
Carnegie Middle East Center
Beirut, Lebanon

ISSN 2945-7017   ISSN 2945-7025 (electronic)
Middle East Today
ISBN 978-3-031-05101-2   ISBN 978-3-031-05102-9 (eBook)
https://doi.org/10.1007/978-3-031-05102-9

© The Editor(s) (if applicable) and The Author(s), under exclusive license to Springer Nature Switzerland AG 2022
This work is subject to copyright. All rights are solely and exclusively licensed by the Publisher, whether the whole or part of the material is concerned, specifically the rights of translation, reprinting, reuse of illustrations, recitation, broadcasting, reproduction on microfilms or in any other physical way, and transmission or information storage and retrieval, electronic adaptation, computer software, or by similar or dissimilar methodology now known or hereafter developed.
The use of general descriptive names, registered names, trademarks, service marks, etc. in this publication does not imply, even in the absence of a specific statement, that such names are exempt from the relevant protective laws and regulations and therefore free for general use.
The publisher, the authors, and the editors are safe to assume that the advice and information in this book are believed to be true and accurate at the date of publication. Neither the publisher nor the authors or the editors give a warranty, expressed or implied, with respect to the material contained herein or for any errors or omissions that may have been made. The publisher remains neutral with regard to jurisdictional claims in published maps and institutional affiliations.

Cover credit: Aanas Lahoui/shutterstock.com

This Palgrave Macmillan imprint is published by the registered company Springer Nature Switzerland AG
The registered company address is: Gewerbestrasse 11, 6330 Cham, Switzerland

To my daughter, Sophiah

Acknowledgments

This book would not exist without the interviews conducted with Algerians from different backgrounds ready to talk to me and discuss, sometimes for hours, to help me with my research. I am thankful to everyone abroad, but especially in Algeria, who accepted to talk despite repression and the fear it created, and this is why I promised anonymity to everyone. I am thankful to everyone who helped me on the field in Algeria. I want to thank all my friends and colleagues who helped me and encouraged me in the most difficult moments of the writing process that have sometimes been more arduous than expected due to the difficult conditions in Lebanon where I was living at the time, coupled with the global pandemic. These scholars/friends include my dear friend Dr. Loulouwa Al Rachid, who has been here every step of the way with valuable comments and warm, encouraging words, and Ahmed Nagi, with whom I talked for hours about the book and its chapters. A special thanks go to Martha Higgins, Library Director at Carnegie Endowment for International Peace who helped me every time I asked for a reference, a book, or an article. My dear sister, Faiza, friends Katy, Judith, Myriam, Loubna, and Muriel, extended continuous support during the book's writing. One person deserves special thanks: friend and colleague Rayyan Al-Shawaf and his divine editing. Finally, a special thanks to my parents, Anissa and Mostepha, who pushed me to follow my passion for Algeria, my country, and always supported me unconditionally.

Praise for *Understanding the Persistence of Competitive Authoritarianism in Algeria*

"A very rich and useful research on Algeria, merging historical and political perspectives. It paves the way to a very stimulating and comparative concept, as the Algerian regime is conceived as a 'competitive authoritarianism', stressing the role of army as a powerful institution, and functional practices like cooptation, pluripartism and limited liberalization. Hirak is properly described as a very inclusive social movement that highlights the fragility of competitive authoritarianism. To be absolutely used both by political scientists and historians, as well as all those who are keen on the Algerian puzzle!"

—Bertrand Badie, *Professor Emeritus of Universities at Sciences Po Paris, France*

"Excellent insights for students and seasoned political scientists into the functioning of a competitive authoritarian system that for decades has managed to weather substantial challenges through fine-tuning of its "toolkit" rather than overhauling of its foundations. This book impressively dissects how the regime has used competition within authoritarianism to thwart civil society and, of course, the Hirak – and it convincingly concludes that by 2021 the regime no longer needed or wanted competition."

—Isabelle Werenfels, *Senior Fellow and Maghreb Expert, Stiftung Wissenschaft und Politik, Berlin, Germany*

"For a long time there has been a need for a book that explains the remarkable resilience and persistence of the political regime in Algeria in the face of huge challenges and the through flow of leading figures. Dalia Ghanem's book fulfils this need perfectly. An established and astute observer of Algerian politics, Ghanem successfully deploys her detailed knowledge to explain how the experience of Algeria informs our broader understanding of the workings of authoritarian political systems. This book will become an essential text for anyone wanting to understand both Algeria and authoritarian resilience."

—Michael J. Willis, *professor of contemporary Maghreb politics, St Antony's College, University of Oxford, UK*

"This is the book everyone waited to understand Algeria's political system. Extremely well researched, documented, and based on interviews conducted during the Hirak, this is a must-read book, Dr. Dalia Ghanem's exceptional work allows us to understand better the political dynamics in Algeria and the resilience of the political system."

—Dr. Djallil Lounnas, *Associate Professor, Al Akhawayn University*

CONTENTS

1	**Introduction**	1
	Algerian Leaders' Political Playbook	3
	The Pillars of the Algerian Regime	7
	References	10
2	**The Military: The Real Broker of Power in Algeria**	13
	At the Beginning, the ALN	14
	The Crisis of the Summer of 1962	15
	Not the Last Military Coup	16
	Boumediene and the Rise of Military Security	18
	Bendjedid and the Advent of Multiparty Politics	20
	The Army, the DRS, and the Years of Lead	24
	Bouteflika in, the Military Back to Their Barracks?	29
	Bouteflika Out, the Men in Uniform Win Again	32
	Resolute Hirak, Tenacious Military	34
	References	36
3	**Hyperpluralism and Co-Optation: The Secrets Behind Turning the Opposition into a Pillar of the Regime**	39
	The 1989 Opening and the "Partification of Politics"	39
	The Main Opposition Parties	41
	The Legislature: The Best Means to Neutralize Opposition	45
	The Islamists and the Art of Co-Optation	54
	Elections at Any Cost: The Need for a Democratic Alibi	56

xi

xii CONTENTS

| | *Nodding and Losing Credibility* | 58 |
| | *References* | 61 |

4 Divide and Conquer: The Atomization of Civil Society — 65
1962–1988: Between Repression and Toleration — 67
CSOs in the 1990s: Totemic Organizations and Agents of Stabilization? — 72
CSOs as Agents of International Legitimation — 77
Bouteflika's Use and Abuse of CSOs — 82
The Regime's Toolkit for the Recalcitrant — 86
   Legal Obstacles — 87
   Cloning Strategy — 90
CSOs: Mirror Image of the Regime — 92
References — 98

5 A Controlled Economic Liberalization — 103
1962–1988: The Monopolization of the Hydrocarbon Industry — 105
   Ben Bella and Autogestion — 106
   Boumediene's Policies and the Rise of Opportunities to "Cash In" — 110
1978–1992: Chadlism, Infitah, and Affairisme — 118
   For a Better Life? — 118
   "Work and Rigor," a Difficult Serenity — 123
   Impossible Reforms — 126
1992–1999: War Economy and the Structural Adjustment — 128
1999–2019: Bouteflika and the Rise of the Algerian Oligarchy — 133
   The Creation of Custom-Made Monopolies — 134
   The Mechanics of Corruption — 137
2019: Yet Another Reset? — 142
References — 145

6 The Policies of Violence and Repression — 153
1962–1988: The Years of Lead — 156
   Violence Against Opponents — 156
   Violence Against Society — 158
   The Repression of Identity and Its Culmination: The Berber Spring — 159
October 1988, the Grapes of Wrath — 162
1989–1992: The Descent Into Violence — 167

The FIS: From Accommodation to Confrontation	169
1992–1998: Repression and the "Total War on Terror"	173
The "Security Centers"	174
The Total War on Terror and Forced Disappearances	176
2001: The "Black Spring"	182
The 2019 Hirak: *Calibrated and Targeted Repression*	187
References	193

7 Conclusion: Algeria's Future Prospects—Less Competitive, More Authoritarian 199
References 205

ACRONYMS

AA	Association Agreement
AACC	National Association to Fight Corruption (Association Algérienne de Lutte Contre la Corruption)
ACB	Béjaïa Citizens Association (Association Citoyenne De Béjaïa)
ACDA	Agir pour le Changement et la Démocratie en Algérie
AD	Algerian Dinar
AFEPEC	Women's Association For Personal Fulfilment And Citizenship (Association Féminine pour L'Epanouissement de la Personne et L'Exercice de la Citoyenneté)
AI	Amnesty International
AIS	Islamic Salvation Army (Armée Islamique du Salut)
AITDF	Independent Association for the Triumph of Women's Rights (Association pour l'Indépendance et le Triomphe des Droits des Femmes)
ALN	National Liberation Army (Armée de Libération Nationale)
ANP	National People's Army (Armée Nationale Populaire)
ANSEJ	National Agency for the Support of Youth Employment (Agence Nationale de Soutien à L'Emploi des Jeunesse)
APC	Communal People's Assembly (Assemblée Populaire Communale)
APN	National People's Assembly (Assemblée Populaire Nationale)
APW	Popular Assembly Wilaya (Assemblée Populaire De Wilaya)
ASSEVET	Association of Support and Solidarity with the Families of Victims of Terrorism (Association de Soutien et de Solidarité aux Familles des Victimes du Terrorisme)
AVV	Green Algerian Alliance (Alliance De l'Algérie Verte)

xv

BMPJ	Mobile Brigades of Judicial Police (Brigade Mobile de la Police Judiciaire)
CASA	Algerian Confederation of Autonomous Unions (Confédération Algérienne des Syndicats Autonomes)
CCE	Committee of Coordination and Implementation (Comité de Coordination et d'Exécution)
CCLAS	Center for Conduct and Coordination of Anti-Subversive Actions (Centre de Conduite et de Coordination des Actions de lutte anti-Subversive)
CCN	National Consultative Council (Conseil Consultatif National)
CFSP	Common Foreign and Security Policy
CIDDEF	Information and Documentation Center on Children's and Women's Rights (Centre d'Information et de Documentation sur les Droits des Enfants et de la Femme)
CLA	High School Council (Conseil des Lycées d'Algérie)
CNAPEST	National Autonomous Council of Professors of Secondary and Technical Education (Conseil National Autonome du Personnel Enseignant du Secteur Tertiaire de L'Education)
CNCPPDH	National Consultative Commission for the Promotion and Protection of Human Rights (Commission Nationale Consultative de Promotion et de Protection des Droits de l'Homme)
CNDDC	National Committee for the Defense of the Rights of the Unemployed (Comité National pour la Défense des Droits des Chômeurs)
CNEH	National Center for Historical Studies (Centre National des Etudes Historiques)
CNES	Economic and Social National Council (Conseil National Economqiue et Social)
CNRA	National Council for the Algerian Revolution (Conseil National pour la Révolution Algérienne)
CNSA	National Safeguarding Committee of Algeria (Comité National pour la Sauvegarde de L'Algérie)
CNT	National Transitional Council (Conseil National de Transition)
CR	Council of the Revolution (Conseil de la Révolution)
CSJ	High Council of Youth (Conseil Supérieur de la Jeunesse)
CSOs	Civil Society Organizations
DCSA	Directorate for Army Security (Direction Centrale de la Sécurité de L'armée)
DDS	Direction of the Security Services (Direction de la Documentation et de la Sécurité)
DDSE	Directorate of Documentation and External Security (Direction de la Documentation et de la Sécurité Extérieure)

DEC	Communal Executive Delegation (Délégation Exécutive Communale)
DGDSE	Directorate-General for Documentation and External Security (Direction Générale de la Documentation et de la Sécurité Extérieure)
DGSN	General Directorate for National Security (Direction Générale de la Sûreté Nationale)
DSI	Department of Homeland Security (Direction de la Sécurité Intérieure)
ENA	Etoile Nord-Africaine
ENTV	Public Television Network (Entreprise Nationale de Télévision)
EU	European Union
FCE	Business Leaders Forum (Forum des Chefs d'Entreprises)
FFS	Socialist Forces Front (Front des Forces Socialistes)
FIDH	International Federation of Human Rights (Fédération Internationale pour les Droits Humains)
FIS	Islamic Savaltion Front (Front Islamique du Salut)
FJD	Front of Justice and Development (Front de la Justice et du Développement/El Adala)
FLN	National Liberation Front (Front de Libération Nationale)
FNTS	National Federation of Health Workers (Fédération Nationale des Travailleurs de la Santé)
GIA	Islamic Armed Group (Groupe Islamique Armé)
GIS	Special Intervention Group (Groupe d'Intervention Spéciale)
GLD	Legitime Defense Groups (Groupes de Légitime Défense)
GPRA	Provisional Government of the Algerian Republic (Gouvernement Provisoire de la République Algérienne)
HCE	High State Committee (Haut Comité d'Etat)
HRW	Human Rights Watch
IMF	International Monetary Fund
LADDH	Algerian League for the Defense of Human Rights (Ligue Algérienne pour la Défense des Droits de l'Homme)
LADH	Algerian League of Human Rights (Ligue Algérienne des Droits de l'Homme)
MAK	Movement for the Autonomy of Kabylia (Mouvement pour l'Autonomie de la Kabylie)
MALG	Ministry of Ammunition and General Connections (Ministère de l'Armement et des Liaisons Générales)
MCB	Berber Cultural Movement (Mouvement Culturel Berbère)
MDA	Movement for Democracy in Algeria (Mouvement pour la Démocratie en Algérie)
MDRA	Algerian Democratic Movement for Renewal (Mouvement Démocratique pour le Renouveau Algérien)

MIA	Armed Islamic Movement (Mouvement Islamique Armé)
MPA	Algerian Popular Movement (Mouvement Populaire Algérien)
MRN	Movement for National Reform (Mouvement pour la Réforme Nationale/El Islah)
MSP	Movement for Society and Peace (Mouvement de la Société pour la Paix)
NGOs	Non-Govermental Organizations
NIP	National Indicative Program
ONDH	National Observatory of Human Rights (Observatoire National des Droits de l'Homme)
ONM	National Organization of Mujahidin (Organisation Nationale des Moudjahidines)
PAD	Parties of the Democratic Alternative (Forces du Pacte de l'Alternative Démocratique)
PAGS	Socialist Vanguard Party (Parti de l'Avant-Garde Socialiste)
PCA	Algerian Communist Party (Parti Communiste Algérien)
PNSD	National Party for Solidarity and Development (Parti National pour la Solidarité et le Développement)
PPA	Algerian People's Party (Parti du Peuple Algérien)
PRS	Socialist Revolution Party (Parti de la Révolution Socialiste)
PT	Worker's Party (Parti des Travailleurs).
RAFD	Algerian Rally of Democratic Women (Rassemblement Algérien des Femmes Démocrates)
RAJ	Rally for Youth Action (Rassemblement Action Jeunesse)
RCD	Rally for Culture and Democracy (Rassemblement pour la Culture et la Démocratie)
RND	National and Democratic Rally (Rassemblement National Démocratique)
SATEF	Autonomous Union of Education and Training Workers (Syndicat Autonome des Travailleurs de l'Education et de la Formation)
SIT	Islamic Labour Union (Syndicat Islamique du Travail)
SM	Military Security (Sécurité Militaire)
SNAPAP	Autonotomous National Union of Public Administration Personnel (Syndicat National Autonome des Personnels de l'Administration Publique)
SNAPEST	National Autonomous Union of Secondary and Technical Teachers (Syndicat National Autonome des Professeurs de l'Enseignement Secondaire et Technique)
SNATA	Autonomous National Syndicate of Algerian Workers (Syndicat National Autonome des Travailleurs Algériens)
SNOMMAR	National Union of Officers of the Merchant Navy (Syndicat National des Officiers de la Marine Marchande)

TAJ	Rally for Hope for Algeria (Le Rassemblement de L'espoir pour l'Algérie/Tajamu' Amel el Jazair)
UGE	General Union of Students (Union Générale des Etudiants)
UGEA	Union of Algerian Students (Union Générale des Etudiants Algériens)
UGFA	General Union of Algerian Women (Union Générale des Femmes Algériennes)
UGTA	General Union of Algerian Workers (Union Générale des Travailleurs Algériens)
UNDEF	United Nations Fund for Democracy
UNEA	General Union of Algerian Students (Union Générale des Etudiants Algériens)
UNEP	National Union of Public Contractors (Union Nationale des Entrepreneurs Publics)
UNFA	General Union of Algerian Women (Union Générale Des Femmes Algériennes)
UNJA	National Union of Algerian Youth (Union Nationale des Jeunes Algériens)

CHAPTER 1

Introduction

There is little dispute among Algerian scholars regarding the nature and course of Algerian history from 1962 until 1989. In 1962, the country gained independence following a hard-fought eight-year war against colonial power France. By this time, the army had gained the upper hand, politically speaking, over the National Liberation Front (Front de Libération Nationale, or FLN), a phenomenon that accelerated with time. The FLN's slow decline would turn it into a front for what was essentially a military regime. To make matters worse, the parties and associations that existed pre-independence were dismantled, and all opposition was banned. Deprived of political sovereignty, Algerian society was also closely controlled by the Military Security (SM), an arm of the military.

Yet such a situation was untenable in the long run. Millions of Algerians born after 1962 found it difficult to relate to a regime that relied solely on the war of independence for legitimacy. The fall of hydrocarbon prices in the mid-1980s struck a deadly blow to the system of rent distribution and patronage networks, one already under strain due to growing urbanization and population growth. As a result of the fiscal imbalance, the quality of public services rapidly deteriorated, leading to a huge downscaling of the state's provision of basic services. The demagogic buzzwords of equal opportunity, social justice, egalitarianism, and the magnanimous state increasingly failed to mollify the populace. As a

© The Author(s), under exclusive license to Springer Nature Switzerland AG 2022
D. Ghanem, *Understanding the Persistence of Competitive Authoritarianism in Algeria*, Middle East Today,
https://doi.org/10.1007/978-3-031-05102-9_1

1

result, on October 5, 1988, riots erupted in Algiers and quickly spread to other cities. Rioters attacked state symbols to show their disgust at a leadership that remained deaf to their demands.

In 1989, the Algerian government, responding to such domestic agitation, which in turn brought international pressure to bear on Algiers, appeared to embark on a course of political liberalization. Indeed, the government promulgated a new constitution that established a multiparty system. Yet here is where a major divergence of opinion occurs. Many Algeria experts maintain that developments that year, not least the promulgation of a new constitution, put the country squarely on the road to democracy. As argued by this book, however, Algeria's transition in 1989 from single-party rule to a multiparty system did not lead to democracy. This book, *Algeria: Understanding the Persistence of Competitive Authoritarianism*, which is aimed at Algeria observers of all kinds and written in an accessible style, argues that the Algerian regime went from the outright authoritarianism that had characterized it since independence in 1962 to what is known as "competitive authoritarianism." Under such a hybrid regime, which mixes elements of democracy with authoritarianism, opposition forces admittedly enjoy access to democratic institutions and can contest power (Carothers, 2002; Diamond, 2006; Ottaway, 2003; Schedler, 2006;). Nevertheless, the political arena remains tilted in favor of state-backed entities and individuals. For example, state-supported electoral candidates, whether incumbents or challengers, rely on unfair media access, abuse of state resources, various degrees of intimidation and violence, and outright electoral fraud to retain or acquire power.

Since 1989, many studies of Algeria have fallen prey to the lazy bromide that the country is in the process of democratizing. Over the past three decades, several scholars, analysts, and journalists have characterized Algeria as a sort of flawed democracy (what democracy isn't?) that has failed to consolidate and is in what amounts to a state of permanent transition. The truth, as recognized by the more astute Algeria experts, is quite different. Algeria fits into a category that Levitsky and Lucan determined, in a seminal study of post-Cold War political dispensations, included 35 states in the Americas, Eastern Europe, Asia, the former Soviet Union, and Africa. "[R]ather than 'partial,' 'incomplete,' or 'unconsolidated' democracies," the authors argued, "these cases should be conceptualized for what they are: a distinct, nondemocratic regime type" (Levitsky, 2010: 4). As for Algeria specifically, its political changes have been described by Roberts as "pluralism without enfranchisement" (2003), by Zakaria as "illiberal democracy" (1997), and by Brumberg as "liberalized autocracy" (2002:57). According to Brumberg, liberalized autocracies "provide a kind of virtual democracy," whereby the promotion of "a measure of political openness in civil society, in the press, and even in the electoral system" is coupled with the state's unrelenting control over the security establishment, the media, and patronage networks (Brumberg, 2003: 3).

The work of Roberts, Zakaria, and Brumberg has led to a better understanding of political change in the Arab world, including Algeria, and a re-examination of the regime's aspirations, yet even their analyses have not gone far enough. In large part, this is because of their insistence that a transition is underway. Instead of assuming that Algeria is muddling through a never-ending transition to democracy, this book, which is based on frontline research that includes interviews with people in the army, the police, the business sector, politicians, civil society organizations, and ordinary citizens between 2016 and 2021, takes the country's political system as it is. There is no trend toward democratization. In fact, Algeria today is more a continuation of its pre-1989 iteration than it is any sort of precursor to democracy. Despite periodic changes in government, including the ostensibly all-important presidency, Algeria is for all intents and purposes still run by a military-backed regime that assumed power when the country gained independence in 1962.

Algerian Leaders' Political Playbook

In 1989, the regime declared its intention to overhaul the country's political system by allowing for a multiplicity of political parties and free and fair elections. Despite skepticism in many quarters, the regime appeared to make good on its promises, and to do so quickly, legalizing parties and setting parliamentary elections for December 1991. Ironically, the process was interrupted by the politico-military elite itself in 1992 in order to stave off a crushing Islamist victory in the second round of that year's parliamentary elections, but it was resumed in 1995. Since then, elections (presidential, legislative, and local) have been held regularly. The political arena has opened up, and opposition actors and parties have come to occupy a place in the political landscape. The extension of political resources even reached the Islamists, who participated in the 1995 presidential election, entered parliament in 1997, and have since been part of government coalitions. The regime allowed greater freedom of speech, and a dynamic press thrived; the country's newspapers, which numbered a mere 13 in 1989, reached 160 in 1991 and 269 in 2015. Finally, civil society organizations (CSOs) went from 12,000 in 1988 to 57,400 in 1998 and 92,627 in 2011.

Nevertheless, as this book demonstrates, the political opening up was controlled, and had its limits. For instance, CSOs were allowed to operate on the assumption that they could be co-opted or at the very least manipulated into fragmenting civil society. Those that spent most of their time criticizing the government came to pay a hefty price for their course of action. They were demonized, marginalized, or repressed outright. The result was almost always the same. The organizations in question became too weak to challenge the government's policies and actions.

The situation was similar when it came to political parties. Some proposed parties were never granted a license to begin with, owing to their would-be founders' refusal to commit to the rules of the game, by which they were expected to serve as nothing more than a democratic fig leaf, as opposed to real challengers. Those that obtained a license and proceeded to behave in too independent a manner were subsequently faced with a dilemma: change tack and toe the government line on critical issues or fail to win anything approaching a substantial number of seats in the next parliamentary elections. The co-optation and fragmentation of the major opposition parties in Algeria was so thorough that these parties ended up losing credibility in the eyes of the general population and even their own constituents.

A second method of control exercised by the regime was a carefully calibrated utilization of the country's economic resources to tie the upper stratum of Algerian society closer to the state. Selective liberalization of the economy saw the distribution of rents to the country's coastal elites, who dominate private enterprise and—since 1989—occasionally establish or fund business-friendly political parties to gain more leverage in parliament. From the regime's perspective, this upper stratum of society, if properly compensated, could serve as an effective mediator with the masses, particularly if it could provide them with opportunities for work. To that end, the regime transformed economic sectors such as defense and hydrocarbons into sources of political patronage that benefited the elites, who in turn dispensed favors and jobs to members of the working class.

When it appeared that disaffection was increasing among working-class Algerians, the regime reoriented its economic largesse so that it targeted such people directly. This is what took place during the early days of the Arab Spring, which began in neighboring Tunisia in 2011 and threatened to engulf Algeria along with the rest of the region. The regime in Algiers had benefited from high oil prices throughout the 2000s, so much so that Algeria, with $194 bn in exchange reserves in 2013, ranked eighth in the world by that metric. This very comfortable financial cushion allowed the regime to expend economic resources to steer potentially disaffected segments of society toward complacency and buy social peace. Indeed, the government spent massive sums of money on public-sector wages, infrastructure, social housing, and job creation.

For instance, to reduce unemployment among youths aged 15 to 34 (38 percent of the population, or 14.3 million people) (Safir, 2012), the government set up the National Agency for the Support of Youth Employment (ANSEJ). Much of the funds distributed between 2011 and 2019, which cost no less than $20bn (Maghreb Emergent, 2020), were distributed as bank loans, providing the unemployed with opportunities to create startups and attain economic security. For good measure, the government even put together a reform package that included a more open political arena, the enhancement of women's political participation (law 12–01), and the lifting of Algeria's nineteen-year-long state of emergency.

The strategy worked. Algeria's regime and its extensions—political leaders, key military personnel, and business tycoons—mitigated opposition, hampered mobilization, and secured much of the populace's obedience and even loyalty. One after the other, the regimes of Tunisia, Egypt, and Libya fell. Yet Algeria's remained standing. And today, a decade later, it is still standing. One of this book's key themes is that the markers of change that we have seen in Algeria qualify as such in the outward sense, but function as cleverly concealed enablers of regime continuity, of regime self-preservation. The regime's prime decision-makers—the *décideurs* or le *pouvoir*, as Algerians call them—comprise the army, the National Liberation Front (FLN), and increasingly the Democratic National Rally, or RND, and the country's coastal elites. Through judicious and timely political openings and economic interventions, they have succeeded in preventing the politico-economic system's total transformation. It is change without change.

The Algerian regime's resilience was tested once again in 2019. That year, the press office of President Abdelaziz Bouteflika announced that he, who had been in power for twenty years and was clearly ailing, announced that he would run for a fifth term. In response, hundreds of thousands of protesters took to the streets all over the country in spontaneous demonstrations. *Bouteflika mekech el khamsa* [Bouteflika, there will be no fifth term] was their rallying cry. This *Hirak*, Arabic for "movement," was born out of the exasperation of millions of Algerians with their out-of-touch president, but also with the regime behind him.

Although the traditional political parties made to join the movement in order to capitalize on the widespread discontent, their representatives, including party leaders, were often publicly shamed by the demonstrators, who called them *chiyatin* [sycophants], as they perceived them as instruments of the regime. Rank-and-file members of these traditional political parties who were dissatisfied with the country's stage-managed politics joined the protests in droves and scoffed at their leaders' newfound opposition to Bouteflika. The protests caught the regime off-guard and impressed the world with their scale and nature. Learning from the experience of the 1990s—which was particularly violent, as demonstrations turned into clashes with the police—the participants kept their movement leaderless. And above all, their protests remained *Silmiya* [peaceful] and *Hadhariya* [civilized] (Ghanem, 2019).

The *Hirak* transcended sociodemographic and ideological milieux, as participants were from all backgrounds: youth, old, educated, employed, unemployed, women, men, Islamists, secularists, democrats, liberals, higher-income groups, the well-off middle class, and less privileged classes. In bigger cities, the first year was the most intense phase of the *Hirak*. After the Covid-19 pandemic hit Algeria in February 2020, the movement had to suspend its marches to avoid mass contamination. Once it had recovered from its initial shock, the regime swung into action. Low on funds, owing to oil prices having plummeted from an apex of $111 per barrel in June 2014 to around $32 in March 2020, and declining exchange reserves, it could not buy off the demonstrators. Instead, the regime, already stung by the chilly reception accorded Bouteflika's replacement as president, Abdelmadjid Tebboune, following a stage-managed election, instructed Tebboune to enact political reforms. In August 2020, his government did just that, announcing a raft of measures. These included a referendum on 73 constitutional amendments promising a clearer separation and balance of powers, the respect of fundamental rights and public freedoms, the establishment of an Independent National Electoral Authority, the independence of the judiciary, the prevention of and fight against corruption, and the abolition of the

Constitutional Council and its replacement by a Constitutional Court. In an attempt to render the *Hirak* moot, the government stated explicitly that it was enacting the reforms in response to "the will of the people," as expressed through the "authentic, blessed *Hirak*."

With the lifting of most pandemic-related restrictions in February 2021, the *Hirak* returned to the streets. While participation in these revived weekly demonstrations remained more or less the same in terms of numbers, the participation of women and the middle class gradually declined throughout 2021. Organizational weaknesses and ideological differences in the *Hirak* were essential factors in this change, but regime interference was crucial (Ghanem, 2020). To ensure that those still taking part in *Hirak* demonstrations received the message that their movement was now superfluous, the regime organized several nation-wide counter-demonstrations in which participants showed their support for the government and tried to clash with peaceful anti-government protesters. The authorities also launched a media campaign to tar those who maintained that the *Hirak* had yet to achieve its aims as people calling for separatism, hate, and even terrorism.

There followed the criminalization of street demonstrations and the use of the Covid-19 pandemic and confinement measures to silence the last voices of dissent. Throughout this period, one thing the regime did not do is resort to outright violence. Indeed, calibrated coercion was the order of the day. This differed drastically from 1988, when the regime used a heavy-handed response and troops shot protesters on sight, killing dozens, and the 1990s, when it interrupted parliamentary elections, which the Islamist FIS party was poised to win, and violently and often indiscriminately repressed Islamists and even those suspected of Islamist sympathies. The result, as we all know, is that many of those Islamists and unaffiliated people turned into jihadists.

The Pillars of the Algerian Regime

The regime's reliance on political patronage and economic clientelism in order to neutralize opposition, all the more so in the decades since 1989, when opposition parties were finally allowed, should be viewed as part of a larger picture. This book identifies five pillars sustaining the Algerian regime, without which it would have crumbled long ago. The first pillar is the real locus of power: the army. The second is the co-optation of the opposition. The third is the fragmentation of civil society. The fourth is rent distribution, patronage, and corruption. The fifth pillar is repression.

The first chapter of this book discusses the most significant pillar: the Algerian military. The People's National Army (ANP), as it is known, is the most powerful political institution in the country and wields extensive influence beyond the confines of the military. The army sees itself as the distilled essence of the nation, meaning that, in the eyes of its leadership, it is inconceivable that the institution be restricted to the security sector and cut off from politics (Bünte, 2021; Hlaing, 2009; Kühn & Wolf, 2010). The army makes the major decisions, and its civilian façade, the government, implements them (Cook, 2007). This has been demonstrated time and again, most recently during the 2019 political crisis. Under Chief-of-Staff and Vice-Minister of Defense Ahmed Gaïd Salah, the army pressured Bouteflika to step down, appointed Abdelkader Bensalah as an interim president with a caretaker government, and arrested dozens of politicians and business tycoons, all to placate the *Hirak* and give the impression of change and transition to a more transparent system and a more democratic regime. At the same time, however, the army set an early date for a presidential election, despite widespread calls within the *Hirak* for an extended transition period. Gaïd Salah lived long enough to see the army's candidate, Abdelmadjid Tebboune, "elected" on December 12, 2019. Ten days after Tebboune's stage-managed election, Salah died at 79 of sudden cardiac arrest. The show went on, Tebboune entered *El Mouradia* Palace, and, in line with the wishes of the military's upper echelon, he appointed Major-General Saïd Chengriha as the army's new chief-of-staff. Its work done, the army returned to the barracks, but of course continued to monitor political goings-on with a view to intervening when necessary.

Although the army wields tremendous influence, in order for it not to have to govern the country outright, it was necessary for the regime to co-opt the country's opposition. This is the second pillar upon which regime rule rests, and is the subject of Chapter 2. For obvious reasons, co-optation has emerged as a vital regime-survival strategy since 1989, when opposition parties were finally allowed. In co-opting opposition parties, the regime not only sustains itself, but also provides itself with a democratic fig leaf. This is crucial, given Algeria's foreign policy orientation. Algeria has never pursued an isolationist policy of the sort that, for example, long characterized Myanmar and continues to characterize North Korea. Moreover, its close ties to France and the fact that many

Algerian opposition figures have historically resided there has made it imperative that Algiers maintain good ties with Paris, among other European capitals.

Chapter 3 explores the Algerian regime's tactics to fragment the civil society sector, control its activities, and minimize its activism. Civil Society Organizations (CSOs) in Algeria are characterized by a lack of financial and material resources, a dependency on funds disbursed by the state, limited access to international funds, and a deficiency in networking on the national and regional levels. They are consequently vulnerable to the government's tactics, which include co-optation, litigation, marginalization, scapegoating, and coercion. Several CSOs that initially showed promise as monitors of the state's authoritarianism and corruption wound up unwilling or unable to challenge the government's policies and actions.

The fourth chapter examines rent distribution as yet another pillar of the regime. Oil-extracted rents have long served as the regime's favored tool to buy social peace and even people's political allegiances. The regime has used oil money to manipulate the democratic process, for example funding pro-regime incumbents during elections and thereby helping them to enhance economic opportunities for their clients and supporters. Essentially, in Algeria, the regime's corruption has a political dimension, in that a portion of ill-gotten gains are earmarked for patronage networks. This chapter investigates how the regime goes about all this and how it sometimes even bribes those it excludes from the system so that they refrain from speaking up.

While patronage networks have shrunk due to the economic crisis, the fifth and final pillar propping up the regime, coercive capacities, remains important and is the focus of Chapter 5. The regime's coercive capacities are such that it does not need to resort to extensive violence in order to, for example, thwart opposition protests. The authorities proved as much in March 2020, during the *Hirak*, when they employed low-intensity coercion consisting of the arrest of youth activists, opposition figures, students, lawyers, and journalists, the shuttering of media outlets, and in May 2021 the wholesale sealing off of Algiers to prevent the capital from swelling with demonstrators flocking to it from elsewhere. These coercive measures triggered a muted response in Western capitals, which is likely to encourage Algiers to continue its repression.

The system's capacity to respond quickly by sacrificing Bouteflika, jailing his clique, choosing a new president, and amending the constitution, all while using the Covid-19 pandemic and various coercive tactics to stifle voices of dissent, allowed it to stymie the *Hirak* and consolidate its rule at a critical historical moment. But for how long? Today's youth, whose expectations for democracy and transparency are high, seem adamant about changing the rules of the game and drafting a new social contract. The *Hirak*, despite its modest achievements, succeeded in raising awareness and encouraging people to call for change. Also, Tebboune and his government's lack of legitimacy is likely to exacerbate an already fragile social contract. Moreover, buying social peace is no longer really possible. Algeria's exchange reserves have been depleted owing to the drop in oil prices and its consequences on the mono-dependent Algerian economy, coupled with the effects of the Covid-19 pandemic. The rise in oil and gas prices caused by the war in Ukraine led the Algerian authorities to abandon their austerity measures, which included reducing subsidies and raising taxes. Nontheless, the regime's *modus operandi* may no longer prove effective. If so, the regime will at some point have to do what it has long put off: effect real change.

References

Brumberg, D. (2002). The Trap of Liberalized Autocracy. *Journal of Democracy., 13*(4), 56–68.

Brumberg, D. (2003). Liberalisation Versus Democracy: Understanding Arab Political Reform. *Carnegie Endowment for International Peace*, Middle East Working Papers (37). Democracy and Rule of Law project.

Bünte, M. (2021). Ruling but not Governing: Tutelary Regimes and the Case of Myanmar. *Government & Opposition: An International Journal of Comparative Politics.* 1–17. Accessed January 24, 2022.

Carothers, T. (2002). The End of the Transition Paradigm. *Journal of Democracy., 13*(1), 1–21.

Cook. S. (2007). *Ruling But Not Governing: The Military and Political Development in Egypt, Algeria, and Turkey.* JHUP.

Diamond, L. (2006). Is The Third Wave Over? *Journal of Democracy., 7*(3), 20–37.

Ghanem, D. (2019). Photo Essay, A protest Made in Algeria. *Carnegie middle east center.* April 2. https://carnegie-mec.org/2019/04/02/protest-made-in-algeria-pub-78748. Accessed January 24, 2022.

Ghanem, D. (2020). Algeria's Hirak: Why Such a Mass Movement Achieved so Little?. *Manara Magazine.* December 15. https://manaramagazine.org/2020/12/15/algerias-hirak-why-such-a-mass-movement-achieved-so-little/. Accessed January 24, 2022.

Hlaing, K. (2009). Setting the Rules for Survival: Why the Military Regime Survives in an age of Democratization. *The Pacific Review., 22*(3), 271–291.

Kühn, A., & Wolf, D. (2010). Beyond the Fallacy of Coup-Ism: Conceptualizing Civilian Control of the Military in Emerging Democracies. *Democratization., 17*(5), 950–975.

Levitsky, S, Way. L. (2010). *Competitive Authoritarianism: Hybrid Regimes after the Cold War*. Cambridge University Press.

Maghreb Emergent. (2020). Emploi: Combien a coûté le dispositif ANSEJ-CNAC-ANGEM à l'Algérie depuis sa création ?. *Maghreb Emergent*. August 22. https://bit.ly/32zu8Nd. Accessed January 24, 2022.

Ottaway, M. (2003). *Democracy Challenged: The Rise of Semi-Authoritarianism*. Carnegie Endowment for International Peace.

Roberts, H. (2003). The Battlefield: Algeria 1988–2002. *Studies in a Broken Polity*. London: Verso.

Safir, N. (2012). La jeunesse algérienne: Un profond et durable malaise. *Confluences Méditerranée., 81*(2), 153–161.

Schedler, A. (2006). *Electoral Authoritarianism: The Dynamics of Unfree Competition*. Lynne Rienner.

Zakaria, F. (1997). The Rise of Illiberal Democracy. *Foreign Affairs., 76*(6), 22–43.

CHAPTER 2

The Military: The Real Broker of Power in Algeria

In Algeria, the People's National Army (ANP) wields enormous influence in the political arena. In essence, the Army views itself as a guiding force without which Algeria would go astray. For the military's upper echelon, political neutrality is inconceivable, and ceding ground to civilians, even democratically elected ones, would endanger the nation. While it is true that the Algerian military has supported civilian presidents, it has since the country's attainment of independence in 1962 rejected efforts to have the parliament or the government oversee internal military affairs, define security policies, and make military personnel accountable for their deeds in civil courts (Ghanem, 2014).

During Algeria's first three decades as an independent state, the Army consistently manipulated the political arena from behind the scenes. Though it never governed the country, the Army exercised, to varying degrees, supervision and even outright control and sometimes intervened directly in matters of state. The Army's actions in 1992 marked a qualitative change in its approach to Algerian politics. That year, it intervened to scrap parliamentary elections that the FIS was poised to win, and arrested thousands of party members.

Yet this was not to be the brief sort of intervention of old. The Army's actions prompted several factions within the FIS to resort to arms and launch an all-out rebellion against the regime. For the next seven years,

© The Author(s), under exclusive license to Springer Nature Switzerland AG 2022
D. Ghanem, *Understanding the Persistence of Competitive Authoritarianism in Algeria*, Middle East Today,
https://doi.org/10.1007/978-3-031-05102-9_2

13

even as it battled Islamist groups across the country, the Army took its most hands-on approach to date in managing Algerian politics. Only in 1999, with the jihadists almost wholly defeated and the Army having engineered the election of Bouteflika, did the military resume its traditional role behind the scenes. In 2019, the Army intervened to oust Bouteflika, whom a growing national protest movement vehemently opposed, before once again retreating into the background.

At the Beginning, the ALN

The process by which the military went from the armed wing of a political party to an autonomous entity, and ultimately became the locus of power, is not a uniquely Algerian phenomenon. Indeed, the transformation recalls that of several national liberation movements in Africa and Latin America. In Algeria's case, the struggle against French colonialism (1954–1962) conferred upon the *Armée de Libération Nationale* (National Liberation Army or ALN), the FLN's armed wing, a vital role and turned it into a centerpiece of the Algerian political system's architecture even before the country attained independence. By 1962, the ALN, now on the verge of evolving into the Algerian Army, had overtaken the FLN as the most powerful political—not just military—force in the land. How did this happen?

The FLN was formed in 1954 and established the ALN the same year. In the Soummam Congress of 1956, the ALN agreed to the primacy of the political over the military and the primacy of the interior over the exterior. The National Council for the Algerian Revolution, or CNRA, was created during this Congress. The CNRA, composed of 34 members, was empowered to take political, military, economic, and social orientation decisions. The CNRA divided the national territory into six *wilayas* [provinces], established units and ranks, and set up a command structure (battalions, companies, sections, and groups). It created an entire administrative organization for the health, liaison, equipment, intelligence, finance, war material, press, and information services. The CNRA also created the Committee of Coordination and Implementation (CCE) as the executive body of the Revolution (Harbi, 1992).

The second CNRA meeting, held in Cairo in August 1957, formally invalidated the Soummam Congress principles by adopting three critical decisions. First, the CNRA announced that all those who participated in the Liberation struggle, with or without uniform, were equal. Consequently, there was no primacy of the political over the military, nor any difference between the interior and the exterior. Second, the CNRA expanded its membership to reach 54 members, and the military's hegemony was apparent: only 18 politicians, as opposed to 36 ALN officers, among them 27 in the interior. Third, the CCE appointed five colonels to take charge of the country's five wilayas: Mahmoud Cherif (wilaya I), Lakhder Bentobal (wilaya II), Krim Belkacem (wilaya III), Amar Ouamrane (wilaya IV), and Abdelhafid Boussouf (wilaya V). The ascension of the military became inevitable (Ouaissa, 2010: 78–79). The CNRA's decision in 1960 to create a single General Staff and entrust Colonel Houari Boumediene with leading it accelerated the military's control of the Revolution.

Under Boumediene's command, corruption was curtailed, and almost all the money that flowed to the border army was used to purchase weapons and support the FLN and its members' families. This strengthened the confidence of the *Mujahidin* in Boumediene. The well-armed, disciplined, and motivated border army went on to notch one victory after another against French forces. Thanks largely to its efforts, Algeria obtained its long-sought independence in 1962.

The Crisis of the Summer of 1962

The signing of the Evian Accords and the going into force of the ceasefire on March 18, 1962, created new dynamics within the FLN. The recovery of Algerian sovereignty accentuated divisions from the war years. In fact, a crisis erupted between various Algerian revolutionary factions, one from which the ALN would emerge more powerful than ever.

After being pragmatic during the war period, a strategy by which it avoided imploding, the FLN was undermined by internal disagreements (Mohand-Amer 2014a). Its core political institutions, meaning the GPRA and the CNRA, failed to ensure the transition to independence due to the shrinking of their role and influence, and the provisions of the Evian Accords reduced their missions. During the extraordinary session of the CNRA in Tripoli, held between May 25 and June 6, 1962, the GPRA's role was strongly contested, and it, along with the CNRA, was forced to play a secondary role. The Tlemcen Group, led by Ahmed Ben Bella, an influential FLN leader who had spent much of the war in French captivity, the Border Army, and the *wilayas*, replaced the GPRA and called for a power transfer to their benefit. The impossibility of achieving a *modus vivendi* before independence revealed the precariousness of institutions that had proven their worth during the war.

On June 30, 1962, the GPRA, which had returned to Algiers to take control of the country, dismissed Boumediene and the ALN's General Staff. Boumediene rejected his dismissal and was supported by Ben Bella. In September, an armed conflict broke out between, on the one hand, the Boumediene-led ALN, supported by Ben Bella's FLN faction, and with him three wilayas (I, V, and VI) out of six, and on the other a rump FLN/ALN loyal to the GPRA (Mohand-Amer 2014b: 65–66). The towns of Boghari (today Ksar el Boukhari), Brazza, Médéa, Sidi Aïssa, Orléansville (now Chlef), and Aumale (now Souk El Ghozlane) experienced the deadliest violence (Haroun, 2000: 194).

The General Union of Algerian Workers or UGTA, the General Union of Students (UGE), and the Algerian Red Crescent organized demonstrations against this drift. The people demonstrated in the capital and elsewhere, calling for the end of the violence, chanting: *seb'a snin baraket!* [Seven years is enough!].

On September 10, Boumediene, having routed the rump FLN/ALN loyal to the GPRA, entered the capital amid much fanfare. With his support, elections for a National Constituent Assembly were quickly organized. There was a single list of names imposed as a "choice" for Algerians. On September 20, 196 candidates were elected, only six of whom were members of the GPRA. On September 25, the National Constituent Assembly proclaimed the birth of the People's Democratic Republic of Algeria and appointed Ben Bella head of the first Algerian government. Ferhat Abbas was appointed president of the Assembly, Mohamed Khider FLN secretary-general, and Boumediene Minister of Defense. The following year, Ben Bella was elected by referendum as the first president of independent Algeria. This marked the culmination of an extraordinary turn of events that had seen Boumediene and Ben Bella essentially mount a coup, albeit a popular one, against the GPRA.

Not the Last Military Coup

Ben Bella quickly set about concentrating all power in his hands. To that end, he suspended the 1963 constitution, which provided for a balance of powers, a mere month after it was enacted. Ben Bella used the Army, which had evolved out of the ALN and was headed by Boumediene, to stifle voices of dissent and opposition. He banned the Algerian Communist Party (PCA) and arrested its leader, Bachir Hadj Ali, on November 29, 1962. The Socialist Revolution Party (PRS) was outlawed in August 1963, and its president, Mohamed Boudiaf, was kidnapped by the political police on June 21, 1963, in the heart of Algiers. Boudiaf was sequestered for more than five months in Tsabit (Wilaya of Adrar) and then sent into exile for twenty-eight years. Ben Bella dismissed Mohamed Khider from his post of FLN secretary-general. Khider left for Europe, where he died in obscure circumstances. Abderrahmane Farés, former president of the provisional executive, was arrested on July 7, 1964, and deported to Bechar. Finally, on August 19, 1964, Ferhat Abbas, former president of the provisional government, was arrested and deported to Adrar—for ten months—for having challenged the authorities.

Cognizant of the Army's growing power under the charismatic Boumediene, Ben Bella decided to bring the institution firmly under his control. He saw his chance when Mohamed Chabani, head of the fourth military region of Biskra launched a mutiny. Chabani's forces were defeated, and he was arrested, aled, and convicted of conspiring against the FLN and launching the mutiny. Chabani was executed on September 3, 1964 (Haroun, 2005: 311–313). Ben Bella next moved against Boumediene himself, who was defense minister. Ben Bella installed Colonel Taher Zbiri, whom he perceived as personally loyal to him, as Chief-of-Staff in October 1963, attempting to undercut Boumediene while the latter was on an official visit to Moscow. In May 1965, Ben Bella was planning to take the Ministry of Foreign Affairs portfolio from Abdelaziz Bouteflika, a Boumediene protégé, and assign it to a loyalist. This move sealed his fate. Boumediene, who had control of the Army and had grown closer to the anti-Ben Bella faction within the FLN, decided to depose the president. In the early hours of June 19, 1965, Ben Bella was arrested at his home. Ironically, his appointee, Zbiri, presided over the arrest.

Upon discovering tanks stationed in Algiers' streets, many Algerians believed that they were witnessing scenes being filmed for "The Battle of Algiers," which Gillo Pontecorvo was then shooting in Algeria amid much media publicity. However, at noon, Boumediene appeared on television and announced the end of what he termed Ben Bella's "personal regime." He also denounced the toppled president's "adventurism," "political narcissism," and his "morbid love of power." (Le Monde diplomatique,

1965). He did not describe what had occurred as a coup, but rather as *el Islah el thawri* [revolutionary reform].

Boumediene came up with the Council of the Revolution (CR), born on June 20, 1965. The CR was composed of twenty-six individuals, sixteen of whom were senior military officers (Leca & Vatin, 1975: 501). It dissolved the National People's Assembly (APN) and granted itself complete government control. Boumediene himself became president of the CR, prime minister, and defense minister. By extension, the Army became the ultimate arbiter of all political issues.

Nevertheless, the 1965 coup did not give rise to a government by the Army. Having gained the final say on political decision-making and coercion, the Army was content to share power, at least outwardly, with civilians. This did not always prove quite as clever as Boumediene and his top brass thought it was because a number of "civilians" who ascended to political positions of influence had only just left the military and were acting in its interest. But it was effective. If under Ben Bella, the Army participated in power, under Boumediene, it took power (Yefsah 1982, Yefsah, 1990). Moreover, by virtue of its popularity and its continued role in rebuilding a war-devastated country, the Army met with little resistance.

Under Boumediene, the most significant change was the intensification of the military's support for state authoritarianism. Owing to his independent streak, Ben Bella's increasingly authoritarian measures had aroused the Army's ire. Now, however, authoritarianism in Algeria was the doing of a man who had emerged from the military and coordinated closely with its leadership. From the latter's perspective, this made all the difference.

Boumediene and the Rise of Military Security

In 1967, Boumediene was faced with increasing criticism about his authoritarianism and his reliance on officers who had launched their careers in the French army. Within the Army, tensions erupted, and old rivalries and clan struggles contributed to the deepening of the crisis. Arguably the greatest rivalry was between the "Army of the Border," composed of soldiers stationed during the war in Tunisia and Morocco, and the "Army of the Interior," composed of soldiers called *maquisards* [Resistance fighters]. The latter feared the former because of their good technical training and worried about the Army's transformation into a modern outfit that would no longer need them. Keenly aware of these divisions, Boumediene did not want the Council of the Revolution to convene until a majority could be obtained in his favor. These tensions were exposed in broad daylight during the commemoration of the fifth anniversary of the outbreak of the Algerian Revolution. During these commemorations on November 1, 1967, Chief-of-Staff Zbiri was absent, and Boumediene described this as "an act of very serious indiscipline" on the part of a "brother" (Viratelle 1969). Despite mediation attempts, the discussion between Zbiri and Boumediene reached a stalemate, and Zbiri moved to the Lido armored camp at Fort-de-l'Eau, near Algiers. Rumors of a coup were circulating in the capital.

Boumediene took the offensive with two measures that precipitated events. He placed a new general secretary at the head of the FLN and purged its executive secretariat of Zbiri's allies. More importantly, he transferred to Orléansville (Chlef), 200 km from Algiers, the armored unit of Fort-de-l'Eau, commanded by Captain Haousnia Layachi, brother-in-law of Colonel Zbiri, to deprive the latter of critical support. On December 14, Zbiri ordered 1,500 men and around 30 tanks and armored vehicles to march toward Algiers. But they never reached the capital, as Boumediene was informed of the insurrection by those of Zbiri's allies who were planning to abandon him, among them a certain Commander Chadli Benjedid. Zbiri's rebellion was nipped in the bud, in part thanks to Boumediene's use of the air force to bomb armored columns advancing on the capital. On the 15th, Boumediene announced that he had taken command of the Army. No fewer than 184 Algerians were tried for their participation in Zbiri's failed coup (Viratelle 1969).

Zbiri's failed coup allowed the army to consolidate its hold on the system. The Army became the best-organized and best-managed institution in the country. The Army's Military Security wing (SM), created in September 1958 under the Ministry of Ammunitions and General Connections, became its strike force. Through its networks, the SM infiltrated newspapers, universities, administrative bodies, conferences, public debates, the police, and the FLN, playing a vital role in co-opting elites and controlling society (Harbi, 1992: 187). The powers granted to the SM facilitated arbitrary arrests, the extension of detention periods, and abetted torture. The SM was used to stifle or purge the regime's opponents. Those who criticized the president or the regime were systematically discredited as "counter-revolutionaries" and "saboteurs of socialism." Sometimes, they were exiled or even killed.

20   D. GHANEM

Yet the economy was failing, with the pauperization of large social classes and the enrichment of the politico-military bourgeoisie. The latter amassed colossal fortunes under the guise of socialism. Boumediene realized as much. In a speech delivered in Constantine in 1973, he invited "the billionaires" in the country to "leave state bodies" if they wanted to continue to make billions and "leave the Revolution to the revolutionaries." (Yefsah, 1992: 84). Yet Boumediene could not afford to alienate the military. He was a prisoner of the Army's most influential members, the CR, which controlled the military regions, the bureaucracy that managed the oil rent, and the SM.

Bendjedid and the Advent of Multiparty Politics

When Boumediene died in December 1978, the military mediated between two civilian factions battling for succession. The rivalry pitted the Minister of Foreign Affairs, Abdelaziz Bouteflika, against the FLN's General Secretary, Mohamed Salah Yahiaoui. A faction of the military, led by the head of its powerful intelligence branch, Kasdi Merbah, intervened to avert conflict and protect the regime's stability. Both Yahiaoui and Bouteflika were sidelined in favor of a compromise candidate, Colonel Chadli Bendjedid. He became head of state, head of the Army, and head of the FLN. Having brought Bendjedid to power, the military retreated to its preferred position behind the scenes. From the beginning, however, it was clear that Bendjedid would not govern as he saw fit. At the military's behest, his cabinet included many of its senior members—several of whom were also members of the FLN's political bureau.

Chadli also used the SM to stifle opposition, starting with those close to former president Boumediene. He modernized and reorganized the Army according to Soviet models of organization and doctrine. For instance, in 1984, he created the rank of General for the first time. In less than three years, the Army, composed of 150,000 men with very uncertain operational skills, became a conventional Army organized around several forces. The air and naval forces were established in 1985, the land forces in 1986, and the National Gendarmerie and the National Defense of the Territory in 1988. These forces were headed by the General Staff, which reported to the president of the Republic, who also held the position of Defense Minister.

From the beginning, Chadli understood that he would not govern alone. Since his appointment in 1979, he had to compete with the senior military officers who had appointed him head of state (i.e., Colonels Kasdi Merbah, Ahmed Belhouchet, Mohamed Attaïliah). He managed to free himself from their grip, only to fall under the control of those whom he promoted to the rank of General, created in 1984, and on whom he relied to assert himself as commander-in-chief of the Army—which he was, according to the constitution. Larbi Belkheir became an adviser to Chadli and established himself as the strongman, the "godfather" of power. Belkheir's maneuvers led, in 1986, to the dismissal of General Belhoucif (the first Algerian officer to be awarded this rank when it was created), chief-of-staff of the Army, and his deputy for operations, Kamel Abderrahim, and to the promotion, among others, of Khaled Nezzar, who was given the command of the land forces, and would become later Defense Minister. Chadli promoted Nezzar and others because he was afraid of the *maquisards* likely to oppose his inclination for political and economic reforms. Belkheir, supported by his *protégé* Colonel Mohamed Mediène, known as "Toufik," whom he placed at the head of the Central Directorate of Security of the Army, convinced Chadli to evict the *maquisards* from the upper military hierarchy. However, the day after the December 1991 elections, which were won by the Islamic Salvation Front (FIS), his most loyal subordinates, Generals Larbi Belkheir and Khaled Nezzar, among others, pushed him to resign.

Nevertheless, Bendjedid's main problem, at least initially, was not friction with the Army but a doddering economy. The development plans put in place under Boumediene in the 1970s had failed. The priority given to heavy industry—to the disadvantage of agriculture and the production of consumable goods—made the country reliant on imports for 60 percent of its needs. An attempt to rectify the imbalance with a five-year plan (1980–1985) characterized by the development of the private sector, privatization of agriculture, slowing industrialization policy, and providing credit to developers in the industry, services, and the agricultural sector—proved belated and ineffective.

The sudden drop in the price of oil, Algeria's main export, in 1985, when the barrel dropped from $40 to less than $10, caused a full-blown recession. This was of particular concern given the rapidly growing population. Algeria had gone from 11 million inhabitants in 1962 to 24 million in 1988 (Stora, 2006: 63–64). And rapid urbanization, which reached 50 percent in 1988, hampered the country's social development strategies. Unemployment approached 30 percent, living conditions deteriorated,

22 D. GHANEM

and food shortages became common (Stora, 2006: 64). The era of the so-called magnanimous state, able to supply food and medicine and provide housing, had come to an end.

Meanwhile, Bendjedid had been in crisis with the FLN since the extraordinary Congress of 1986, due to opposite views on reforms. Back then, Bendjedid had criticized the FLN's "inertia" and "stagnation" (Le Monde diplomatique, 1986). The president was convinced of the need for reforms and had in his circle Mouloud Hamrouche, then-General Secretary of the presidency, and the "reformers" under his wing. Yet most FLN members and a faction of the military were against reforms. Bendjedid's ruling coalition, the presidency, and his cabinet marginalized the FLN. Then Bendjedid's cabinet director, Major-General Larbi Belkhir, who helped appoint Bendjedid in 1979, imposed himself and his team as a force in the face of the government. On September 19, 1988, President Bendjedid called an executive meeting and delivered a vehement speech at the *Palais des Nations* which none of the 2,000 participants (government officials, military, FLN members, executives of mass organizations, state, and business executives) expected. Bendjedid criticized the FLN and its leaders' incompetence, mismanagement, carelessness, and failed management. This emboldened ordinary Algerians to vent their own frustrations. On October 5, 1988, hundreds of thousands of youths took to the streets all over the country to express their *dégoûtage* [disgust] with the regime (Rarrbo, 1995). The people were frustrated with the centralization of power in the hands of a small bourgeois elite. They saw this politico-military elite as entirely uninterested in their needs, using corruption, clientelism, nepotism, and tyranny to remain in power. The riots expressed the population's political, economic, cultural, and social revulsion. Over ten days, the rioters attacked ministries, the headquarters of the ruling FLN, post offices, public transport, telephone booths, and almost everything else that represented the state. The social contract between the masses and its leadership had ruptured, and the regime's discourse could no longer conceal the dismal social realities (Zoubir, 1993).

The Army intervened, shot many rioters on sight, and arrested many more to restore order. The official death toll stood at 176, while unofficial figures stood at 500, and dozens of young people were tortured after their arrest. All this shocked Algerian society. The riots destabilized the regime, but it reacted quickly. Instructed to do so by the Army, Bendjedid loosened his grip on power and introduced economic and political reforms. Chief among these was *El Infitah* [the economic opening] and *El*

Ta'adudiya el hizbiya [multiparty system]. The country appeared to have embarked on a democratization drive. Bendjedid succeeded in purging many military commanders following criticism of how the Army dealt with the riots. A new generation of technocratic officers, younger and less politicized, emerged, and the Army returned to its barracks. The sidelining of the Army was formalized in the 1989 constitution, where it was referred to only in terms of its defense capacities (Art.24). Yahia Rahel, head of the Army's influential policy department, declared that the ANP would stand "above the political debate" (Rouadjia, 1995: 160).

With the advent of the multiparty system, Algeria witnessed a proliferation of political parties, and elections were set for 1991 (local) and 1992 (parliamentary). The ruling FLN no longer monopolized the political landscape; it had a serious challenger in the Islamic Salvation Front (FIS). The latter emerged triumphant in the local elections of June 12, 1990, taking control of 853 out of 1,551 municipalities and 31 wilayas out of 48 (Cubertafond, 1999: 8; Kapil, 1990: 31). Caught off-guard, the authorities promulgated a new electoral law in April 1991 that gerrymandered electoral districts so that parliamentary elections scheduled for December 1991 would result in the FLN securing a majority of seats. The next month, however, the FIS called a general and open-ended strike to attempt to force the repeal of the new electoral law, and gave President Bendjedid a week to set a date for early presidential elections. The strike was widely observed—until the military intervened to end it just over a week after it had gone into effect. Clashes ensued, resulting in nearly 50 deaths, with 300 people injured. On Wednesday, June 5, 1991, the government declared an *état de siège* for four months (Benchikh, 1992). The government resigned by the president's order, and the legislative elections were postponed. On June 30, 1991, FIS leaders Abassi Madani and Ali Belhadj were arrested for "armed conspiracy against state security," and FIS newspapers were banned from publishing.

Yet the FIS was not banned or prevented from contesting the elections. Despite the gerrymandering of districts, which worked against it, the FIS obtained 188 of the 232 seats in parliament. To avoid a crushing victory by the FIS in the second round, scheduled for January 16, 1992, and in which 198 seats were up for grabs, the Army, with its chief-of-staff, General Khaled Nezzar, forced Bendjedid to dissolve the parliament, where the speaker—his constitutional successor—sat, and subsequently compelled Bendjedid to resign on January 11, 1992. The electoral process was interrupted, the country was left without an executive branch, and the Army deployed in the streets. This was the "rape of the ballot box" (Stora, 2001).

The Army, the DRS, and the Years of Lead

Three days after Bendjedid's resignation, and worried about displaying its omnipotence in broad daylight, the military leaders created a five-member Haut Comité d'État (HCE) to act as a collective transitional executive until the end of Bendjedid's mandate in 1993. The HCE, a sort of provisional political authority, helped by a National Consultative Council, a body acting as parliament, was composed of Khaled Nezzar (Minister of Defense), Ali Kafi (President of the National Organization of Mujahidin), Ali Haroun (Minister of Human Rights), Tedjini Haddam (former Rector of the Paris mosque), and Mohamed Boudiaf. Boudiaf, one of the few remaining *chefs historiques* [historical leaders] from the war of independence, was asked to return from his 28-year exile to lead the HCE. Boudiaf held the HCE presidency from January 16, 1992, until his assassination on June 29 of the same year. Ali Kafi replaced him until the HCE's dissolution on January 30, 1994, with the election of President Liamine Zeroual.

On January 24, a Friday, demonstrations outside mosques in cities across the country, which had become a common weekly occurrence following the Friday sermon, were met with military force. In several instances, the Army opened fire, causing the death of some 30 people in total. The Army went on to occupy the mosques and launched a campaign of arrests targeting activists and supporters of the FIS. In February, the HCE announced the opening of seven detention centers in Algeria's southern desert region to accommodate those detained. The HCE press release reported that 6,786 individuals were jailed across seven detention centers in the Great South (Reggane, El Homr, Tsabit, Ain M'guel, Ain Salah, Ouargla, bordj Omar Driss) (Barik, 1996). On February 9, 1992, the HCE declared a twelve-month *état d'urgence* [state of emergency]. It would last for nineteen years.

This new round of repression accelerated a nascent Islamist insurgency, the initial, scattered signs of which had come late the previous year. Although the first armed assault occurred as early as November, it was in December, when the second round of parliamentary elections was canceled, that attacks began to take place with greater frequency. Following the early 1992 campaign of repression, more and more FIS members who had either managed to elude arrest or who were too low-ranked to have been targeted in the first place took up arms. Unaffiliated individuals who were unfairly arrested, jailed, and sometimes tortured by zealous members of the security forces strengthened the ranks of the jihadist groups. They tended to join the newly formed military wing of the FIS, called the Islamic Salvation Army (AIS) or the even more extreme Armed Islamic Group (GIA), which was hostile to both the government and the FIS.

The AIS, GIA, and other jihadist groups began launching murderous attacks against anybody they deemed opposed to establishing an Islamic state. This category included army conscripts and their families, intellectuals, doctors, lawyers, university professors, writers and journalists, trade unionists, and foreigners. One of the bloodiest chapters of Algeria's modern history, the Black Decade, had begun. By the time it had ended, the casualty toll would stand at 150,000 people killed, 7,000 disappeared, and one million internally displaced.

When the HCE was dissolved in January 1994, the military chose to appoint a consensus candidate, one who could bridge the gap between the hardliners, known as the "eradicators," who saw no compromise with the Islamists, and the "dialoguers," who called for negotiations with the Islamists and the rehabilitation of the FIS in the political game. This candidate was General Liamine Zeroual. Brought to power by the Army in 1994, Zeroual was comfortably elected on November 16, 1995, with more than 60 percent of votes. This legitimization by the ballot did not translate into more democracy. Algeria remained, behind its democratic façade, ruled by a handful of senior military officers.

In 1994, following two years of stalemate, the balance of power began to shift in favor of the military. The reasons for this included the IMF's acceptance of Algeria's request to reschedule its debt, the opening of the Algerian hydrocarbon sector to foreign investments, and the rise in oil prices. The corresponding increase in state revenue enabled the regime to invest in development projects that alleviated popular discontent—and therefore deprived the jihadists of recruits. More importantly, flush with money, the regime embarked on a drive to modernize its security and defense apparatuses in preparation for the *guerre totale* [total war] on terror envisaged by the Army's most hardline faction. The latter, at whose head stood none other than Chief-of-Staff General Mohamed Lamari, had significant allies among civilian groups with close ties to the state, including the General Union of Algerian Workers (UGTA), the

National Union of Public Contractors (UNEP), the National Organization of Mujahidin (ONM), as well as the self-styled opposition Rally for Culture and Democracy (RCD) political party (Roberts, 1994).

These hardliners had from the start refused any dialogue or negotiation with the Islamists and had gathered under the National Safeguarding Committee of Algeria (CNSA) on December 30, 1991, calling for the direct intervention of the Army to stop the FIS. They were counterbalanced by those that emphasized dialogue and reconciliation between the state and mainstream Islamists (i.e., not jihadists). Such groupings included the Front of Socialist Forces (FFS), the Movement for Democracy in Algeria (MDA) led by former president Ahmed Ben Bella, the Workers' Party (PT), reformist members of the FLN, Ennahda, and a faction of the FIS itself. Brought to Rome in January 1995 by the Community of Sant'Egidio, a worldwide Catholic lay association headquartered in Italy's capital, representatives of these dialogue-minded groupings released a platform calling for a peaceful political solution to the crisis, the reintegration of the FIS into Algeria's political system, and the withdrawal of the Army from the political sphere (Le Monde diplomatique, 1995).

Keen to press ahead with the military option yet simultaneously wary of appearing jingoistic, President Zeroual and the Army's top brass launched their own reconciliation effort, which the government promptly adopted. Even as the Army kept up its pressure on jihadist groups, a "Clemency Law" was passed on February 25, 1995. The law guaranteed forgiveness for "those who went astray" as long as they laid down their weapons and reintegrated into society under certain conditions. Some 2,000 jihadists accepted the deal and disarmed between 1995 and 1996, but the vast majority would have no truck with it (Ghanem, 2018).

Lamari and his hardline faction in the military expected as much and were able to consolidate their position as a result. In 1996, the Army's leadership announced a total war on terror. It had long taken to preparing for just such a hoped-for eventuality. The military corps assigned to fighting jihadist groups had numbered 15,000 in 1993, but reached 80,000 in 1996. During the same period, the number of gendarmerie troops doubled, reaching 50,000. Additionally, at Major-General Mohammed Touati's suggestion, civilians were enlisted in the campaign. The government, which at the time was helmed by Prime Minister Redha Malek, established three types of militias, for which some 200,000 men were recruited.

2 THE MILITARY: THE REAL BROKER OF POWER IN ALGERIA   27

Ironically, increased militarization served to strengthen a state that otherwise appeared weak. As Theda Skocpol has pointed out, even after a substantial loss of legitimacy, a state can remain relatively stable—and certainly immune to internal mass revolts—especially if the repressive apparatuses retain their cohesion and effectiveness (Skocpol, 1979). Thus it was with Algeria. The Army, on the strength of a string of victories it notched against the GIA and other groups, described itself in its official organ as an "impregnable fortress against which all maneuvers, all plots aimed at bringing Algeria to its knees will be broken." (Marchés tropicaux et méditerranéens 1995).

The militarization of the state did not simply serve to turn the tide against the insurrectionists, but had significant sociopolitical ramifications. In order to uncover plots both real and imagined, the Army's intelligence branch, now called the Department of Intelligence and Security (DRS), which Tewfik Mediène headed, grew quite intrusive in the political arena. The DRS's arrogation to itself of more and more power mirrored the self-aggrandizement of the military as a whole. For example, Lamari essentially transferred most responsibilities and prerogatives of the Ministry of Defense to the Army's General Staff, in which he placed officers who were loyal to him. The Ministry was reduced to managing the administrative services of the Army, while the General Staff would command its operational services.

Divergences between the real power (the Army's General Staff) and the formal power (presidency and government) intensified in 1997. Generals Lamari and Médiene disagreed with President Zeroual over his negotiations with the FIS and his amnesty formula for the AIS (Martinez, 1997). The outcome, as expected, was the victory of the military. The Army and DRS used the local networks of General Ahmed Gaïd Salah in the region of Djidjel, a stronghold of the AIS, to approach the group's leaders. The military and the DRS then opened secret lines of communication with the AIS's leader, Madani Mezrag, based on the view that the AIS had superseded the FIS in importance (Ghanem, 2018). On September 21, 1997, the AIS declared a unilateral ceasefire.

The ceasefire was heralded as having brought to an end the conflict between the state and one of the largest rebel groups. From the military's perspective, it was just as important because it rendered moot the talks between Zeroual and the FIS. Had those talks been allowed to take their natural course, they might have culminated in a truce. Zeroual would have emerged from such a truce as an architect of peace and strengthened his position vis-à-vis the military's high command.

The affair further soured relations between Zeroual and the Army, which eventually removed him from office. In September 1998, at the instigation of generals Lamari and Médiene, Zeroual called early presidential elections for February 1999, ostensibly due to his wish to leave political life and retire. That the military instructed Zeroual to call early elections is significant. Had he resigned, he would have been replaced by Bachir Boumaza, president of the Council of the Nation (the Algerian parliament's upper house). Boumaza was not beholden to the military, which suspected him of wanting to strengthen the FLN at its expense. The departure of Zeroual at the behest of Lamari and Mediène confirmed once again what the Army had always denied—that it was an institution above the presidency and that it rejected the government's authority. In seven years, the Army had sacked three heads of state: Chadli Bendjedid in 1992, Ali Kafi in 1994, and Liamine Zéroual in 1999.

To conceal its control of the presidency, the Army resolved not to draw the next president from its ranks. Zeroual's successor would be a civilian—albeit one loyal to the military. He would receive formal legitimacy through elections and real legitimacy through the Army's support. The man for the job was Abdelaziz Bouteflika, minister of Foreign Affairs for sixteen years under Boumediene. He was also the latter's *protégée* and even delivered Boumediene's funeral sermon in 1978. Since 1981, Bouteflika had languished in a sort of self-imposed exile, most of it spent in Switzerland, owing to a falling out he had had with the military leadership. Now, in 1999, he was invited to return to Algeria.

From the Army's perspective, things were looking up. Some 7,000 jihadists had laid down their weapons to benefit from the ceasefire the military had declared, and Algeria seemed poised to emerge from the semi-isolation it had suffered on the international stage following its scuppering of the 1992 elections. The presidential election was held in April 1999. The Army successfully encouraged several parties (FLN, RND, Ennahda) to announce their support for Bouteflika, even before announcing his intention to run for the presidency. The DRS, led by Mediène, also backed Bouteflika and is believed to have pressured one of the candidates, former head of the government between June 1991 and February 1992, Sid Ahmed Ghozali, to withdraw his candidacy to avoid causing trouble for Bouteflika (Tuquoi, 1999). Eventually, Ghozali's candidacy was rejected by the constitutional council. Also, on the eve of the election on April 14, 1999, citing fraud, the six candidates in the presidential election withdrew from the race. Bouteflika was the only candidate to remain in the race. He was elected with 73 percent of the vote.

BOUTEFLIKA IN, THE MILITARY BACK TO THEIR BARRACKS?

The military brought Bouteflika to power within the framework of a pacted transition. In exchange for ceding partial political power to a civilian president and government, the military received guarantees regarding its political prerogatives and economic interests. For example, the military would retain complete discretion over its colossal budget and resources. Moreover, through Bouteflika's "Charter for Peace and National Reconciliation," the military secured full amnesty for members of the security forces involved in human rights violations during the Black Decade.

This was significant. During the Black Decade, the Army and the DRS were at the forefront of the "war against terror" and were widely believed to have been responsible for extensive repression, torture, extrajudicial killings, and forced disappearances. Bouteflika's Charter did not mandate that the state investigate such serious human rights abuses, let alone prosecute those suspected of perpetrating them. Instead, the Charter proposed financial compensation for the families of individuals whose "disappearance" was suspected to have been engineered by the state.

For all his concessions to the military, Bouteflika did not intend to share governing duties with it or anyone else. This was partly because he was still smoldering with resentment against the men in uniform who had prevented him from taking his rightful place as successor to Boumediene following the latter's death. Almost as soon as he was elected, Bouteflika announced that he would govern the country without the Army. In July 1999, on the sidelines of Crans Montana Forum in Switzerland, he declared, "I am the representative of the Algerian people, and no institution of the Republic can take a bite out of me, even if it be the People's National Army. I am all of Algeria. I am the embodiment of the Algerian people, so tell the generals to eat me if they can."

However, Bouteflika knew he could not discount the Army entirely. His strategy was to try to curry favor with the powerful DRS and drive a wedge between it and the rest of the military. He appointed current and former DRS men to strategic positions, which allowed the security agency

30   D. GHANEM

to preserve its sphere of influence even as the role of the Army as a whole was in retreat. The appointment of Noureddine Yazid Zerhouni is a case in point. Zerhouni had been number two at the DRS for many years, back when it was called the Sécurité Militaire (SM), before becoming an ambassador in the 1980s, and he continued to exercise much sway at the organization. Bouteflika entrusted him with the Ministry of Interior in 1999. Zerhouni would remain Minister of Interior for ten years and was a Bouteflika loyalist throughout his tenure.

Bouteflika's gambit worked. His alliance with the DRS enabled him to keep the military at bay, despite its leadership's growing unease with his independent streak. Furthermore, the DRS itself proved a durable ally. In 2004, the DRS organized and backed Bouteflika's re-election, despite considerable opposition from the military's upper echelons, including Chief-of-Staff Mohamed Lamari. Bouteflika was re-elected with 84 percent of the votes. This strengthened his position further; he took advantage of the situation to ease mid-ranking officers with suspect loyalties into early retirement (he could not afford to do this with the higher-ups) and promote loyalists. Bouteflika's grip on power was secure for the next several years, and he was re-elected—again with DRS backing—in 2009, despite his candidacy for a third term having necessitated a constitutional amendment.

Cracks in Bouteflika's mutually beneficial alliance with the DRS began to appear in 2013. That year saw the In Amenas fiasco, which was the culmination of an irregular series of terrorist attacks on soft targets by jihadists, who had become active again in 2011. For almost four days, jihadists held dozens of foreigners hostage at a natural gas facility near In Amenas. A botched rescue operation by the Algerian military led to the death of thirty-seven hostages and twenty-nine jihadists (Chrisafis & Borger, 2013). Bouteflika blamed the DRS, which he had charged with overseeing the rescue effort. His ties with the DRS were already strained owing to his suspicion that it opposed his planned candidacy for a fourth presidential term and was plotting against him and his circle by pushing the judiciary to pursue cases against his clan and supporters.

Bouteflika strengthened his ties to the military's top brass, particularly Generals Athmane Tartag and Gaïd Salah, and proceeded to ease into early retirement several DRS leaders. The dismissals included General Mohamed (Toufik) Mediène's right-hand man and head of the Central Directorate for Army Security (DCSA), Major-General Mhenna Djebbar, whom Major-General Lakhdar Tirèche replaced. Djebbar was reassigned to head a DRS sub-department called the *Bureau d'organisation*. As for General Abdelmalek Guenaïzia, his position as Minister Delegate to the Ministry of National Defense now came under the oversight of the president and was changed to vice minister of defense; Guenaïzia himself was replaced by the Chief-of-Staff of the Army, General Ahmad Gaïd Salah.

General Athman "Bachir" Tartag and General Rachid "Attafi" Lallali, who headed the Department of Homeland Security (DSI) and the Directorate of Documentation and External Security (DDSE) were replaced by General Abdelhamid Bendaoud and General Mohamed Bouzit, respectively. "Tartag" reappeared in 2016 when he replaced "Toufik" Mediène, who was himself dismissed. He held this position until 2019, when he was arrested and jailed in military prison.

Despite Bouteflika's position as president, these decisions had to be approved by the Army's Supreme Council. The latter was happy to oblige, seeing such measures as a way to reduce the power of a security organ—the DRS—that had broken free of the military's grasp, as well as a means to reassert its influence over Bouteflika. When, despite his frail health, Bouteflika ran for an unprecedented fourth presidential term in 2014, the military gave him its full backing, ensuring his victory. By this time, he had lasted longer than all of his predecessors. Given the military's history of political interference and his self-crafted image as a strong civilian president who refused to kowtow to the Army, this was a supreme irony. As an army colonel said of Bouteflika in a 2021 interview:

> He would never have lasted as long as he did without the military and the DRS. The military brought him to power, and they removed him. [...] True, over the years, some divergences culminated in serious accusations from one side or another and ended up printed in national newspapers. Since his arrival, Bouteflika played a tough chess party with the military and the DRS. He scored several times but, in the end, checkmate for the military and its intelligence agency. (Author's interview, May 8, 2021)

In January 2016, Bouteflika went even further, issuing a presidential decree dismantling the DRS. This passed without significant opposition from the military. As the DRS's replacement, Bouteflika announced the creation of the Direction of the Security Services (DSS). In theory, the DSS would fall under the presidency's direct authority. However, the military was angling to control the new body from the start. Essentially, Bouteflika had come full circle. Having attained power through the

32   D. GHANEM

military, he managed for a time to limit its political role by playing it off against the DRS, only to fall back on its leadership's backing when he decided to clamp down on and then dissolve the DRS. Indeed, in replacing the DRS with the DSS, he had left the Army an opening to monitor the latter's creation and ensure that it fell firmly within its control. During Bouteflika's fourth term, the military's say in domestic affairs was stronger than ever (Ghanem, 2015).

Bouteflika Out, the Men in Uniform Win Again

According to several interviewed insiders within the politico-military establishment, the military's leadership had planned to back Bouteflika for a fifth term, despite his poor health and the fact that certain factions of the Army wanted him sidelined. As explained by a retired military officer at the time (February 2019), "In their calculus, Bouteflika was still a valid candidate who was going to be accepted by a fatigued population that would not dare to object." The opposite was true. Across the country, demonstrators—sometimes joined by emboldened opposition political figures—took to the streets in what was quickly dubbed the *Hirak*, or "movement."

The demonstrators called on the Army to intervene and for the Chief-of-Staff, General Ahmed Gaïd Salah, to call on the Constitutional Council to apply Article 102 of the constitution, declaring Bouteflika unfit for office. This spooked the Army, which feared a repeat of the mass disorder of 1988. The military leadership understood that any crackdown would undermine its credibility, national image, and internal cohesion. Exceptions aside, the security forces were instructed to respond to the protests with restraint, the better to ensure the military establishment's interests and protect its image. Protesters were allowed to vent their frustration and anger in Algiers, Constantine, Oran, and other cities. A military insider explained the decision thus: "The situation was tense. [...] Yet the choice of the majority was that things had to be done without violence, as violence would create schisms within the army." (Author's interview, February 26, 2019).

Nevertheless, the protests continued. In early April, just six weeks into the *Hirak*, the military relented, forcing Bouteflika to step down and appointing Abdelkader Bensalah, President of the Council of the Nation, the upper house of parliament, as interim president in charge of a caretaker government. A former commander of a military region explained the military's thinking in these words: "In April 2019, we had to intervene again to save the republican institutions. We did not want things to fall apart like in Libya." (Author's interview, February 18, 2021).

To signify a break with the Bouteflika era, the military proceeded to dismiss top generals, including some in the secret services, reshuffled magistrates and judges of military courts (Boufassa, 2019), and used the judiciary to remove from the ruling elite several influential yet unpopular figures who were accused of corruption (Alilat, 2019). This went some way toward placating protesters, but the Army made the mistake of upstaging Bensalah. After months of watching General Gaïd Salah deliver weekly televised speeches on the state of the country, people began to dismiss interim president Bensalah as the Army's stooge. Protesters now called for "a civilian state and not a military one." (Author's observations during protests in Algeria in 2019).

Gaïd Salah and his fellow generals quickly realized that remaining at the forefront of the political stage would exact a heavy price. Moreover, there was scant appetite among the military leadership to inherit the country's socioeconomic challenges and assume responsibility for governing in the long term. The military needed to ensure a speedy presidential election to minimize damage to its image, maintain internal stability, and keep its grip on power. On September 15, Bensalah announced that the first round of this election was set for December. Gaïd Salah and his clique chose Abdelmadjid Tebboune as their candidate. Sure enough, he was elected president in the first round. This enabled the military to withdraw backstage. As in the past, the institution retained power and influence over crucial economic and political matters; Tebboune was yet another civilian façade of a government dependent on and steered by the military.

Tebboune's election also guaranteed the military's immunity and economic interests, and secured certain influential generals' private interests. High-ranking military members have been involved in the private sector since the 1990s. They have built economic monopolies and enriched themselves and their allies. Once Tebboune and the civilian façade were in place, the military removed from its ranks certain figures of whom it had grown suspicious. The reason for this had to do with the recently concluded election. A faction of the military had broken ranks and supported the candidacy of Azzeddine Mihoubi, the acting general secretary of the Democratic National Rally (RND) and a former minister of culture under Bouteflika. Under its new chief-of-staff, Saïd Chengriha, who had replaced Gaïd Salah following the latter's sudden death, the military leadership wanted to clean house. Between May 2020 and August 2021, three of the country's leading intelligence and security units were restructured. These were the Internal Security Directorate (DGSI), the Central Directorate for Army Security (DCSA), and the Directorate-General for Documentation and External Security (DGDSE). Their heads were dismissed, and the DGSI's General Wassini Bouazza was imprisoned.

The removal of these high-ranking officers indirectly reveals the thinking animating the military leadership. In collaboration with the intelligence branch, the military's high command sought to prevent internal conflicts within the Army regarding the recent election of Tebboune and to eliminate any potential future threats against him. These high-ranking officers and their networks could have organized a coup amid a popular uprising demanding leadership change, a deteriorating economy affected by the oil crash, and the Covid-19 pandemic. Additionally, prevailing conditions on the "Algerian street" could have facilitated public support of such a move. As a preventative measure, the military used the 2019 crisis as an opportunity to coup-proof the new government and ensure that it would steer Tebboune with a single and steady hand.

Resolute Hirak, Tenacious Military

The military may have consolidated its position, but the *Hirak* showed no sign of abating. Protestors were unwilling to compromise on their desire for civilian rule. Crucially, however, the *Hirak* did not disavow the military as an institution and instead directed its criticism at the Army's ruling clique or "the generals." The *Hirak* not only took up a long-standing accusation implicating the generals in economic embezzlement that allowed for the proliferation of corruption, but also called into question their involvement in politics and, in particular, in the appointment of presidents of the Republic. Hence the *Hirak*'s flagship slogan, "*dawla madaniya machi askaria*" (Civil state, not a military one).

For a majority of Algerians, including the *Hirak*, this distinction was important. As the inheritor of the legacy of the ALN, which fought and ultimately defeated the French occupier, the Algerian Army as an institution enjoys great prestige. Additionally, ordinary Algerians have long felt that the Army is the guarantor of the country's unity and internal cohesion. The tumultuous post-Arab Spring environment seems to have reinforced such a feeling. This is why, despite the aforementioned slogan that repudiates the idea of a military state in favor of a civil alternative, the

Hirak also popularized the chant, *djich chaab, khawa khawa* (The people and Army are brothers).

Whether Tebboune could have ridden the *Hirak*'s wave and asserted control over the politically activist leadership of the military is difficult to ascertain. What is clear is that he did not show the slightest inclination to attempt such a thing. Instead, Tebboune and the Army's top brass sought to tamp down the *Hirak* without resorting to outright violence. Subtle tactics to silence dissent became the order of the day. Co-optation, blackmail, and convictions of activists meted out by a judicial system over which the government (and by extension the Army) exerts significant influence were used to weaken the *Hirak*.

At the time of writing, it was unclear how long the government would continue with such an approach, particularly if protests escalated. And escalate they well might, given that the socioeconomic consequences of the Covid-19 pandemic include increased unemployment and poverty, creating further resentment against the Algerian leadership. When the cost of tolerating mass protests exceeds that of repression, the Algerian government may decide that coercive measures are the best option. In this regard, the depletion of exchange reserves and other severe fiscal challenges take on greater significance. Algeria is experiencing a major economic crisis, meaning that it is probably only a matter of time before the government's patience for widespread demonstrations and sit-ins, which further paralyze the economy, wears thin.

Given its considerations, the military looks increasingly unlikely to oppose a decision by the government to quash the *Hirak*. It may even encourage the government to do so—and may also, if necessary, participate in the repression alongside the security services. The reasons for this are not difficult to pinpoint. Stung by the *Hirak*'s criticism and call for democratization, the military leadership has been further alarmed by the volatile security situation in Libya, Tunisia, and the Sahel, as well as the omnipresent jihadist threat.

International fallout would be minimal were the government/military to instruct the security services to move against the *Hirak*. In light of the tenuous security situation and numerous attacks by jihadists in Europe, especially France, the EU's financial and political support of the current regime is unwavering. The EU fears the outcome of an uncertain democratization process that might lead to the advent of a radical Islamist regime, a refugee crisis, and a subsequent spillover of terrorism into

Europe (Ghanem, 2019). Moreover, the Algerian military will remain Algeria's most powerful political actor.

References

Ali Yahia, A. (2007). *La dignité humaine*. Alger: INAS éditions.

Alilat, F. (2019). Algérie : Le procureur Belkacem Zeghmati, cheville ouvrière de la purge orchestrée par Gaïd Salah?. *Jeune Afrique*. July 12. https://www.jeuneafrique.com/mag/799297/societe/algerie-le-procureur-belkacem-zeghmati-cheville-ouvriere-de-la-purge-orchestree-par-gaid-salah/. Accessed January 24, 2022.

Alilat, F. (2021). Algérie: Comment le pouvoir tente d'étouffer le Hirak?. *Jeune Afrique*. May 28. https://www.jeuneafrique.com/1179607/politique/algerie-comment-le-pouvoir-tente-detouffer-le-hirak/. Accessed January 24, 2022.

Archives videos. (1999). Bouteflika au Forum de Crans Montana. *Youtube*. https://youtu.be/_BlBRjvmG1Y

Barik, A. (1996). L'Algérie et les droits humains dans les camps d'internement. *Le Monde diplomatique* (archives). March. http://www.monde-diplomatique.fr/1996/03/BARIK/2460. Accessed January 24, 2022.

Benchikh, M. (1992). Obstacles to the Democratization Process in Algeria. *Revue Des Mondes Musulmans Et De La Méditerranée.*, *65*, 106–115.

Boufassa, L. (2019). Des juridictions clés, dont Blida, Constantine et Oran concernées par le mouvement dans les tribunaux militaires. *Le Courrier d'Algérie*. September 19. http://lecourrier-dalgerie.com/des-juridictions-cles-dont-blida-constantine-et-oran-concernees-mouvement-dans-les-tribun aux-militaires/. Accessed January 24, 2022.

Chrisafis, A, Borger, J. (2013). Algeria Hostage Crisis: The Full Story of the Kidnapping in the Desert. *The Guardian*. January 25. https://www.theguardian.com/world/2013/jan/25/in-amenas-timeline-siege-algeria. Accessed January 24, 2022.

Cubertafond, B. (1999). *L'Algérie contemporaine*. Presses Universitaires de France.

Ghanem, D. (2014). The Devoted Guardians of Algeria's Power. *Sada: Carnegie Endowment for International Peace*, April 16. https://carnegieendowment.org/sada/55359

Ghanem, D. (2015). Despite Shake-Ups, Algeria's Security Apparatus Stronger than Ever. *World Politics Review*. September 17, 2015. https://www.worldpoliticsreview.com/articles/16714/despite-shake-ups-algeria-s-security-appara tus-stronger-than-ever. Accessed January 26, 2022.

Ghanem, D. (2018). Algeria's Peace Process: Spoilers, Failures, and Successes. *POMEPS* Studies 30. The politics of post-conflict resolution.

September 18. https://pomeps.org/algerias-peace-process-spoilers-failures-and-successes#_ednref19. Accessed January 24, 2022.

Ghanem, D. (2019). *Algeria: The EU's Real Partner or a "Tough Suburb of a Prosperous EU Metropolis"?, in Adel Abdel Ghafar*. Prospects and Challenges. Brookings Institution Press.

Harbi, M. (1992). *L'Algérie et son destin, Croyants ou citoyens ?*. Paris: éditions Arcantère.

Haroun, A. (2000). *L'été de la discorde. Algérie 1962*. Alger: Casbah éditions.

Haroun, A. (2005). *Algérie 1962: La grande dérive*. L'Harmattan.

Kapil, A. (1990). Algeria's Elections Show Islamist Strength. *Middle East Report.*, *166*, 31–36.

Le Monde Diplomatique (1995). La Plate-forme de Rome. *Le Monde Diplomatique* (archives). March. https://www.monde-diplomatique.fr/1995/03/A/6228. Accessed January 24, 2022.

Le Monde Diplomatique. (1965). Houari Boumédiène. Proclamation du conseil de la révolution du 19 juin 1965. *Le Monde Diplomatique* (Archives). October. https://www.monde-diplomatique.fr/1965/10/BOUMEDIENE/26873. Accessed January 24, 2022.

Le Monde Diplomatique. (1986). La riposte à la crise est l'affaire de tous. *Le Monde Diplomatique* (archives). November. https://www.monde-diplomatique.fr/1986/11/A/39636. Accessed January 24, 2022.

Leca, J., & Vatin, J. C. (1975). *L'Algérie politique. Institutions et régime*. Presses de la Fondation Nationale des Sciences Politiques.

Marchés tropicaux et méditerranéens (1995). April 21. No 2580.

Martinez, L. (1997). Les enjeux des négociations entre l'AIS et l'armée. *Politique Étrangère.*, *4*, 499–510.

Mohand Amer, A. (2014a). Les wilayas dans la crise du FLN de l'été 1962. *Insaniyat* (65): 105–124. http://journals.openedition.org/insaniyat/14796. Accessed January 24, 2022.

Mohand-Amer, A. (2014b). *Les crises du FLN, 1954–1954. L'Algérie d'aujourd'hui entre poids du passé et exigences de l'avenir*. Paris: Bouchène.

Ouaissa. R (2010). *La classe-État algérienne. 1962–2000. Une histoire du pouvoir algérien entre sous-développement, rente pétrolière et terrorisme*. Paris: Publisud.

Rarrbo, K. (1995). *L'Algérie et sa jeunesse. Marginalisation sociale et désarroi culturel*. L'Harmattan.

Roberts, H. (1994). Algeria Between Eradicators and Conciliators. *Middle East Report.*, *189*, 24–27.

Rouadjia, A. (1995). Du nationalisme du FLN à l'islamisme du FIS. *Les temps modernes*(580): 115–136.

Skocpol, T. (1979). State and revolution: Old Regimes and Revolutionary Crises in France, Russia, and China. *Theory and Society.*, *7*(1), 7–95.

Stora, B. (2001). *La guerre invisible. Algérie, années 90*. Paris: Presses de Sciences Po.

Stora, B. (2006). *Histoire de l'Algérie depuis l'indépendance*. La Découverte.

Tuquoi, J. P. (1999). Une fraction de l'armée algérienne soutient Abdelaziz Bouteflika. *Le Monde*. February 18. https://www.lemonde.fr/archives/art icle/1999/02/18/une-fraction-de-l-armee-algerienne-soutient-abdelaziz-bouteflika_3537902_1819218.html. Accessed January 24, 2022.

Viratelle, G. (1969). Cent quatre-vingts Algériens sont jugés pour leur participation à la rébellion de décembre 1967. *Le Monde* (archives). July 11. https://www.lemonde.fr/archives/article/1969/07/11/cent-quatre-vingts-algeri ens-sont-juges-pour-leur-participation-a-la-rebellion-de-decembre-1967_2411 560_1819218.html. Accessed January 24, 2022.

Yefash, A. (1982). *Le Processus de légitimation du pouvoir militaire et la construction de l'État en Algérie*. Éditions Anthropos.

Yefsah, A. (1990). *La question du pouvoir en Algérie*. Alger: ENAP.

Yefsah, A. (1992). L'armée et le pouvoir en Algérie de 1962 à 1992. *Revue Des Mondes Musulmans Et De La Méditerranée.*, 65, 77–95.

Zbiri, T. (2012). *Un demi-siècle de combat. Mémoires d'un chef d'état-major algérien*. Alger: éditions Echourouk.

Zoubir, Y. (1993). The Painful Transition From Authoritarianism in Algeria. *Arab Studies Quarterly.*, 15(3), 82–115.

CHAPTER 3

Hyperpluralism and Co-Optation: The Secrets Behind Turning the Opposition into a Pillar of the Regime

In 1989, the Algerian regime scrapped the single-party political system in place since independence. This move enabled the emergence of political opposition and competition between parties. Yet such democratization proved to be largely surface deep. Today, the Algerian regime is characterized by what is variously known as "electoral authoritarianism" (Schedler, 2006) and "competitive authoritarianism" (Levitsky & Way, 2002). It is a hybrid regime, one that mixes elements of democracy and authoritarianism. In countries governed by such hybrid regimes, even if opposition parties avail themselves of democratic mechanisms and participate in elections, the playing field is severely tilted in favor of state loyalists, whether incumbents or challengers. As a result, competition exists but is unfair. In the Algerian case, the regime's allowance of multiparty elections enables it to project an image of openness to the world even as it vitiates electoral representation by co-opting independent political actors.

THE 1989 OPENING
AND THE "PARTIFICATION OF POLITICS"

The country's *glasnost* in 1989 and its subsequent experience with party politics must be understood in the context of the regime's increasing loss of legitimacy and the stratagems it used to preserve power. The end of the

© The Author(s), under exclusive license to Springer Nature   39
Switzerland AG 2022
D. Ghanem, *Understanding the Persistence of Competitive Authoritarianism in Algeria*, Middle East Today,
https://doi.org/10.1007/978-3-031-05102-9_3

40 D. GHANEM

FLN's monopoly on political representation did little to transform Algeria's political system; the party had long served as a façade for the real power structure, the military. The introduction of pluralism replaced a monolithic façade with a pluralistic one, but this did not result in a significant change in the form of government (Roberts, 1999: 386). Rather than representing specific segments of society, several Algerian parties cater to the state's various factions, which retain control over their activities. Elections, rather than serving as a forum for political competition, are viewed by the regime as a means of legitimizing and re-legitimizing itself, a democratic alibi that comes in handy when it is accused of authoritarianism. The regime views political parties that are ostensibly opposed to it not as rivals, but rather as potential partners whom it might coerce into presenting Algeria to the world as a democracy. In this context, the outcomes of elections reflect the battles taking place at the heart of the state, more than in the public sphere (Addi, 2002).

The techniques employed by the state to regulate parties' capacity, including their practice of tampering with the ballot box during elections, have actively contributed to the general public's loss of confidence in their ability to perform their functions effectively. In the eyes of many Algerians, political parties are everything but instruments for articulating their political choices. As a result, there is widespread skepticism and cynicism about the electoral process and, consequently, about political parties. The parties' inability to compete has rendered them particularly vulnerable to manipulation by the government. This has to do with the state's rentier character. The opaque public financing distribution system incentivizes parties to connect with the government rather than their electoral bases. Paradoxically, by hindering the political parties' ability to establish social roots, the state undermines the exact function that it gave these parties in the first place: maintaining their legitimacy.

A large number of parties causes the party system to fragment, with multiple parties creating confusion over which cleavages that shape the political spectrum are real. Several narrowly focused issue-based parties spring up and seem to operate without relying on any specific segment of society, adding to political parties' inability to form strong bonds with social groupings (Huntington, 1968). Hyperpluralism, or the process of "partification of politics" (Arato, 1994), leads to the demobilization of an increasingly apathetic or cynical general public. This is what has happened since Algeria's political opening in 1989. Hyperpluralism has emerged as a distinguishing feature of the country's political culture and institutions, and the regime has co-opted parties across the spectrum.

The regime's strategy notwithstanding, ostensibly independent politicians and parties are responsible for allowing themselves to be co-opted. These new actors on the political scene adapted to the implicit rules of the game introduced by the regime in 1989. Faced with the grim reality that pursuing an independent line would consign them to the political wilderness, they chose to sacrifice much of their autonomy in return for relevance. In co-opting disparate political parties, most of which are led by coastal elites, the regime has succeeded in fostering a cohesive political class out of people with outwardly differing agendas. This class is dependent on the regime for its (limited) power and understandably resistant to attempts by independent-minded political parties to broaden their support base at its expense. Indeed, to forestall any sort of electoral breakthrough from anti-establishment parties, the political class operates extensive patronage networks that secure ordinary citizens' loyalty. These networks can obtain jobs for their supporters and discounted housing and land allocation. By facilitating all this, the regime cements its relationship with a political class to which it has subcontracted the task of securing ordinary Algerians' quiescence.

With the regime's backing, the Algerian political class has repeatedly thwarted the ambitions of anti-establishment parties, most of which lack the means to operate extensive patronage networks and are therefore able to rely on no more than a small group of core supporters. That said, these anti-establishment parties deserve criticism for their failure to establish a coalition that, through a united front, might present a credible challenge to the reigning political class and the regime propping it up (Ait-Hamadouche & Zoubir, 2009). As a result, there is little incentive for the political class, much less the regime, to open the political arena and allow for a genuine and fair opposition. On the contrary, the Algerian political class will continue to serve as the regime's pillar.

The Main Opposition Parties

A plethora of opposition parties characterize the Algerian political landscape. The most important have branches in several regions, regularly win seats in parliamentary elections, and are featured in the state-controlled media. The potential resistance of the opposition is enclosed and neutralized by incorporating it into an organized forum where the opposition may raise its voice and concerns while also giving the regime credibility (Gandhi, 2008: 181). From the regime's perspective, opposition actors in parliament allow the ruling elite to co-opt potential opposition forces and make policy concessions that benefit the regime's clientele and large segments of society, thereby reducing the sources of popular discontent and social protest.

The irony is that these nationwide and seemingly politically successful opposition parties are beholden to the regime. Indeed, the latter has co-opted them. Co-optation takes several forms and depends largely on the resources available to the regime, which is keen to continue controlling established parties and neutralizing up-and-coming ones from the start. A good metric to measure the co-optation of opposition parties is the number of ministerial portfolios and seats in the People's National Assembly (APN), the Algerian lower house of parliament, that they obtain in each election, all of which are rigged (Roberts, 1998). An overview of Algeria's main "opposition" parties is useful to understand this phenomenon.

The Rally for Culture and Democracy (RCD), founded by Saïd Saadi in 1989, is one of the largest opposition parties. The RCD has branches across Algeria but is particularly strong in the Berber-dominated districts of Algiers and the Berber hinterland of Kabylia. The party is staunchly secular and maintains that Algerian society needs radical change through an overhaul of educational programs it claims are dominated by Islamist ideas and conservative narratives. In 1992, with Islamist parties on the verge of winning a majority in the country's parliamentary elections, Saadi called on the army to intervene and scupper the elections to "protect democracy." (This is what ended up happening—though not because Saadi had any influence on the military). The RCD continued to court the army and backed the government's all-security approach in the 1990s. It was rewarded with 19 seats in the 1997 parliamentary elections. The party boycotted elections in 2002 to distance itself from the government's heavy-handed management of the crisis in Kabylia during the 2001 riots. In 2007, it obtained 19 seats. In 2012, the RCD boycotted the elections; the reason was a suspicion on its part that the regime would use fraud to reduce its number of seats, but defections of important figures had weakened the party, and this may have played a more significant role, as it was afraid to lose legitimately by losing seats to the other Berberist party, the Socialist Forces Front (FFS). The RCD won nine seats in 2017. The party boycotted the controversial legislative election of June 2021, accusing the regime of "being unable to open a serious dialogue to achieve a real democratic transition" (Algeria-Watch, 2021).

The Workers' Party (PT) is Algeria's largest leftist party. Trotskyist in orientation, and long led by Louisa Hanoune, the PT opposes any reforms that might liberalize Algeria's state-managed economy. The party advocates strengthening the public sector to better cater to people's needs. The PT has consistently declined to accept ministerial portfolios various governments have offered. However, as of 1997, the party has fielded candidates in parliamentary elections. The PT won four seats in 1997, 21 in 2002, 26 in 2007, 24 in 2012, and 11 in 2017. In June 2021, the PT boycotted the legislative elections, describing them as a "masquerade" and a "circus" (Amir, 2021a).

The FFS, founded in 1963 by Hocine Aït Ahmed, is another major opposition party. Aït Ahmed had played a leading role in the FLN but broke with the latter after it established a one-party political system when Algeria gained independence in 1962. Like the RCD, the FFS draws support from the Berbers of Kabylia and Algiers. In 1989, with the confrontation between the army and Islamists already looming, the FFS memorably held demonstrations in which its members called for an Algeria that was "neither a police state nor a fundamentalist one." In the 1991 parliamentary elections, the FFS attempted to bring under its wing all parties that opposed the Islamic Salvation Front (FIS). The FFS firmly condemned the army's scuppering of elections in 1992 and called on it to cease intervening in politics. The FFS held two ministerial portfolios, one in trade and one as Delegate Ministry of Universities, in 1987 and 1989, respectively. It obtained 20, 20, 28, and 14 seats in the parliament in 1997, 2002, 2012, and 2017, respectively. The FFS joined the RCD and the PT in boycotting the 2021 elections, claiming that "the party refuses to act as a 'stepping stone' for the 'masquerade' of the regime" (Amir, 2021b).

The Movement for Society and Peace (MSP) was created in 1989 by Mahfud Nahnah and initially operated under the name Hamas. The MSP was supposed to serve as the Muslim Brotherhood's Algerian branch and had the establishment of an Islamic state as its goal. However, after what happened to the FIS, the MSP concluded that to avoid the same fate, it would have to forswear its revolutionary approach and instead engage the regime in dialogue. To that end, the party declared its opposition to the Islamist insurgency and backed the establishment of the National Transitional Council, which exercised legislative functions in the absence of an elected parliament. The MSP even took part in the 1995 presidential elections. In 1999, the party rallied behind Abdelaziz Bouteflika, the army-backed candidate who went on to become president that year, and supported his reconciliation policy. Over time, the MSP has clinched several parliamentary seats and wielded ministerial portfolios, most significantly the Ministry of Industry and the Ministry of Public Works. During the 2021 legislative elections, the MSP participated and obtained 64 seats, yet it decided not to be part of the government. The reason cited by the MSP leader, Abderrazak Makri, was that the party "wants to be in power and not a facade of power" (Amir, 2021c).

During the 2019 political crisis, the putative opposition was unable to generate support among the masses of ordinary citizens who had taken to the streets. After trying unsuccessfully for weeks to curry favor with the demonstrators and ending up denounced as *chiyatin* [sycophants] and kicked out of every weekly protest, leading figures of all four parties avoided such gatherings altogether. In what amounted to a candid admission of its unpopularity, the RCD went so far as to suggest a roadmap for a democratic transition that would replace all political parties' candidates, including their own, with civil society figures, technocrats, academics, and constitutional experts.

The negative popular reaction to the traditional opposition parties' attempt to ride the wave of protests stemmed in part from their history of servility to the regime. However, it also had to do with their behavior at a critical moment. The parties' inability to forge a coalition that might pose a challenge to the regime meant that even among people who were in theory open to such parties playing a role alongside the protesters in opposing the regime, few saw them as a viable means to press the uprising's demands. Some political parties did see an opportunity to peel themselves away from the regime and consequently entered into alliances with one another, but these were dictated by old ideological cleavages and, as such, a far cry from the broad-based opposition coalition that so many people seemed to want. Divisions that amounted to little when these parties were all beholden to the regime resurfaced as soon as they began to experiment with the possibility of mounting a robust opposition.

For instance, several progressive parties joined forces to create the Parties of the Democratic Alternative (PAD). However, the PAD coalition was weakened by internal disagreement regarding the role of Islamist parties and the refusal of staunchly secular parties to engage with them (Ait Ouarabai, 2019). Meanwhile, conservative parties MSP, Ennahda, El

Bina, FJD (*El Adala*), *El Fadjr El Jadid* [The New Dawn], *Talaie El Hourriyet* [The Vanguard of Freedoms], and the National Party for Solidarity and Development (PNSD) joined forces in 2019 and signed the Aïn Benian platform, calling themselves the "Forces of Change for the Triumph of the People's Choice." Yet despite having excluded progressives, they proved unable to find common ground. A few weeks afterward, the coalition broke up and was excluded from the regime-backed "Panel of Dialogue and Mediation," led by Karim Younes (Moula, 2019).

Scrambling to stave off marginalization at the hands of the regime and aware that they had little support among the protesters, a clutch of opportunistic parties within the now all-but-dead "Forces of Change for the Triumph of the People's Choice" made a final, desperate move. *Talaie El Hourriyet, El Bina,* and Future Front announced their willingness to field candidates in the presidential election of December 12, 2019, even though the regime had refused to meet the Ain Benian platform's condition for its signatories to participate: the release of prisoners of conscience and the establishment of a genuinely independent body for the organization and control of elections.

As for civil society organizations, their attempts—led by the Coordination of Autonomous Trade Unions—to coordinate and join forces with political figures (Karim Tabbou, Abdelaziz Rahabi, Mustapha Bouchachi) and parties (FLN, RND, MPA, MSP, FJD) did not have the expected success. They managed to bring together progressive and conservative actors for a consultation held on August 24, 2019. However, nothing came of this, and the expected coalition was stillborn.

THE LEGISLATURE: THE BEST MEANS TO NEUTRALIZE OPPOSITION

Although the regime has, for obvious reasons, traditionally focused on co-opting the major opposition parties, it has not disregarded the smaller ones. On the contrary, when resources were available, the regime used them to absorb into its orbit parties that posed no significant challenge. Such was the case in 2014, during Bouteflika's fourth term in office (2014–2019). At the time, the regime had a comfortable financial cushion, with $178bn in foreign reserves and $37bn in its sovereign wealth fund. These resources were used to co-opt no fewer than 30 parties, which then supported the ailing president's bid for a fourth term (AFP, 2014). The reward was not the same for everyone. While many parties were rewarded with positions in the administration and promised parliamentary seats, two major parties, the FFS and the PT, were offered ministerial positions. This was meant to deter challenges to the regime's rule, and has generally proven effective. Parties do not obstruct the regime and even advocate on its behalf in exchange for such positions and other privileges such as direct economic benefits. For opposition parties, career opportunities and resources are the best deal they can obtain, as no one can offer better patronage deals than the regime.

While the regime is tempted to let opposition parties gain legitimacy through the ballot box, it is also interested in having a docile and malleable parliament, which explains regular fraud and ballot-stuffing. Without such measures, the regime could end up facing a scenario similar to that of 1990–1991. On that occasion, the regime let the ballots choose and consequently had to deal with the impending victory of the FIS, a radical Islamist party. The FIS performed very well in the municipal elections of 1990 and then in the first round of the parliamentary elections of 1991. The second round of parliamentary elections, supposed to occur in January 1992, never took place because the regime could not take the risk of integrating into its system an independent party such as the FIS, all the more so given the latter's radical Islamist orientation. As envisaged by the regime, the parties' role was to stabilize and strengthen the system by endowing it with electoral legitimacy. The FIS would never have done this, as its goal was to remake the country in its image. In refusing to play the regime's game, the FIS would have exposed the military as the major power behind the scenes.

As it happened, the army ended up exposing itself by halting the elections, banning the FIS, and jailing thousands of its members and sympathizers in camps in the Sahara Desert. A civil war ensued, from which the army emerged victorious and in even firmer control of the country. Today, as then, the military-backed regime is unwilling to integrate into the political system autonomous political parties. The parties are still meant to strengthen the system and not challenge it. To be part of the game, they have to accept the rules that the FIS refused to play by.

Following the FIS debacle, the regime determined that it needed to control parliament as tightly as possible. This meant determining which parties were granted a seat at the parliamentary table. The Algerian parliament, newly opened up to the newly legalized multiplicity of parties, became part of the larger authoritarian structure of the state, and has remained so. For the Algerian regime, control of the legislature is critical.

It enhances the executive branch's capacity to manipulate parliament. For example, when Bouteflika called on parliament to modify the constitution and eliminate presidential term limits, it did just that. Today, MPs have no say in colossal military expenditures and other budgetary matters, cannot conduct high-profile investigations into government abuse, and cannot even ensure a modicum of accountability for high-ranking government officials. While it is true that MPs ask questions, most of the time, these questions remain unanswered. In 2017, for instance, according to a local media, deputies asked 8,888 questions to representatives and members of the government and received only 449 responses (El Watan, 2017).

As a result, winning seats in parliamentary elections has come to mean co-optation at the hands of the regime. Opposition parties are the regime's democratic fig leaf (Addi, 2006). The results of parliamentary (and municipal) elections tell us much about where things stand at any given moment. In 1997, at the height of the civil war, the regime decided to resume the electoral process that it had suspended in 1992 and demonstrate that Algerian democracy had not collapsed in the face of the Islamist threat. Parliamentary elections were scheduled for June 5. As always, the regime—the titular head of which was President Liamine Zeroual, who was elected two years earlier in 1995 and continued to enjoy the army's backing—wanted to restore public trust in the state. This mission would fail were the FLN to emerge triumphant in the elections. The FLN, after all, was the symbol of what many Algerians termed the Years of Lead; it embodied authoritarianism, mismanagement, and corruption. The FLN was the object of demonstrators' wrath in 1988 and the big loser against the FIS in the first pluralist elections in 1990–1991. In a somewhat rich turn of events, the FLN was now depicting itself as an opposition party. Nevertheless, the regime wanted, as always, a docile parliament, meaning that free and fair elections were out of the question.

Four months before the legislative elections, the regime established a new political party to cut this Gordian knot. This is how the National Rally for Democracy (RND) was born (Djerbal, 1997). To ensure a smooth voting process amid a civil war, 300,000 troops were deployed throughout the country. A smooth process, of course, does not mean an honest one. Though it was not saddled with the FLN's historical baggage, the RND did not prove especially popular, and fraud was needed to secure the sort of outcome the regime wanted. The RND won 156 seats out of 380, the biggest share of any political party.

In second place was the MSP (Hamas). With 2,907,857 votes, the MSP came close to the 3,260,222 votes won by the FIS in the first round of the 1991 legislative elections and won 69 seats. The regime had quite strategically allowed a co-opted Islamist party to win nearly as many seats as the FIS was on the verge of winning back in 1992. In return, the MSP undertook to support the regime's planned Civil Concorde Law, an extension of the Clemency Law initiated by Zeroual in 1995. The civil Concorde Law was voted in 1999 under Bouteflika and turned under his auspice to a full amnesty voted in a 2005 referendum. The Law was called the Charter for Peace and National Reconciliation.

In third place was the FLN, with 64 seats. The FFS got 20 seats, the RCD 19, and the PT four. Interestingly, the FLN, FFS, and PT had decided to participate in the elections despite having committed to the St. Egidio platform, which was fully rejected by the regime and for which the regime answered by putting in place the Clemency Law the same year the St. Egidio took place. Their about-face may have indicated a lack of integrity, but the rationale behind it was logical enough. Boycotting the elections would almost surely have increased their popularity but would have decreased their power and influence. Limited representation, even in a game whose results are fixed, was in their eyes the best outcome. This was especially true of the FLN, which became part of a coalition government that included the RND and MSP.

Regime-sponsored parties once again monopolized effective political representation, except now there were two of each: the Arab/nationalist family with the FLN and its twin, the RND; the Islamists with the MSP and Ennahda; and the Berberists with the RCD and the FFS. This cloning maximized the regime's room for maneuvering and its ability to play off the parties against one another. This is not unique to the 1997 elections; throughout the years, the state has supported clone parties for every polit- ical cleavage (Islamist, Berberist, nationalist, etc.) in an attempt to weaken each party's particular appeal. Since the dissolution of the FIS in 1992, the state has consistently supported more than one party appealing to the Islamist voters, or at least its more moderate components, such as Hamas, Ennahda, and Islah. When it came to Berberists/secularists, the founding of the RCD in 1989 and the support it gained from Chadli Bendjedid's circles at the time was purposefully intended at challenging the FFS's hold on the electorate. Similarly, the establishment of the RND on the eve of the 1997 election contributed to eroding the FLN's monopoly on representation of the Arab/nationalist family.

This hyperpluralism contributed to the parties' weakness, which in turn damaged the broader institutionalization of the party system due to their inability to establish solid class bases, and create weak links with social groups. Hyperpluralism can also explain these parties' tendency to engage in highly dogmatic debates rather than focus on concrete policy issues such as the economy to mobilize the electorate (Liverani, 2008: 102).

The parliament configuration changed five years later, in 2002. This allows us to track changes in the balance of power and distinguish between actors on good terms with the regime and those marginalized due to their refusal to play the game (Hachemaoui, 2003: 42). On May 30, 2002, the parliamentary elections took place in a charged political atmosphere. The death of Massinissa Guermah, an 18-year-old high school student, killed while in police custody on April 18, 2001, provoked protests in the Berber regions. It was the beginning of what came to be called the "Black Spring." Riots spread across Kabylia and quickly became lethal, with 126 people killed. Government buildings and political parties' offices were burnt to the ground. President Bouteflika's promise to set up an independent commission to investigate the killings of civilians did not assuage protesters. It was in this fraught situation that legislative elections took place.

The RND's reputation had been weakened due to massive fraud in the 1997 elections and internal disputes that were making the headlines. Also, several RND mayors were indicted for corruption and mismanagement. As such, the regime no longer viewed the RND as a useful tool to manage the population and decided to rearrange the parliamentary chessboard's pawns. Sure enough, the RND lost its position as the largest parliamentary bloc, going from 156 seats to 47, which placed it third overall. The FLN, now back in favor, staged a massive comeback, winning 199 seats, as against 64 in 1997. This meant that, thirteen years after the FLN lost its position as the country's sole legal political party, it improbably succeeded in becoming the most popular party and won a majority of seats in parliament. As though that were not enough, it registered big gains in the municipal elections in October of the same year.

For the FLN to make its way back into the regime's good graces, it was not sufficient for the RND, its erstwhile replacement, to have failed to resonate with the people. The regime pressured the FLN itself to institute changes. Under a new secretary-general, Ali Benflis, who took the helm in 2001, the party improved its national image. Benflis replaced the old guard with more educated and younger party members, including women, and fashioned a more modern discourse that targeted youth. While in 1997, 11% of MPs had belonged to the generation born after independence, in 2002, this number reached 25%. The rejuvenation of the parliament, which was in its majority FLN, was orchestrated by party leaders (Werenfels, 2007: 69).

In return, the regime ensured the party's rehabilitation and electoral triumph. As before, patronage and vote-buying were used to secure an overwhelming victory. Indeed, ultimately, it was the regime, not ordinary party members, that decided who would make the FLN slate, and it helped for prospective candidates' credentials to include relationships with important regime figures (army generals, minsters). However, even then, the prospective candidate had to convince the regime that he could serve as an effective mediator between it and the people and convince the latter that they would benefit from generous handouts, subsidies, and other social benefits (i.e., housing and land allocation) (Hachemaoui, 2013: 151–153).

After supporting successive governments, the FFS and the RCD lost their credibility and constituencies to a leaderless movement called the *Aârush*. The *Aârush* was born during the Kabylia crisis and claimed to speak on behalf of all Berber hinterland inhabitants. The very existence of the *Aârush* deepened the fragmentation of both the FFS and the RCD. To save what was left of their regional and national image, the RCD left the government it had joined in 1999. The party had been co-opted, in part, through three ministerial positions: the Ministry of Health and the Ministry of Public Works, both held by Amara Benyounes, and the Ministry of Transport, headed by Hamid Lounaouci. The RCD removed its two ministers from the government to avoid endorsing the latter's policies and the security forces' violence. The FFS, for its part, criticized the authorities for their management of the crisis but did not endorse the *Aârush*. The FFS suspected the *Aârush* of being the work of the security services themselves—in order to thwart the FFS presence in Kabylia, its traditional bastion. Nevertheless, this episode seriously eroded the FFS and RCD electoral and activist bases. The spectacular decline of the RND–which in five years, went from 109 seats to have only 47 representatives in parliament out of 389, provides a good example of how the regime protects, abandons, rewards, or punishes its party clients.

The distribution of seats in parliament changed again with the elections of 2007. The context was challenging, with a new round of suicide attacks perpetrated by armed Islamist groups against the security forces and a spectacular return to bombings in Algiers. Additionally, several financial scandals had tarnished the government's image. The El-Khalifa scandal was the most notorious of these, which caused an estimated $2.5 bn in losses and dramatically undercut Algerians' confidence in their rulers and representatives (Hachemaoui, 2007). The latter had grown greedy and begun to act with impunity due to the country's comfortable financial cushion; thanks to the high oil prices, Algeria had accumulated $110bn in foreign exchange reserves.

To many observers, the results of the elections were predictable: a low turnout (35.67%) and a solid performance on the part of the regime's three biggest pawns, the FLN, RND, and MSP. A revamped FLN (Benflis and his supporters were purged) won 136 seats, the RND 62, and the MSP 52. Opposition parties showed little to no concern about the possibility of the regime rigging the elections. Even the fact that the Commission for the Preparation of Elections was chaired by Abdelaziz Belkhadem, head of the government and the FLN general secretary, generated little criticism.

The FFS boycotted the elections, while the RCD, which had boycotted them in 2002, presented candidates in all constituencies and even declared that it was amenable to the idea of participating in government. It should be said that several leaders of the *Aârush*, which spearheaded the "Black Spring" protests in Kabylia, ran for parliament on the RCD's lists. This was surprising. After having served as the voice of disfranchised youth who trusted neither the FFS nor the RCD, these *Aârush* leaders had allowed themselves to be co-opted by the regime. The RCD was rewarded with 19 seats.

The elections of 2012 took place during a tumultuous time marked by the Arab Spring. The regime, which sought to forestall an uprising in Algeria, wanted mass participation in the elections to (re)legitimize itself and did not hesitate to engage in scaremongering to steer people away from protest and toward the ballot box (Ait-Hamadouche, 2012). For example, the FLN and the RND used the term "riots" in a calculated effort to depoliticize the uprisings and depict them as a negative phenomenon. The regime was particularly anxious about the possibility that Algerians' exasperation with the country's leadership, much of it fueled by unprecedented media coverage of corruption among the president's coterie, would manifest itself on the streets. Already, demonstrations had taken place. The regime deployed its economic arsenal to buy social peace, offering generous handouts and encouraging people to make their views known through the ballot box.

Ultimately, the participation rate was low, standing at just under 43 percent, but the FLN and the RND were rewarded for parroting the regime line on the uprisings and maintaining that the ballot box was where change could be achieved (Tlemçani, 2012). The FLN won 221 seats out of 462, followed by the RND with 70 seats. The MSP, which was emboldened by the Arab Spring and concomitant Islamist resurgence, decided that it wanted to be more than simply a regime-beholden Islamist party and joined fellow Islamist parties Ennahda and the MRN to create the Green Algeria Alliance (AAV). They overplayed their hand, as the regime did not feel sufficiently threatened to allow them a greater share of the pie. The AAV succeeded in securing only 47 seats, even fewer than what the MSP achieved alone in 2007, when it won 52 seats. The FFS, which had boycotted elections in 2002 and 2007, participated following the government's promise to allow Western observers to oversee the voting process and give the next parliament an important role in rewriting the constitution. It was rewarded with 26 seats. This, together with the RCD boycott, allowed the FFS to position itself as the main representative of Kabylia. The PT followed the FFS with 24 seats.

The elections were notable for the participation of newly licensed parties. The Algerian Popular Movement (MPA) and the Rally for Hope for Algeria (TAJ) were two such parties. Former RCD vice-president Amara Benyounes created the MPA in 2012. Benyounes, who, as mentioned, had held ministerial portfolios during his time with the RCD, broke with the party in 2001 following infighting with its leader, Saïd Saadi, and became a critic of Bouteflika. He then turned around and supported Bouteflika's candidacy for a second term (2004–2009) and, later, his candidacy for a fourth term (2014–2019). It is not difficult to divine what accounts for the flip-flopping. After years of waiting to obtain the necessary permits to create a new party, Benyounes got what he wanted in the run-up to the 2012 elections. Despite the newness of this party and its lack of a social base, the MPA obtained six seats in parliament, and Benyounes became Minister of Regional Planning, Environment, and the City (Dris, 2018).

The other newcomer and winner was TAJ, established by Amar Ghoul, formerly a high-ranking member of the MSP, in 2012. Essentially, when the MSP grew emboldened by the Arab Spring and adopted a more independent line, the regime sought to pry away some of its leaders. Ghoul was granted a license for a proposed party in 2012. The Rally for Hope for Algeria (TAJ) was born. Ghoul held several ministerial portfolios: Public Works in 2012–2013, Transportation in 2013–2015, and Regional Planning, Tourism, and Handicrafts in 2015–2016. Moreover, he succeeded in convincing MSP and FNA freshly elected MPs in the 2012 election to join him right after the election. They had been elected as MSP and FNA candidates but subsequently proclaimed their allegiance to TAJ.

The 2017 elections saw more pluralism without diversity. The participation rate barely reached 35% (similar to 2007). The FLN won 161 seats, some 60 fewer than the previous elections. This may have had to do with the regime wanting to punish the party for an internal crisis caused by corruption charges against some of its deputies. The RND was allowed to win 100 seats to adjust the power balance further. The MSP came in third position with only 34 seats, as the regime no longer felt the need to trot the party out as proof it was not repressing moderate Islamists. TAJ participated for the first time in the legislative elections, winning 20 seats in parliament—and later 31 municipalities in the local elections of the same year.

Besides TAJ, other parties that functioned as clients or stooges of the regime registered gains (Dris, 2018). The Future Front (Front El Mustakbal), founded in 2012 by Abdelaziz Belaïd, a former FLN stalwart, won 14 seats, as against two in 2012. Similarly, the MPA won 13 seats in 2017, as against 7 in 2012. The MPA, TAJ, and the Future Front are examples of co-opted parties that were offered benefits in exchange for following the regime's line, mobilizing support for it, and helping it cover its authoritarianism and occupation with a democratic veneer. Unsurprisingly, the three did well in municipal elections and went on to support Bouteflika for a fifth term as president (Hamdi, 2019).

With all this in mind, it is safe to say that elections are the means by which the regime (re)legitimizes itself. There is no alternation of political power through elections; rather, the regime manipulates elections to strengthen itself while posing as democratic. The regime sees political parties, including the opposition, as auxiliaries through which it can ensure the appearance of representation even as it maintains the reality of repression. Within this controlled political arena, opposition parties are integrated into the machinery of an authoritarian system. They are, in theory, committed to democratizing, but are rewarded or punished based on their loyalty to a regime they are meant to oppose.

The Islamists and the Art of Co-Optation

The case of the Islamists is particularly enlightening. As part of the regime's strategy to buy itself new popularity and legitimacy as an open, inclusive regime, not only did it allow the Islamists to participate in the political game, but it also encouraged some—Ennahda and Hamas—to do so. This move contributed to the beginning of a deep fragmentation between those who refused any cooperation with the regime and those willing to negotiate.

The case of Ennahda is particularly instructive. Established in 1989, Ennahda witnessed a terrible split in 1995 because of infighting between two of its leaders: on the one side, there was Lahbib Adami, who called for dialogue with the government, and on the other side, Abdallah Djaballah, the party founder who refused any rapprochement with the government. The fight ended with the expulsion of Djaballah and his replacement by Adami, who steered the party toward the corridors of power. Djaballah and his supporters created a party called El Islah, from which he would be ousted and replaced by Djahid Younsi. Djaballah then created another party in 2012 called the Front for Justice and Development (FJD, or El Adala).

Similarly, the main Islamist party, the MSP, witnessed internal schisms due to its collusion with the regime. Its participation in parliamentary elections and acceptance of ministerial portfolios in several governments diluted its oppositional identity (Ghanem, 2015). Much of the MSP's electorate came to see its strategy as naked opportunism, despite being critical to the party's survival, as parties have limited access to resources. For the MSP, and other cited parties, joining the government is the only viable means of securing the resources and media access necessary to remain a viable political force. Furthermore, joining the government is the best means of preserving their parties to play another day and survive on a skewed playing field. Co-optation of the Islamists in Algeria started as far back as 1992, when the FIS was outlawed and the regime needed an Islamist card to show that it was inclusive and democratic. In exchange for its participation, the regime provided the MSP with ministerial positions, parliamentary seats, and the opportunity to benefit from the redistribution of oil revenues.

The MSP's first serious split occurred during the 2004 presidential election. The party's leader, Aboujerra Soltani, decided to back Bouteflika's candidacy for a second term. This incensed many party members, who subsequently resigned. A second crisis shook the MSP in 2008 and revolved around much the same issue. Soltani decided to support President Bouteflika's candidacy for a third term, which necessitated a constitutional amendment lifting a two-term limit on the presidency. The party's second-in-command, Abdelmadjid Menasra, accused Soltani of making key concessions to the government without consulting party members. Menasra ultimately left the party and was joined by 28 of the MSP's 51 members of parliament and several mayors, members of local councils, presidents of local assemblies, and rank-and-file members. He created the Movement for Preaching and Change (MPC). This crisis harmed the MSP's credibility and obliged it to compete with the MPC for much the same popular base (Ghanem, 2015).

As we have seen, the MSP, emboldened by the Arab Spring, decided to dispense with its image as a stooge of the regime and contested the 2012 parliamentary elections as part of a larger Islamist grouping called the AAV. In response, the regime ensured that the AAV performed poorly. Nevertheless, with the Arab Spring still a source of inspiration, the MSP did not revert to quietism. In May 2013, Abderrazak Makri took over the party's presidency. Makri portrayed himself as the leader who would finally break the system and make the MSP a true opposition force. He joined other parties in an umbrella opposition group called the National Coordination for Liberties and Democratic Transition (CNLTD). The latter protested against Bouteflika's plans for a fourth term in 2014 and called for a democratic transition of power. However, following intense pressure from former president Soltani, who retained much influence within the party, the MSP returned to its tradition of dialogue and compromise with the regime.

This would not be the last instance of the MSP backtracking on an initially forthright oppositional stance. Something similar happened during the 2019 political crisis. The MSP initially expressed its support for the popular *Hirak*, which opposed the regime and Bouteflika. However, by this time, with the Arab Spring having lost much of its luster, the party's leadership seemed skeptical of the *Hirak's* chances of limiting the regime's power even if Bouteflika were obliged to step down. From the party leadership's perspective, it would be foolish for the MSP to sever its links to the regime.

With this in mind, Makri met secretly with the president's brother, Said Bouteflika, in an attempt to broker a deal that would satisfy both the regime and the *Hirak*: the president would extend his term by one year before stepping down. When the contents of this proposal were made public, there was an outcry on the part of many elements of the *Hirak*. Makri and the MSP attempted damage control by refusing to participate in the 2019 presidential elections, even after Bouteflika signaled he would not run for a fifth term. However, when those elections resulted in Abdelmadjid Tebboune ascending to the country's presidency in December, the party immediately pledged to back him and urged all Algerians to do the same, owing to a supposed urgent need for national consensus. A few months into Tebboune's tenure, the MSP was indistinguishable from a pro-regime party. For example, in March 2020, the MSP's leader Makri described the *Hirak's* leadership as "radicals" recruited by international freemasonry.

The MSP seems to have calculated that criticizing the government and demanding a change in direction yet stopping short of calling for regime change is the best strategy to adopt. The criticism is meant to cast the MSP as a challenger in the eyes of the party's rank-and-file. The party's oppositional discourse is intended to remind its electorate that the party is on the side of the people. By opposing the government and some of its decisions, the MSP hopes to play up the distance between it and the government, especially when the latter makes decisions that adversely affect ordinary Algerians.

Nevertheless, many Algerians have seen the party as "a party of the regime." During the 2004 presidential elections for Bouteflika's second term, the Ministry of Industry and Restructuring came to be heavily staffed by MSP officials. This was not a coincidence. The Minister of Industry and Restructuring himself, El-Hachemi Djaâboub, was an MSP cadre. Djaâboub received free rein to appoint individuals to key positions in this ministry, and the MSP declared its support for Bouteflika's candidacy in the upcoming election. It is worth noting that Djaâboub remained Minister of Industry under Ouyahia governments III and IV and was Minister of Trade under Ouyahia governments VI, VII, VIII. He was appointed Minister of Labor, Employment, and Social Security by Tebboune under the government of Djerad in September 2020.

ELECTIONS AT ANY COST: THE NEED FOR A DEMOCRATIC ALIBI

The Algerian regime's emphasis on holding parliamentary elections on June 12, 2021, amid a deep political impasse and legitimacy crisis, can be understood as a manifestation of its attitude toward elections since the 1989 opening. Having so-called opposition groups and allowing them to compete simplifies discussions between them and the leadership. For the competitive authoritarian regime that is the Algerian one, elections are a time for bargaining, negotiating, and gaining credibility. Allowing old parties to compete and new ones to enter the political arena and compete for seats in parliament allows such parties to raise their demands, and this flow of demands facilitates the government's responsiveness and even compromise. Additionally, by allowing these groups to participate in the political game, the regime lessens their motivations to rebel and resort to dissent or violence, as the FIS did in 1992 (Willis, 1999). Despite Tebboune's lack of legitimacy and social protests, the regime's tenacity in organizing parliamentary elections makes sense within this framework.

Parties can make requests, and the state can make concessions without appearing to give in to public outcry and the *Hirak's* demands through the legislature. Seemingly robust legislatures boost the chances of a regime's survival by reducing the risk of more civil upheaval and soci-etal turmoil. In the 2021 legislative elections, opposition parties such as the RCD, FFS, and the PT boycotted the elections for the reasons cited above. Their boycott did not constitute a problem for the regime. Cognizant of the difficulties inherent in selling the concept of a "new Algeria" to established institutional parties, the authorities opened the political field to new players, particularly youth, to whom it provided financial support to launch parties and run campaigns. This allowed the regime to appear open to change, accepting "fresh blood," while in reality, it was prepared only to welcome a new clientele.

The rush to establish independent lists and register new candidates for the elections demonstrated that the regime was still capable of convincing large sections of the population, potential leaders, and elites that their best chances for advancement lay in continuing to work with the regime and its leadership rather than organizing against it and antagonizing it. Additionally, despite the president's many controversial decisions (i.e., closing the borders for over 19 months, which involved hundreds of Alge-rians stuck abroad under the guise of shielding the country against the Covid-19 pandemic; dissolving the lower house of parliament, and using low-intensity repression more often), none of these decisions prompted any top government officials to criticize Tebboune, the military or the police publicly. This impression of uniformity, solidarity, and elite cohe-sion (which was very low during the first weeks of demonstrations) was bolstered by state-run media and newspapers, which either discontinued coverage of the weekly marches or resumed coverage with misleading assertions. This was the case during the November 1, 2020 huge rally of the *Hirak*, which the media portrayed as evidence of Algerians mobilizing to celebrate their new constitution. Later on, misconceptions gave way to blatant misrepresentations, such as the *Hirak* being infiltrated by the Movement for Autonomy of Kabylia (MAK) or by Islamists of *Rashad*, who were supposedly calling for violence.

Nodding and Losing Credibility

Political parties, politicians, and parliament members have lost credibility and legitimacy in most Algerians' eyes. Asked to rate politicians' honesty on a seven-point scale, with one representing the most dishonest, more than half of the 1,200 respondents in a 2017 Arab Barometer poll rated them a one (28%) or two (25%). Political parties and parliament were the least trusted political institutions. Only 14 percent of the respondents trusted parties, and only 17% trusted the parliament (The Arab Barometer, 2017).

Predictably, nothing had changed by the time of the 2019 protests. Only 19% of respondents to an Arab Barometer poll conducted at the start of the *Hirak* said they had voted in the 2017 parliamentary elections. Among those aged between 20 and 29, it was 9%. And only one in ten rated the 2017 elections as free and fair. Parliamentarians have been intensively criticized by Algerian bloggers and artists. In a viral video, they were called "*kharlamaniyin*" or in French "Merdéputés." Parliamentarians are seen at best as incompetent and truant when it comes to attending parliamentary sessions and at worst as opportunistic thieves whose only motivation is to secure large salaries, bonuses, and other benefits. Sofiane, a secondary school teacher, explains:

> They are *béni oui oui*; they have been nodding for years […]. They say yes to any law without reading it. All that matters is the money. Did you see those idiots in parliament? It is a rarity, but when they are present, they just vote and say yes to the finance law without reading it, to the amendment of the constitution even if it means that we will have a president for life. […]. How can I even reach them when they do not even have a committee room where you can go and talk to the parliamentarian who is supposed to represent you? […] Anyway, how can these people represent us while their

salaries are insanely indecent! They earn $3,000 a month! How can they represent me while my peers and I earn $180? How can they represent me while my salary has been almost the same for the last decade while theirs is skyrocketing? (Author's interview, Algiers, December 2016)

What the interviewee is referring to is the salary raise those parliamentarians received in 2008. One month before the constitutional amendments by which President Bouteflika removed the two-term limitation, the MPs' salaries were raised by 300% to reach $3,000, the equivalent of 30 times the Guaranteed Minimum National Salary (SNMG). The motion was adopted by a show of hands and without debate by 500 votes in favor (Algeria-Watch, 2009). Besides these generous salaries, parliamentarians are offered a general expenses bonus, a vehicle allowance, a telephone allowance, a monthly accommodation allowance and another for catering, as well as other advantages such as zero-rate loans and other benefits for *Eid* or *El Hadj*, plus a departure bonus at the end of their term. All these perks are given out in exchange for the MPs never holding the government accountable for anything.

This lack of confidence and disgust in parliamentarians is likely to have deepened since the revelations of former FLN deputy and former vice-president of parliament Baha Eddine Tliba. During his 2020 trial for corruption, Tliba revealed that, during the legislative elections of 2007, parliamentary seats were bought (Meddi, 2020). Tliba disclosed that seats were expensive and that to head the FLN list in the region of Annaba, he paid seven billion centimes of Algerian dinars [approximately $440,000]. Tliba explained during his trial that it was a well-known practice and that no less than 300 billion centimes ($24 million) were collected by those who prepared the lists of the FLN for the 2007 election. These revelations lifted the last veil on the extent of political corruption in the political arena in Algeria. Several parties called for the dissolution of parliament. President Tebboune eventually did just that in February 2021, in a desperate bid to appease the *Hirak*.

A seat in parliament grants the MP parliamentary immunity from prosecution and allows him/her to weave a politico-economic network of influence, particularly with the business community (Hachemaoui, 2003). To be part of the parliament allows them and their political parties to safeguard their electoral base and network of clients, but also their wider social group, tribe, or people who come from the same region, by providing them with benefits in exchange for their support. These benefits include jobs, goods, financial aid, tax reduction, and even rent allocations during election campaigns. For his 2004 campaign, President Bouteflika visited 16 provinces and spent over $450 million on programs for local development.

Similarly, for his third term (2009–2014), even before the beginning of his presidential campaign, Bouteflika had marshaled the support of the FLN, the RND, the MSP, the General Union of Algerian Workers (UGTA), the National Organization of Mujahidin (ONM), the National Association of Zaouïas, and the Forum of Business Leaders (FCE), nearly 30,000 NGOs, and 1,000 women's associations. In Algiers alone, out of 6,933 associations, more than 5,000 supported Bouteflika's candidacy. During that election, it was widely rumored that $186bn was to be distributed during his third term as kickbacks to those who supported his re-election, so all manner of parties and organizations wanted to collect the rent money (Tlemçani, 2012).

For many interviewees spoken to between 2017 and 2020, things were clear: the only objective of politicians, including supposed opposition figures, is attaining power. In the eyes of such interviewees, the politics of opposition in Algeria is not a struggle for democratization and a better future for Algerian citizens. Rather, the opposition parties engage in posturing of the sort meant to elicit party-specific concessions from the regime: ministerial portfolios, parliamentary seats, high positions in the bureaucracy, and other rent distribution benefits (Hachemaoui, 2003: 44). With time, these benefits have deepened parties' loyalty to the regime. The opposition parties have become so tamed and co-opted that they can no longer serve as an oppositional force or even a counterweight to the regime.

Indeed, political parties have a weak operational structure outside of elections. Moreover, when elections roll around, the parties turn into clubs where opportunistic people of all kinds jostle for positions of influence without paying heed to political values. This results in an even more disappointing scenario than the one they denounced. As a result, the parties are discredited among wide swaths of the population and increasingly unable to mobilize citizens. This became readily apparent with the *Hirak* in 2019. During the first weeks of the protests against Bouteflika's fifth term, many opposition party leaders joined the movement and took to the streets. Yet protesters denounced them as "sycophants" and "lackeys of the regime," and kicked them out of the protests. The impression is that these parties are dormant and come to life only at the prospect of an electoral victory. During the 2019 protests, interviewees explained that they felt the opposition parties had no intention to change the system. In their view, the parties wanted to use the widespread anti-regime sentiments and demonstrators to extract better conditions for their continued machinations within the political arena.

Ultimately, the weakness of Algerian opposition parties lies in their lack of commitment to democratic principles and their unwillingness to compete with the regime. Their leadership, as well as their programs, have often remained unchanged for decades. Most Algerian parties have one dominant figure, either a founder or a co-founder, whose re-election is systematic and without any contestation, or one who continues to wield power behind the scenes. Unlike the 1990s FIS, which had a broad appeal with a nationwide agenda and could bridge the fractures (geographic, ethnic, and linguistic) of Algerian society, the current parties cannot replicate such a scenario. Their co-optation runs deep, and their fragmentation even deeper (Lowi, 2009: 124).

Indeed, not one of the major opposition parties has presented a credible alternative to the regime. They have not presented a new societal project or new values, nor have they presented new modes of political action. Instead, they have adapted to the rules of the game (Ait-Hamadouche & Zoubir, 2009). And they have reproduced the same patterns as the ones they have denounced: the lack of a democratic mechanism within parties, the absence of alternation and open dialogue, the expulsion of detractors, the struggle for leadership, and the cult of personality. The political class, including the opposition, is as anti-democratic as the regime it decries.

References

Addi, L. (2006). Les partis politiques en Algérie. *Revue des mondes musulmans et de la Méditerranée*, (111): 139–162. https://journals.openedition.org/remmm/2868. Accessed January 24, 2022.

Ait Ouarabai, M. (2019). Il refuse de pactiser avec le courant islamiste: Le PLD explique les raisons de son retrait du PAD. *El Watan*. November 11. https://www.elwatan.com/edition/actualite/il-refuse-de-pactiser-avec-le-courant-islamiste-le-pld-explique-les-raisons-de-son-retrait-du-pad-11-11-2019. Accessed January 24, 2022.

Algeria Watch. (2009). Augmentation des salaires des parlementaires: Les députés narguent la population. *Algeria Watch*. December 13. https://algeria-watch.org/?p=27832. Accessed January 26, 2022.

Algeria-Watch. (2021). Le RCD boycott les législatives du 12 juin. *Algeria-Watch*. March 21. https://algeria-watch.org/?p=76909. Accessed January 24, 2022.

Amir, N. (2021a). Le Parti des travailleurs opte pour le boycott. *El Watan*. March 16. https://www.elwatan.com/edition/actualite/le-parti-des-travailleurs-opte-pour-le-boycott-16-03-2021a. Accessed January 24, 2022.

Amir, N. (2021b). Le FFS se rejoint au front du boycott. *El Watan*, April 4. https://www.elwatan.com/edition/actualite/des-legislatives-sans-lopposition-04-04-2021c. Accessed January 24, 2022.

Amir, N. (2021c). Le MSP explique son refus de participer au gouvernement. *El Watan*. July 1. https://www.elwatan.com/edition/actualite/le-msp-explique-son-refus-de-participer-au-gouvernement-01-07-2021b. Accessed January 24, 2022.

Arato, A. (1994). The Rise, Decline and Reconstruction of the Concept of Civil Society, and Directions for Future Research. In A. Bibic, & G. Graziano, G (Eds), *Civil Society, Political Society, Democracy*. Ljubljana: Slovenian Political Science Association.

Djerbal, D. (1997). Les élections législatives de juin 1997 en Algérie: Enjeux politiques logiques et acteurs. *Maghreb-Machrek*, (157): 149–180.

Dris, C. (2018). Algérie 2017: De quoi les élections législatives et locales sont-elles le nom?. *L'Année du Maghreb*, (19): 169–183. http://journals.opened ition.org/anneemaghreb/4258. Accessed January 24, 2022.

Dris-Ait Hamadouche, L. (2012). L'Algérie face au printemps arabe: L'équilibre par la neutralisation des contestations. *Confluences Méditerranée*, (81): 55–67. https://www.cairn.info/revue-confluences-mediterranee-2012-2-page-55.htm

Dris-Aït Hamadouche, L., & Zoubir, Y. (2009). Pouvoir et opposition en Algérie: vers une transition prolongée ?. *L'Année du Maghreb*. http://jou rnals.openedition.org/anneemaghreb/535. Accesses January 24, 2022.

El Watan. (2017). Députés de la nation, combien ça coûte?. *El Watan*. February 9. https://www.elwatan.com/edition/actualite/deputes-de-la-nation-combien-ca-coute-09-02-2017. Accessed January 24, 2022. Accessed January 24, 2022.

Gandhi, J. (2008). *Political Institutions Under Dictatorship*. Cambridge University Press.

Ghanem, D. (2015). The Future of Algeria's Main Islamist Party. *Carnegie Middle East Center*. April 14. https://carnegie-mec.org/2015/04/14/fut ure-of-algeria-s-main-islamist-party-pub-59769

Hachemaoui, M. (2003). La représentation politique en Algérie entre média-tion clientélaire et prédation (1997–2002). *Revue française de science poli-tique*, (1): 35–72. https://www.persee.fr/doc/rfsp_0035-2950_2003_num_53_1_395688. Accessed January 24, 2022.

Hachemaoui, M. (2007). La corruption en Algérie: un système politique informel. *El Watan*. February 10. https://www.elwatan.com/edition/contri butions/la-corruption-en-algerie-un-systeme-politique-informel-10-02-2007. Accessed January 24, 2022.

Hachemaoui, M. (2013). *Clientélisme et patronage dans l'Algérie contemporaine*. Karthala.

Hamdi, R. (2019). Présidentielle en Algérie: les soutiens se multiplient autour d'un 5e mandat d'Abdelaziz Bouteflika. *Jeune Afrique*. January 31. https:// www.jeuneafrique.com/728772/politique/presidentielle-en-algerie-la-mac hine-pour-un-5e-mandat-dabdelaziz-bouteflika-se-met-en-marche/. Accessed January 24, 2022.

Huntington, S. (1968). *Political Order in Changing Societies*. Yale University Press.

Levitsky, S, & Way, L. (2002). The Rise of Competitive Authoritarianism. *Journal of Democracy*, (13)2: 51–65.

Liverani, A. (2008). *Civil Society in Algeria*. Routledge.

Lowi, M. (2009). *Oil Wealth and the Poverty of Politics*. Cambridge University Press.

Meddi, A. (2020). Algérie : faut-il dissoudre le Parlement (et le FLN) ?. *Le Point*. September 8. https://www.lepoint.fr/afrique/algerie-faut-il-dissoudre-le-parlement-et-le-fln-08-09-2020-2390935_3826.php. Accessed January 26, 2022.

Moula, H. (2019). La plateforme de Aïn Benian, le virage raté. *Reporters*. August 5. https://www.reporters.dz/la-plateforme-de-ain-benian-le-virage-rate/. Accessed January 24, 2022.

Robbins, M. (2019). Arab Barometer. Wave V. The 2019 Algerian Protests. *Arab Barometer*. https://www.arabbarometer.org/wp-content/uploads/ABV_Alg eria_Protests_Public-Opinion_Arab-Barometer_2019.pdf. Accessed January 26, 2022.

Roberts, H. (1998). Algeria,s Contested Elections. *Middle East Report*, (209): 21–24. https://merip.org/1998/12/algerias-contested-elections/. Accessed January 24, 2022.

Roberts, H. (1999). Algeria's Veiled Drama. *International Affairs.*, 75(2), 383–392.

Schedler, A. (2006). *Electoral Authoritarianism: The Dynamics of Unfree Competition*. Lynne Rienner.

The Arab Barometer. (2017). Algeria: Five years after the Arab uprisings. *The Arab Barometer*.

Tlemeçani, R. (2012). Algérie: Un Autoritarisme électoral. *Tumultes*, (38): 149–171. https://www.cairn.info/revue-tumultes-2012-1-page-149.htm. Accessed January 24, 2022.

Werenfels, I. (2007). Managing Instability in Algeria. *Elites and Political Change Since 1995*. Routledge.

Willis, M. (1999). *The Islamist Challenge in Algeria: A Political History*. New York University Press.

CHAPTER 4

Divide and Conquer: The Atomization of Civil Society

In the late 1980s, Civil Society Organizations (CSOs) proliferated in Algeria. Their number grew from nine officially recognized organizations between 1976 and 1988 to 13,000 in 1991, to 57,000 by 1997 (Liverani, 2008: 9–10), and reached 92,627 in 2011. CSOs had an active presence in political life and worked on advancing agendas that included human rights, women's rights, and minority rights, among others. Yet this phenomenon, which several scholars, analysts, and academics interpreted as indicative of a "dynamic" and "vibrant" associative life that bode well for democracy, was, in fact, a controlled opening from above. The Algerian regime was grappling with a substantial legitimacy deficit, and to preserve itself and its institutions, it allowed the birth and growth of associational life in a very restricted form of democratization. The regime opened up the political arena to improve its legitimacy nationally and its standing internationally, but it made sure to calibrate the opening so that it did not lose significant power.

The regime let CSOs multiply but not prosper, keeping the associative sector on a tight leash. The state manipulated and fragmented the associative sphere to control the politicization of social grievances and also to mobilize groups likely to support the government's goals. The regime used legal means and financial stratagems to enhance the government's ability to regulate, control, and restrict CSOs' influence and obstruct

© The Author(s), under exclusive license to Springer Nature Switzerland AG 2022

D. Ghanem, *Understanding the Persistence of Competitive Authoritarianism in Algeria*, Middle East Today, https://doi.org/10.1007/978-3-031-05102-9_4

their activities. While allowing space for pluralism, the regime narrowed the space for democratization. It used the expansion of the associative realm from the 1990s onward to portray itself as liberal and forging a path to democracy with robust civil rights. As a result of this top-down approach, CSOs became agents for stabilizing the social and political status quo instead of keeping the state in check (Cox, 1999). They aided the regime in maintaining itself and its political system. In other words, the associative sector enabled the regime to survive domestically through progressive pluralization with controlled democratization. Internationally, CSOs became the face that cemented the image of a country in transition to democracy (Liverani, 2008: 161–162). Instead of facilitating and hastening Algeria's transition to democracy, CSOs provided the basis for restoring regime control following a period in which it was shaky (Liverani, 2008: 167).

The regime used various tactics and strategies revolving around cooptation to absorb new actors, fragment the civil society sector, control its activities, and undermine its capacity to challenge political powers. Repression, marginalization, and scapegoating, coupled with a complex and opaque regulatory system, further fragmented and weakened civil society organizations. Fragmentation was such that in 2011, Algeria was one of the densest countries in terms of associations in the MENA region, with 1,027 national and 92,627 registered local associations (Human Rights Watch, 2014). In addition, the lack of democratic management within these organizations, combined with the lack of financial and material resources, the dependency on public funds from the government, the limit of access to international funds, and the deficiency in networking on the national and regional level, weakened the autonomy of Algerian CSOs. Consequently, they became vulnerable to manipulation at the hands of the government and unable to challenge its policies and actions. This, in turn, rendered them ill-suited to mediate between state and society. The associative sector had little to no effect on the advent of democracy in Algeria; on the contrary, it was central to the survival of the Algerian regime. Moreover, CSOs' inability to pierce the armor of competitive authoritarianism in Algeria is likely to continue.

1962–1988: Between Repression and Toleration

Historically, the colonial power's repressive actions, backed by the vast majority of the French of Algeria (*Pieds-Noirs*), impeded the emergence of an indigenous civil society. Civil society was primarily reserved for French people and became increasingly reliant on the colonial authority's political, military, and economic protection. However, this did not mean that there was no indigenous civil society. Beginning in the 1920s, Algeria experienced a proliferation of the kind of association called *Nadi* [circle or society] in big cities such as Algiers, Oran, Constantine, and Tlemcen, as well as small towns in the country's interior. By the end of the 1930s, the *Nadi* became the main center of socialization for the Algerian intelligentsia and a hub for a rapidly developing Algerian nationalism, which helped transform the political opportunities of upper-middle-class Muslims (Carlier, 1995: 43–45). This network of associations would benefit the two main political formations: the *Etoile Nord Africaine*, or ENA, and its successor, the *Parti du Peuple Algérien*, or PPA, led by Messali Hadj, which would lay the groundwork for the FLN.

Once independence was proclaimed in 1962, the Algerian state engaged in a top-down reconstruction of civil society over the next decade and a half. As early as December 1962, the Algerian authorities reinstated the 1901 law (*Loi Waldeck-Rousseau*) on freedom of associations. However, as Ben Bella was not enthusiastic about it and wanted to restrict liberties while ensuring the FLN's hegemony, the law was amended through a series of decrees and circulars. For example, the Ministry of Interior's circular of March 2, 1964, instructed *Walis* [prefects] to determine "the real aims" and activity of each association "to prevent the constitution of associations which, under the guise of social, cultural, or artistic activity would undermine the internal or external security of the state" (Izarouken, 2004). This made it harder for associations to obtain the authorization necessary to operate. Between 1962 and 1971, the regime dissolved dozens of associations or prevented them from launching in the first place.

Under Boumediene, the state imposed further restrictions, such as Ordinance 71/79 of December 3, 1971, to guarantee its control. Associations were now subject to a dual authority/agreement: the agreement of the Ministry of Interior for associations with a national vocation and that of the *Wali* in the case of associations with a local vocation. The approval issued by the *Wali* or the Minister of the Interior, depending on the case, had to be preceded by a recommendation from the ministry concerned with the association's primary purpose. As such, even before obtaining the agreement of the *Wali* or the Minister of Interior, any proposed new association had to obtain the preliminary agreement of the ministry responsible for its sphere of activity.

Moreover, the government could unilaterally and without the possibility of an appeal on the part of the association, refuse approval; article 7 of the ordinance stipulated that "associations which undermine political, economic, social and cultural options of the country" would not be allowed to operate. This allowed the authorities to control associative life. Most approved associations revolved around sports (for example, cycling, basketball, football) and professional activity (tourism union, social action committees) during this period. Others were time-specific affairs, such as ad hoc groups formed to construct mosques. Friendship associations extended Algeria's official diplomatic activity, such as the "Algeria - USSR" friendship association. The most important thing was that, as the sole source of authority, the state could not allow any form of organization that was truly autonomous. Boumediene's metaphor for the Algerian state is a good illustration of this. In a 1977 speech, he spoke of "a coherent system of sectors which cover all national activities and extend their ramifications to the most remote places of our country, reflecting the presence and concern of the authority of the state, like the human body whose vascular system conveys and breathes life to its ultimate extremities" (Babadji, 1989: 233).

As such, throughout this period (1962–1978), mass organizations and professional unions were the belts of transmission of the single party-state and its structures of supervision and control of society. This served to submerge grievances and voices of dissent. Until the mid-1980s, civil society was officially represented by FLN mass organizations that represented social categories. Professions were represented by the General Union of Algerian Workers (UGTA), education by the General Union of Algerian Students (UGEA), youth by the National Union of Algerian Youth (UNJA), women's interests by the General Union of Algerian Women (UGFA), and the health sector by the National Federation of Health Workers (FNTS). Their objective was to help deliver the ruling party's official discourse and mobilize Algerians while controlling society. Everything was made for the sake of "national unity with the charms of a discreet Leviathan" (Leca, 1990: 17). The state was the sole representative of a purportedly unified society, and these state organizations supposedly mediated between state and society. The regime used them to absorb, communicate, and channel social demands and respond by combining the ideological capital obtained through the war of independence with the financial capital derived from oil and gas rent, on which the country relied heavily.

However, in 1985–1986, when the price of crude oil fell to about $12 a barrel, the country was hit hard. Oil export revenues collapsed by 36% (*Le Monde*, 1987). The fiscal crisis that followed led the state to disengage from providing health, educational, and even cultural services. Even as it disbanded many smaller associations, the state promulgated Law 87-15 on July 21, 1987, which lifted some restrictions from the 1971 law and allowed for the formation of new associations. The latter were intended to ease state disengagement after the 1985 fiscal crisis but also keep it involved in the field. Essentially, the measure was one of consolidation (Babadji, 1987: 107).

At that time, the institutional equilibrium between the FLN and the presidency was shaky, affecting various factions within the power structure, including the Army. One year before the riots of October 5, 1988, tensions between the FLN and President Bendjedid were at their height. The reformers grouped around Bendjedid and his cabinet were pushing for reforms to counter the FLN's monopoly on political representation. Bendjedid's reformist allies within the military, worried about the deterioration of the relationship between state and society, agreed with the presidency on inventing new intermediaries with greater legitimacy than the largely discredited FLN mass organizations. The 1987 law was meant to counter the FLN's monopoly on political representation by allowing the formation of an associational field overseen by the government but entirely independent of the FLN. This semi-opening was an excellent way for the government to dissociate itself from the discredited FLN, and the idea was that it would give the regime renewed political legitimacy. The proposed law was faced with fierce opposition by the FLN's conservatives, who eventually succeeded in stripping it of its more liberal provisions. By retaining the dual requirements of double recognition (Ministry of Interior and *Wilaya*), the law averted the FLN's downfall by preventing the corporatist system from fully opening up to other associations. Still, new associations were formed, and the state's relationship with the associative sphere shifted from confrontation to cooperation and, preferably, co-optation.

70   D. GHANEM

Many associations motivated by political objectives came into existence, thereby revealing emerging trends. Through its proxies, the state started mimicking the discourse of the most vocal and combative groups in a bid to render them superfluous. For instance, faced with the Algerian Women (UNFA) demands' for more recognition of women's rights, the state created a women's section within the UGTA and the National Union of Students.

Similarly, to stifle the most hostile voices on human rights, the regime created a state-friendly human rights league. The authorities incarcerated Ali Yahia Abdennour, president of an unrecognized hostile league, and used dissension within it to back a splinter group led by Miloud Brahmi. In April 1987, the authorities officially recognized Brahmi's league, the Algerian League of Human Rights (LADH), which functioned as an agent of the government and did not push for genuine change. In 1989, Abdennour's unrecognized league, by then sufficiently weakened due to government infiltration, was itself legalized, and changed its name to the Algerian League for the Defense of Human Rights (LADDH). Throughout the decade, the authorities would use CSOs' internal divisions to atomize the associational sector by creating offshoots of the autonomous organizations. The latter were ostensibly rendered superfluous, as the state-sponsored offshoots were theoretically calling for the same thing.

Independent associations existed, but the more they resisted state interference, the more they remained in constant tension with it. Also, the continued existence of this or that independent association was contingent on the authorities' mood and the nature and mission of the association in question (Liverani, 2008: 18). Non-political associations and those known for their neutrality toward the state were tolerated. In the 1980s, the most numerous associations were cultural Berber grassroots, women's groups, and Islamic charities.

The Berber groups did not remain apolitical for long. In 1980, the "Berber Spring," a politico-cultural awakening, gave birth to the Berber Cultural Movement (MCB). This loose-knit movement denounced state repression and the regime's aggressive cultural policies of Arabization, and called for recognizing the Berber identity and Berber language. The Berberist associative sector born in Kabylia expanded to reach Algeria's coastal towns. Associations mushroomed throughout the country— even in Algiers, which hosted many Berber students in its universities. The regime's crackdown on the Berber Spring failed to stem this phenomenon. The new associations provided the two main opposition parties, the FFS and the RCD, with ideological material and human capital (Chaker, 1989).

There was also the women's movement. Despite its diversity, the women's movement was the most organized, which could have constituted a counter-pouvoir (Remaoun, 1997). Indeed, a decade before the 1989 *Infitah*, women's associations were active; they organized demonstrations (four in 1981) and wrote declarations and *communiqués*. The draft of the Family Code in 1981, which made Algerian women minors for life, pushed the women's movement to fight more openly for women's legal status and equality (Gadant, 1995: 7). In 1981, the first women's committee was created, followed by associations such as *Isis*, *Ahlan*, *égalité et Triomphe* (Equality, and Triomphe).

These early women's groups proved instrumental in uniting feminists of all sorts after the *Infitah* of 1989. They united under the National Coordination, which organized its first meeting on December 1, 1989. The women's movement made Algerian women visible and helped to renegotiate their place and roles in society by occupying public space. They fought for the right of Algerian women to vote and denounced the legal right given to their spouses to vote on their behalf. They also fought for co-education at school and against violence targeting women (Lalami, 2014: 35). In addition, their contribution was vital to the secular arena, providing it with a political agenda and leaders such as Louisa Hanoune (later leader of the Worker's Party, or PT) and Khalida Messaoudi (RCD), among others.

Finally, there were the Islamic charities. They were the most important section of the associative movement in the 1980s. There were 187 religious associations in Algiers alone in 1980 (Dahak, 1982). Their mission revolved around constructing mosques, providing religious education, giving aid to the impoverished, and organizing the pilgrimage to Mecca. Bendjedid's government was more lenient toward organized Islam than were the governments of Ben Bella and Boumediene before him (Lamchichi, 1992: 95–96; Leca & Vatin, 1975: 308). Ironically, these associations, which had strong mobilization networks through their charities and neighborhood committees, would help the FIS, born in 1989 and legalized later that year, create the revolutionary threat that materialized in the 1990s.

CSOs in the 1990s: Totemic Organizations and Agents of Stabilization?

Uncertain about its ability to survive the paroxysm that was the 1988 riots, the regime undertook in 1989 reforms it considered sufficient to assure its political longevity, but that would not alter the core structures of power. It declared multipartyism to give itself a democratic façade, while it put in place mechanisms to keep control. Freedom of association was granted with the 90-31 law of December 4, 1990, but with limitations intended to keep CSOs on a tight leash. This was reflected in particular in the conditions for their creation. For instance, the association had to be founded by at least fifteen adults of Algerian nationality, none of whom had engaged in "behavior contrary to the interests of the national liberation struggle." The requirement to have authorization from the Ministry of Interior or the *Wali*, depending on the nature of the association, was maintained, and constraints relating to funds were significant. Foreign donations/bequests required prior authorization from the Ministry of Interior, and they were prohibited when deemed unrelated to the association's core purpose (Thieux, 2009). Also, while the 1990 law established a 30-day deadline for granting formal recognition, the government's actions and interpretation of the law remained unchanged from the 1970s. Additionally, although it was a significant advance over the previous legal framework, the 1990 law continued to give the government broad discretionary authority to interfere with the functioning and activities of CSOs. Indeed, when the state of emergency was declared in 1992, each police station established a special office charged with investigating newly formed associations immediately upon their application for official recognition, effectively reconstituting one of the primary elements of the restrictive environment established by the 1971 ordinance.

Despite these restrictions, civil society organizations, including charities of an Islamist nature, continued to multiply. According to the Ministry of Interior, between 1990 and 1997, no fewer than 57,000 associations were created, including 11,000 associations of an Islamist nature (Liverani, 2008: 9–10). Yet the multiplication of CSOs during the Black Decade is neither proof of the dynamism of civil society in Algeria nor proof of a democratization process, as many observers interpreted it at the time. First, it should be said that there is a discrepancy between registered CSOs and those that were active as many existed only on paper or had to

4 DIVIDE AND CONQUER: THE ATOMIZATION OF CIVIL SOCIETY

contend with a pending status. Second, less than 2% of these organizations were political; most were cultural, social, or environmental groups.

The multiplication of CSOs during the 1990s and state tolerance toward them has to be put in the context of the civil war. To reacquire the legitimacy it had lost with the October 1988 riots and reinforce itself, the state liberalized the associative sector while preserving a corporatist order based on rent distribution and patron–client networks. Furthermore, selective authorization and co-optation secured the loyalty of several groups in the associative sector (Amarouche, 2012).

Finally, the emergence of the FIS on the political scene, followed by that of jihadist groups, softened many civil society organizations' sentiments toward the state. Rather than enlarging their margin of freedom by shrinking the authority of the state, their priority became ensuring that the latter provided them with physical security, thereby reducing friction between them and the state. Several CSOs, especially women's associations, identified the FIS as an existential threat and openly sided with the regime. A well-known women's rights defender who used to be in the National Union of Algerian Women (UNFA) explained:

> People were dying under the bullets of the Islamists. For many of us, the question of defending more rights for women became secondary because we needed to protect those rights that we had already fought for and acquired. You need to understand our approach in the context of the 1990s. We had FIS leaders claiming that once the party of God was in power, women would return to the home for their natural vocation of procreating and raising small, good Muslims. Later on, we had women being killed just because they were women. We had an obligation to fight this barbarism and protect our achievements in women's rights so as not to fall back where we used to be! We sided with the authorities to denounce Islamism, and we spoke out against it here and abroad because Islamism was a threat to all our achievements. The authorities were our last resort in this fight against these obscurantist forces. (Author's interview, September 19, 2021)

Indeed, jihadist violence offered the regime a chance to use the associational sector to gather support and regain legitimacy domestically. Abroad, the regime used the associational sector to reach out to the international community, provide its version of events, and eventually restore Algeria's relationship with the West, which had deteriorated since the

1992 coup. For the CSOs, jihadist violence necessitated countermobilization and counteraction. As explained by a human rights activist, who used to be active in the LADH in the 1990s:

> We did not have a choice back then. We were scared of the FIS and what Algeria could become with such radicals at the head of the state's institutions. We needed to counter the Islamists, and many of us sided with the *pouvoir* and the military. We mobilized our forces on the ground, and we were taken seriously by the authorities. They let us speak out, even to foreigners, against the violence of the Islamists and what Algeria was going through. Back then, we were very active, speaking up in the media to tell our stories and our fight to the world after years of silence and invisibility. We had a duty to do so […]; it was a civic action to bargain with the authorities for the sake of collective interests. (Author's interview, June 17, 2021)

The state's use of CSOs to strengthen its internal legitimacy worked. At various stages of the civil war, numerous CSOs that used to be a burden on the state allied themselves with it in light of the changed circumstances. The National Committee to Safeguard Algeria (CNSA) is a case in point. The CNSA was established by the RCD and several associations such as the LADH, the National Organization of Mujahidin (ONM), and the National Union of Public Entrepreneurs (UNEP) in 1991 to support the government. In 1992, the CNSA called on the government to suspend the election (Chagnollaud, 2002). It created a women's committee that called for the organization of a women's demonstration to protest against the continuation of the electoral process. Naturally, the CNSA sided with the military when it did scuttle the election. The National Council for Transition (CNT) is another example. On January 26, 1994, the authorities organized the National Consensus Conference to establish the CNT, a transitional unicameral parliament that exercised a legislative function until the 1997 legislative elections. The authorities granted 85 seats out of 192 to civil society organizations during the conference.

The associative sector became less antagonistic toward the regime. The heightened levels of insecurity brought on by daily jihadist attacks, including bombings in public spaces, and killings of both public servants and civilians, led people to concern themselves more with security and less with freedom and individual rights. The Algerian regime used the climate of fear and extreme violence to reformulate the social contract, implement draconian security and economic policies, and repair its relations with several previously antagonistic associations. The subsequent *détente* with the associational sector during the fight against the Islamist insurgency allowed the authorities to tame the associative sector and turn it into a pillar of the regime.

The case of many women's associations is particularly enlightening. Most women's associations fought for women's rights in an attitude of opposition to the Islamists, whom they considered the "main enemy" of women's rights, and sided with the regime. They pleaded for the immediate interruption of the electoral process. Emblematic of this trend was Khalida Messaoudi, close to the communists of the PAGS and the RCD and the so-called modernist wing of the Army. Messaoudi, with the help of Nadia Liassine, created the Independent Association for the Triumph of Women's Rights (AITDF) in January 1990. To broaden the base of "civil society" and fight "green fascism," under the impetus of this trend, Messaoudi created other associations, such as the Algerian Rally of Democratic Women (RAFD). This last was created in January 1992 by Messaoudi with the help of other feminists such as Leila Cheikh, Farida Lesbet, and Khadija Ziani to "block" the Islamist movement and demand that the government avoid any dialogue with it. There was also the Association of Support and Solidarity with the families of victims of terrorism (Assevet), the Women's Commission of the Movement for the Republic, and SOS-Women in Distress.

Women's status was no longer a priority, as the priority was to fight Islamism. The visit of some of these associations to the HCE president on March 8, 1992, demonstrates as much. During this visit, these women's associations explained that abrogating the Family Code, which was inspired by Islamic law and granted women fewer rights than their male counterparts, was no longer on the agenda, as their priority was the fight against Islamism and the maintenance of the state. In return, the authorities offered positions to women from these associations in state institutions such as the National Consultative Council (CCN) and the National Observatory of Human Rights (ONDH), created by the authorities in February 1992. With its newly co-opted activists in the CCN and ONDH, the regime felt no need to push for a change of the Family Code despite the Minister Delegate for National Solidarity and the Minister of State Delegate for Legal Administrative Affairs being women (Fatès, 1994).

In the eyes of many of these associations, the Army was the sole guarantor of democracy, the last bulwark against Islamism. In a letter addressed to President Zeroual on March 24, 1994, the militants of RAFD wrote that "the National Popular Army [...] was the inviolable rampart, the sacred temple of Algerian's dignity" (Rouadjia, 2006). A female researcher and women's rights campaigner active in the 1990s explained:

> Back then, women were being killed, kidnapped, and raped because they were women. It was crucial to fight the Islamists, and to side with the regime was the only way, the rational solution. We succeeded in that fight. We engaged in a merciless fight to get women to know their rights and pressure the authorities to take responsibility and ensure security for women. When jihadist groups started kidnapping girls at schools' gates and threatening them to wear the veil or be killed, we pushed for the security forces to help us, and they did. Women's associations dispatched women activists around schools in 'hot' neighborhoods. We disseminated texts to girls and women, under the protection of the Army or the gendarmerie, to sensitize these women not to wear the veil out of fear. It was a victory for us [...] yes, it was! (Author's interview June 22, 2021)

A women's rights defender who was active in several women's associations at that time in Algiers and Oran further explained:

> We were scared of an Iranian scenario. For us, it was a matter of survival. We were going to be exterminated and so too was Algeria as we knew it. We focused on safeguarding Algeria's and our very existence as citizens, women, and associations [...] The main enemy was no longer the regime but the FIS, with its Islamist ideology, and the jihadist groups. We needed to do that, so we made a pact with the very devil we were fighting [silence]. Many of us spoke out against Islamist violence. However, many of us too remained silent about the regime's violence and all human rights violations [...] Today, when I think about it, yes, the regime emptied us of our substance. Today, we are dispatched here and there, Istanbul, Cairo, Paris, and Madrid, and some of us have become more than ever the voices of the *pouvoir*. [...] At this game, the regime beat us down. (Author's interview July 16, 2021)

This rapprochement between certain (secular) women's associations and the regime reflects the convergence of ideological and cultural interests between the two parties. The regime made much of this rapprochement, both in Algeria and abroad. Many Algerian civil society activists who refused to choose between the regime and the Islamists saw these women's groups' change of stance as proof that the entire women's associative sector had lost its autonomy. This was an exaggeration. In reality, some women's associations refused to follow the example of the "eradicators" and called for the continuation of the electoral process and the integration of the Islamists into the national debate. However, the media paid no heed to these groups, and their voices were eventually relegated to the margins. Such was the case with the previously prominent Association for Equality and Emancipation, founded by Selima Ghezali; Equality, which had operated in Algiers and Oran; Emancipation, of Algiers; Voices of Women, from Boumerdes; *Tighri Net Mettout*, in Tizi-Ouzou; and *Israr*, from Constantine (Rouadjia, 2006).

CSOs as Agents of International Legitimation

On the international level, at least during the first years of the conflict (1991–1994), the regime was isolated. This was due to the fact that many Western countries, without denouncing the 1992 coup, were uncomfortable with the regime's legitimacy. Britain, France, and the United States, among others, were reluctant to admit that they had accepted the lesser of two evils: namely, a regime backed by a military that had interrupted the electoral process and taken effective control of the country, and whose reputation was tarnished by claims of serious human rights violations. Westerners did not have access to much information about Algeria, as the regime had essentially padlocked the country and succeeded in preventing unfiltered news from making its way out. The Black Decade was a war without a face or an image; it was an "invisible war" (Stora, 2001). As such, the international community relied on CSOs for information. It would eventually convince itself that the associational sector was "vibrant" and "dynamic" and, most importantly, not beholden to the regime. As such, the associative sector was proof that the Algerian state, despite having scuttled an election, remained on the path to democracy.

This state of affairs enabled the regime to restore its ties with countries that had downgraded them in the wake of its actions in 1992, which in turn helped Algeria extricate itself from its economic slump. CSOs served as the regime's democratic alibi and a channel through which it filtered information to the West without appearing to do so. Indeed, the authorities periodically trotted out CSOs to show their interlocutors abroad the breadth of Algeria's domestic associative realm and reinforce the notion that the country's journey to freedom and democracy had not been suspended. Women's organizations deemed "modernist" in their notions of women's emancipation, such as the Association of Women for Personal Emancipation and Citizenship (AFEPEC), and women's rights activists such as Khalida Messaoudi, who became the most famous face outside Algeria with her book *Une Algérienne debout* [A Standing Algerian], were placed at the forefront of this campaign. Throughout the 1990s, they were willingly exploited in this manner. The CSOs in question, whether focused on women's rights or human rights, portrayed the conflict as one pitting the forces of "democracy" against those of "obscurantism."

By 1995–1996, the strategy had worked. The visit of the vice-president of the European Commission, Manuel Marin, to Algiers in December 1996 is a case in point. Marin arrived in Algiers four days after the highly contested constitutional referendum of November 1996, which recorded a turnout of 85% of yes. The constitutional revision confirmed Islam as the religion of the state (Art. 2) while prohibiting parties established on a religious, linguistic, regional, racial, gender, corporate, or regional basis (Art. 42). Above all, the constitution increased the concentration of powers in the hands of President Zeroual and granted him the right to legislate by ordinance, with so-called "organic" laws taking precedence over ordinary law and affecting finances, political parties, defense, the judiciary, and information (Art. 123). Also, the constitution provided for the creation in Parliament of a second Assembly, "Conseil de la nation," of which a third of the members would be appointed by the Head of State (Art. 101).

In an interview with the Spanish daily *El Pais*, Marin gave unequivocal support to the Algerian authorities, saying that "it must be recognized that President Zeroual and his government have made considerable efforts in favor of democratic normalization, by holding presidential, parliamentary and municipal elections," and that they have "generally met international criteria for reliability" (*Le Monde*, 1998). Marin also announced that the EU would grant 900 million francs in aid (*Libération*, 1996).

The EU was not in a position to negotiate a better deal. The wide-scale domestic violence in Algeria had already had spillover effects, not only with the refugees' flow, but also with the internationalization of the

4 DIVIDE AND CONQUER: THE ATOMIZATION OF CIVIL SOCIETY 79

conflict. France had witnessed this internationalization first hand with the hijacking of the Air France Airbus in December 1994 and the series of attacks in Paris in 1995. Closing embassies in Algeria and turning down visas for Algerians was not a viable solution. Europe had to act to protect its shores, and it had to help its southern neighbor. As early as 1994, the EU had decided to assist Algeria with its debt. Over $20bn of Algeria's official debt was rescheduled. The EU also assisted organizations with development-oriented programs. To avoid upsetting the Algerian authorities, the aid in question was directed to politically neutral actors. From 1995 onward, the EU delivered a fourfold increase in development funding, making Algeria one of the major beneficiaries in proportional and absolute aid distribution (Youngs, 2005: 96).

Europe remained silent on the violence and human rights violations. Only three statements on Algeria were published by the Common Foreign and Security Policy (CFSP) between 1993 and 1997, out of a total of over three hundred, most of which addressed the Balkans and the Middle East.

When violence heightened with the massacres of civilians in 1996, culminating in 1997, the EU started questioning the Algerian authorities and spoke out for the first time since the early days of the conflict. In 1998, European leaders reiterated "the right of the Algerian people" to be protected. Washington called for an international investigation of mass massacres that started in mid-1996 and culminated in the summer of 1997. The Algerian authorities rejected the US proposal and agreed to welcome a European mission to visit Algeria and debate its state of affairs on condition that discussion of, let alone or investigation into the massacres be taken off the agenda. The Algerian authorities also refused any suggestion of "national political dialogue." Eventually, the Algerians had their way. Algiers offered more cooperation with the EU in the fight against terrorism in Europe in exchange for Europe delivering weapons (Tuquoi, 1998a).

On January 19–20, 1998, the EU sent a European delegation, a "troïka," led by British Minister of State for Foreign Affairs, Derek Fatchett, Austrian Junior Foreign Minister, Benita Ferrero-Waldner, and Junior Foreign Minister of Luxembourg, Georges Wohlfart, to initiate a dialogue with the Algerian authorities. On January 19, 1998, the troïka arrived in Algiers, stayed less than 24 hours, and did not leave the capital to visit the sites of massacres. The troïka had several meetings, including with the Minister of Foreign Affairs, Ahmed Attaf, and civil society organizations. The authorities once again used CSOs activists, prominent newspaper' editors, and opposition figures to prove that the country had a vibrant civil society, a dynamic press, and an outspoken opposition amid violence. It was still on track to democratization. The troïka met with representatives of the National Human Rights Observatory (ONDH) and the Algerian Red Crescent, representatives of prominent private newspapers such as *El Watan*, *Liberté*, *La Tribune*, and *El Khabar*, and leading figures of opposition parties the FFS, the RCD, Ennahda, and the Workers' Party (Tuquoi, 1998b).

Similarly, when a delegation of nine European MPs, led by André Soulier from France, came to Algiers on February 8–11, 1998, the regime used civil society organizations to prove that it was on the path toward democratization. The Europeans met civil society groups centered on human rights, women's movements, and families of victims of terrorism who parroted official government lines. Soulier underlined the "intensity, the frankness of the meetings," explaining that "a new wind was rising in Algeria" (Europe Direct Info, 1998) and that there was a "serious chance of progress on the path to democracy" (EU Delegation Report, 1998). Essentially, these Algerian civil society organizations were for Western countries an alibi that they used to avoid questioning the existing order and suspending cooperation with the Algerian government (Hearn, 2001). The European MPs desisted from formalized contact with the FIS during the visit. They refused to read a letter sent by the FIS transmitted to them by Ali Yahia Abdenour (Aubenas, 1998). The International Federation of Human Rights (Fidh), Human Rights Watch, and Reporters Without Borders spoke out about this visit and regretted the unwillingness of the European Parliament delegation to push for the establishment of an international investigation of the human rights situation in Algeria (Amnesty International, 1998).

The EU approach to Algeria did not change with the end of the civil war in 2000, despite the receding jihadist threat. The EU claimed to support good governance, the rule of law, human rights, democracy, and fundamental freedoms, yet seemed uninterested in these same principles when it came to Algeria. A good example of this is the EU's Association Agreement (AA) with Algeria, which set out a framework for the EU-Algeria relationship in all areas. The AA was signed in 2002 and entered into force in 2005. The AA includes just three articles on politics, but ten on collaboration in the judicial sector. European Union policymakers focused on the latter to avoid advocating political reform.

It is instructive to see how EU regulations excluded giving funds directly to civil society organizations and left the administration of these funds to the discretion of the governing political elite. As a result, the capacity of Algerian civil society groups to regain a measure of independence was constrained. The majority of CSOs rely on limited local resources, and some receive state funds that do not exceed $300 a year, making them ineffective and turning them into empty shells (Benramdane, 2015).

In response to the international excitement about Algeria's associative sector, there was a boom of civil society assistance programs sponsored by foreign state aid agencies, international NGOs, and foundations dedicated to promoting democracy. EU funds tended to go toward boosting the economy and creating employment. The EU allocated between €221 million and €270 million to cooperate with Algeria during the National Indicative Program (NIP) from 2010 to 2014. No less than 60% of these funds were allocated to the labor market and economic diversification changes, and only 30% to reforms to increase citizen engagement in public life (Sutour, 2017). A 2017 EU study found that 88% of Algerians believed EU financial support had been appropriate, but 61% said the EU should have a more prominent role in the nation regarding human rights protections (European Union, 2017).

Looking back, we can conclude that the emergence of CSOs in Algeria, despite all the difficulties, allowed for the advent of a new associative culture and the professionalization of previously loose-knit and largely social groups. Many individual activists turned to advocacy full-time, and their interaction with members of other associations allowed them to network and build alliances. In other words, CSOs in Algeria have gained valuable experience despite unfavorable conditions. In addition, CSOs have gained international visibility after years of anonymity. The MEDA program, part of the Euro-Mediterranean Partnership, for instance, allowed some 300 associations to benefit from training programs at the hands of European counterparts and to strengthen their capacities and modernize them. Similar programs have been launched by international cooperation agencies, international NGOs with offices in Algiers, and many other stakeholders. Algerian associations learned to organize general assemblies, disseminate information, and communicate better. They also learned how to solicit funds and answer proposals from the EU, embassies in Algeria, and international institutions such as the United Nations Fund for Democracy (UNDEF) and UN Women.

Other associations achieved certain of their goals. The committees for the disappeared and the victims of terrorism are good examples of this. They have proven themselves capable of pushing their case on both the national and international levels. A commission was established in 2003 to research the 7,000 missing people from the civil war. On the international level, groups took the case to the UN. The latter expressed its deep concern with the former existence of secret detention centers in Algeria and asked the Algerian authorities to repeal Article 46 of the Charter for Peace and National Reconciliation, which punished whoever "instrumentalizes the wounds of the victim" with imprisonment for three to five years and a heavy fine. Similarly, the Information and Documentation Center on Children's and Women's Rights (CIDDEF), an association advocating for the rights of women and children, was able to ignite a public debate and eventually spur legislative reforms for women's rights, especially in the workplace, as well as the rights of orphans and abandoned children. Wafa, an association that helps parents of intellectually disabled children, also gave rise to an institutional dynamic. The Ministry of National Solidarity and Family took heed and in 2016 adopted Wafa's proposed national plan on autism.

Bouteflika's Use and Abuse of CSOs

With the end of the civil war, the state continued its co-optation and fragmentation strategies. It also sponsored the establishment of various consultative bodies entrusted with advising authorities on contentious issues such as the Family Code, human rights, the Berber question, and youth issues. Additionally, certain organizations were revamped. The National Observatory for Human Rights, or ONDH, had been created in February 1992 to promote human rights while the regime opened security centers in the desert to jail people. The authorities dissolved the ONDH in 2001 and created a new, more pliant organization under the name of the National Consultative Commission for the Promotion and Protection of Human Rights (CNCPPDH). The CNCPPDH's mission was to raise awareness of human rights and undertake related research. The CNCPPDH was also supposed to examine and formulate policy recommendations to improve laws and ensure mediation between state bodies and citizens. It was composed of four members of the president's team, two members of the Council of the Nation, two of the National Popular Assembly, one member of the Supreme Court, one of the Higher Islamic Council, and many others, including one member of each of the following ministries: National Defense, Justice; Interior and Local Authorities; Foreign Affairs; and National Education. Similarly, the Council of Youth (CSJ), created in 1996, at the peak of the civil war, was dissolved a few years later and resuscitated in 2015 to bring together representatives of associative movements according to the then-Minister of Youth, Abdelkader Khomri (Benasseur, 2015).

Significant funds were allocated to these state-friendly organizations. They were used to absorb sensitive issues into the associative realm, which the regime now seemed to trust even more than co-opted political parties. In fact, the regime went further and managed to use the associative sector to support the Army's presidential candidate and avoid relying exclusively on the support of political parties. At the end of the civil war, in preparation for the 1999 presidential elections, the authorities created several *Comités de Soutien* [campaign supporters' committees] to paint an apolitical picture of the Army's candidate: Abdelaziz Bouteflika. Bouteflika was presented to Algerians as the consensus candidate, unaffiliated with political parties, especially the traditional ones (FLN, RND). Hundreds of these supposedly independent support committees were created, and Bouteflika won almost 74% of the vote. Once the election was over, the committees transformed themselves into pro-government civil society organizations but changed back for the elections in 2004, 2009, 2014, and even 2019.

Such was the case with the Civic Association of Béjaïa [Association Citoyenne de Béjaia] or the ACB. Created by the authorities in 1999 as an electoral support committee, the ACB joined with other associations from other parts of the country to form the Coordination of Associations in Support of the Presidential Platform. After Bouteflika's election, the ACB turned to social work, fundraising activities for anti-AIDS campaigns, and organizing events for foreign NGO representatives visiting Algeria (Liverani, 2008: 125).

However, the ACB could never completely separate itself from its political origins. The proof is that during the violence of the Black Spring in 2001, its offices were pillaged and burned in Kabylia. The local population had repudiated it, having understood its political role and connections with the authorities. In 2004, during Bouteflika's second campaign, he sent an emissary to discuss the ACB's potential role in the region to push for Bouteflika's second term, but the ACB's credibility was already buried, and the association could no longer mobilize people (*Liberté*, 2003).

84   D. GHANEM

Nevertheless, for each of Bouteflika's four mandates, the authorities would use and abuse CSOs during the campaigning phase. In 2003, one year before the beginning of the campaign for Bouteflika's second term, and after four years of inactivity, many of these associations were reactivated, once again promoting Bouteflika's run for the presidency. During this election, the FLN split into pro-Bouteflika and pro-Benflis factions. To counter Benflis, who managed to gain the backing of more than 2,500 support committees and several associations (M. H, 2003), the regime reactivated all its associations and created several additional umbrella organizations that grouped hundreds of associations (*Liberté*, 2009). These groups' task was to discuss the benefits of a second term for Bouteflika and secure people's support for the voting day (N. M, 2003). They were particularly active in the country northeast, where Benflis was popular (N. D, 2003).

Not only did the regime play a critical role in impeding the operations of opposition associations, but it also transformed pro-Bouteflika organizations into the transmission belt for the incumbent's financial largesse. Heavyweights such as the Associations of Children of Mujahidin and the Organization of the Zaouias were given generous handouts for their allegiance to the president (Kharoum, 2003). What truly distinguished Bouteflika's committees from those of Benflis was the regime's discriminatory attitude. The government's ministries sided with the regime's incumbent, Bouteflika. For example, the Ministry of Interior allowed pro-Bouteflika groups to gather and organize events while prohibiting Benflis' groups from doing so. When the election took place, and the ballots were counted, Bouteflika was credited with over 80% of the vote. Similarly, many of these associations mobilized people in the 2005 referendum for the Charter for Peace and National Reconciliation in the same way, and they backed Bouteflika's campaign in 2008 in favor of the amendment of the constitution.

The instrumentalization of CSOs for political purposes turned many into a sort of extension of the state and a bridge by which its administrative apparatus redistributed oil revenues to old and new clientelist networks. This was the case, for instance, with the employer's association Forum des Chefs d'Entreprises (FCE), which was created in 2000 to unify all Algerian private and public companies to defend their interests and promote entrepreneurial initiatives. In order to benefit from attractive public procurement contracts, the FCE demonstrated unwavering political loyalty to the president and the government. In 2004, the FCE officially pledged to support President Bouteflika's campaign with contributions ranging from \$4,500 to \$45,000 (Dris-Ait Hamadouche, 2017). It reiterated this support for Bouteflika's fourth term, and those elements that did not, such as the head of the FCE in 2014, Reda Hamiani, were retired (Latrous, 2014). The FCE reiterated its support when the time came for Bouteflika's fifth term.

For helping to legitimize government policies and the incumbent candidate, CSOs, besides obtaining latitude in action and a safe environment to work in, captured rent money in the form of subventions from the communal and *wilaya* budgets and from several ministries. In fact, since the 1990 law, many ministries have established one or more special budget lines to aid friendly associations. Subventions to such organizations accounted for a significant portion of several ministries' available financial resources. For example, funds allocated to charitable organizations accounted for more than 10% of the Ministry of Youth and Sports budget.

Nevertheless, this applies only if groups are supportive of the government. In October 2001, Minister of Solidarity and Social Action Djamel Ould Abbès issued a warning to associations, stating that money was available, and adding that it was substantial, but making it clear that no funding would be available for groups that did not support the government (Naïli, 2001). In fact, during Abbès' trial for corruption in 2020, following the removal of Bouteflika, he admitted that his ministry gave some 22 billion centimes in subsidies to associations without first signing a contract of trust with them (Benali, 2020).

Not only does this show that the distribution methods and criteria for obtaining grants were highly questionable, but it also demonstrates that financial resources ostensibly earmarked for the public good were used for the regime's narrow agenda. The disbursal of funds to CSOs obeyed partisan and political logic. Clamoring for such funds plunged associations into struggles with each other. This only helped further weaken and discredit them in the eyes of citizens. In a 2016 study, the Arab Barometer showed that only 13% of Algerians participated in political meetings or signed petitions. This finding was reinforced in a 2017 study by *Rassemblement Action Jeunesse* (RAJ). Out of a sample of 1,462 people in 41 wilayas, only 2.5% of respondents declared themselves members of an association, and only 0.2% were affiliated with a union.

The Regime's Toolkit for the Recalcitrant

Another tack the regime uses is scapegoating (Thieux, 2009). For instance, during the 2001 torrential rain that caused mudslides and floods, as a result of which 1,000 people died and some 40,000 became homeless, the government attempted to deflect accusations that it was inept by accusing its nemeses among civil society associations of being of no use to people when it mattered. On the other hand, when associations were considered "too successful" in organizing relief and outperforming the authorities, their activities were hindered. Such was the case with SOS Culture Bab El Oued, an association for promoting local culture and the music scene, and which during the flood started distributing food, clothes, and other aid to the neighborhoods hit by the flood. The authorities soon moved to restrict its activities. Similarly, the *Aït Menguellet* association, which collected donations of everything from food to toys in its native Kabylia, was prevented from delivering aid to Algiers during the same period.

When the Covid-19 pandemic hit Algeria, and the Algerian diaspora tried to ship much-needed respirators to the country, the Algerian diplomatic missions abroad erected bureaucratic obstacles and hampered delivery. The Algerian embassy in France, where the most important Algerian diaspora community is located, demanded in a press release on August 6, 2021, that doners contact the relevant embassy/consular representatives to ask for "authorization" to send drugs, which were also much-needed. Additionally, the authorities announced that the material would be received only by an "authorized recipient," namely a division of the Algerian Ministry of Health known as the "Central Pharmacy" (AFP, 2021). The embassy also stipulated that caregivers who wished to travel to Algeria and provide their services would have to obtain permission from the same ministry. Unsurprisingly, when wildfires flared across Kabylia in August 2021, and Algerian associations and individuals abroad mobilized to send humanitarian aid, collecting some $670,000 to help their compatriots, they had to cut through enormous amounts of red tape.

Legal Obstacles

The most blatant use of legal methods to contain civil societies during the 2000s was the 2012 law. The 2012 law on associations (Law 12-06) generated additional restrictions on CSOs in Algeria; consequently, their number dropped from 92,627 in 2011 to 48,957 in 2017. To begin with, the law enhanced the government's power to refuse to register an association or to suspend the activities of an existing one on a vague basis. Though associations had the right to appeal a denial of registration, the government had the power to annul the creation of the association altogether, after which no appeal was possible. The government could do so if it judged the association to be "interfering in the internal affairs of the country or undermining national sovereignty" (Art. 39) or if it did not consider it as "being in the general interest and of public utility" (Art. 34). Associations were called upon to align their governing statutes with the law (Art. 70) by January 2014 or be deemed illegal. As a result, some 59,983 organizations were considered "illegal" by the government, which did not grant them the required authorization. The case of SOS Disparus and *Somoud* is, in this regard, enlightening. These two associations were denied accreditation because their objectives challenged the official narrative. For example, they rejected the 2005 Charter for Peace and National Reconciliation and demanded that the authorities reveal the fate and whereabouts of the thousands of Algerians who were forcibly disappeared during the country's civil war in the 1990s. Another example is the National Association to Fight Corruption (AACC), which was refused accreditation without any justification.

Other requirements included the presence of the association in at least 12 regions out of 48 across the national territory in order to be granted national status—before this law, the requirement was five regions—or the presence of 15 founding members for a regional association and 25 for a national one. There were also restrictions on assembly, as any association/organization had to apply for prior authorization from the Ministry of the Interior at least three days before a "public gathering" and eight days before a demonstration (Art. 5, 15).

Restrictions on funds, with an outright prohibition on receiving funds from foreign groups outside of the "official cooperation agreement," were blatant examples of the regime's plan to limit the actions of civil society by limiting their access to funds that are crucial for their functioning.

The previous legislation allowed Algerian associations to receive donations from foreign groups once authorities had approved their request. The new Law 12-06 made it even more difficult for such requests to obtain approval. And in order to further impede the visibility of Algerian CSOs, the law required approval from the government before a national organization could join an international one. Only associations that were nationwide could do so and not local ones.

As a result of these administrative obstacles, many associations were no longer legal. In Oran alone, no fewer than 346 out of the 760 associations in the province were dissolved in the first six months of 2015 (Saliha, 2015). In 2019, according to then-Interior Minister Noureddine Bedoui, more than 55% of associations registered under Law 90/31, a total of nearly 100,000, were not in compliance with Law 12/06. These organizations were either dissolved or their activities were frozen (Alioui, 2019).

While such dissolutions could happen due to non-conformity with the law, alleged corruption, or alleged misappropriation of funds, it is also true that most of the time, they had political purposes, such as when the association in question opposed alignment with the state. The same treatment was reserved for individuals perceived by the authorities as a threat. A few notorious examples of the use of legal measures to interrupt and disrupt civil rights activists' work are the cases of Djilali Hadjaj, the president of the AACC, who was arrested for "forgery and embezzlement of public funds" in September 2010. Taher Belabès, Coordinator of the National Committee for the Defense of the Rights of the Unemployed (CNDDC), was arrested during a peaceful protest for "obstructing traffic flow and inciting a gathering." In 2013, 96 Algerian activists invited to participate in the World Social Forum in Tunis were prevented from leaving Algeria. In February 2015, eight activists with the CNDDC who were demonstrating for improved labor conditions were arrested for "Unauthorized Gatherings."

In 2019, the authorities dissolved the local ecological association Bariq 21 in the wilaya of Skikda. Bariq 21, an association that campaigned to promote renewable energies and sustainable development, was dissolved under the pretext of violating the law governing partnership agreements with foreign donors. According to the complaint, the president and members of this association organized questionable activities, which led the security forces to monitor them closely. Economic and commercial activities are considered for-profit and thus contrary to the association's statutes. The complaint cited the example of the photovoltaic panels' project financed by the UNDP and "hijacked for personal needs." The *wilaya*'s complaint accused members of this association of participating in national and international events, such as COP 23 in Germany, and also of receiving funding of dubious origin, given that the cost of such participation allegedly exceeded the financial means of the association. The wilaya's complaint also evokes the relationship between members of this association and excursions with foreigners to the wetlands as well as the special relationship between the president and the secretary-general of this association on the one hand and the US embassy in Algeria on the other (Boukarine, 2019).

In 2021, the authorities went further in their fallacious accusations to dissolve associations. SOS Culture Bab El Oued is a case in point. SOS Culture Bab El Oued had been active since 1991, especially during the Black Decade, in helping youth and children in its area. The group offered language lessons, organized field trips, made its premises available to young musicians for their rehearsals, and helped train youth in audiovisual techniques necessary to make feature films and documentaries. In April 2021, the association, and its president, Nacer Maghnine, were accused by the authorities of being "a criminal association made up of eight people aged between 26 and 60 under the guise of an unlicensed cultural association in Bab El Oued." The police raided the association's headquarters, seizing 677 banners, seven computers, a digital camera, and 12 printers, and released images of eight members handcuffed next to a table with the confiscated items, which were considered proof of the criminal activities of the association. The association was accused of attacking national unity, inciting an unarmed gathering, and acquiring modern technological equipment with funds from the diplomatic representation of a large country. According to the authorities, the funds enabled SOS Culture Bab El Oued to "produce provocative films and documentaries" and "leaflets calling for violence" during the *Hirak* protests (Hamdi, 2021).

This was also the fate of Rassemblement Actions Jeunesse (RAJ), an Algerian civil society organization born in 1997 to help youth participate in local governance. The Algiers administrative court sanctioned RAJ for its alleged violation of the law on associations. On October 13, 2021, the court dissolved the association and imprisoned several of its members for "attacking the integrity of the national territory." Several members of RAJ, including its president, Abdelouahab Fersaoui, were prosecuted,

90 D. GHANEM

and up to nine of them were imprisoned. RAJ was essentially punished for being at the forefront of the *Hirak* (Amnesty International, 2021).

Cloning Strategy

The same treatment was meted out to unions. The 1989 constitution established the right to strike and to create autonomous unions. These concepts were expanded upon in Statute 90-June 14, 1990, the December 1991 law, and the 1996 constitution. At the end of the civil war, many unions became vocal about the economic liberalization policies introduced in the mid-1990s, which led to severe degradation of salaried workers' rights, a reduction in the quality of people's living conditions, and the increased likelihood of public-sector layoffs. The regime now saw a need to fragment such unions and punish the recalcitrant.

The UGTA remains the privileged partner of the government, the only one to which it talks. The rigid notion of governance inhibits the authorities from adjusting to the partnership model of governance and administration. The authorities refused to include unions other than the UGTA in any dialogue between the government, enterprises, and labor. The UGTA (and its satellites) was the only interlocutor accepted by the authorities. Meanwhile, the authorities ignored independent unions or accused them of being in "foreign powers' hands." Unions close to the UGTA, such as the National Federation for the Education Workers (FNTE), would be granted the right to negotiate with the government, while independent ones would be refused. The UGTA would barely contest the government's decisions, such as the dismantling of state-owned enterprises and would openly support the regime, as in 2004, when its general secretary Abdelmadjid Sidi Saïd supported President Bouteflika's candidacy for a second term. The UGTA is one example of how unions became a new source of legitimacy for the regime.

Nevertheless, some unions, such as the National Autonomous Union of Public Administration Staff (SNAPAP) and the Autonomous Union of Education and Training Workers (SATEF), tried to protect their autonomy and succeeded in amassing hundreds of thousands of members who regularly participated in demonstrations. As a result, the authorities engaged in all kinds of subterfuges to neutralize them. The authorities prohibited meetings and demonstrations, using blackmail, threats, and all sorts of harassment. They were also able to engage in indirect persecution of troublesome trade unionists in unions the government had infiltrated;

for example, many were brought before the unions' own disciplinary committees, while others were arbitrarily dismissed (Comité national des libertés syndicales, 2005: 11). Sometimes, trade unionists were arrested by law enforcement and imprisoned. Strikes initiated by trade unions were systematically declared illegal by both the authorities and the employers, who were encouraged to break the strike movement. The government, especially through the Ministry of Labor, interfered in the unions' internal affairs by breaking the secrecy of correspondence and even forging correspondence to demoralize the union's base and manipulate the judiciary (Comité national des libertés syndicales, 2005: 11).

In addition, the authorities refused to register unions seen as a threat, such as the Algerian Confederation of Autonomous Unions (CASA), the National Union of Algerian Workers (SNATA), or Algiers High School Council (CLA). The CLA, which had a high mobilization capacity, often conducting strikes for weeks, was prohibited from attending and organizing meetings, and leading members such as Redouane Osmane were arrested and prosecuted in 2006. The authorities persecuted CLA-affiliated teachers, banned them from joining their workstations, and froze their salaries. The National Autonomous Council of Professors of Secondary and Technical Education (CNAPEST) suffered much the same fate. Present in 46 *wilaya*s and with a great capacity for mobilization, CNAPEST frequently saw its members harassed by the authorities, who refused to register the organization.

The authorities also created regime-beholden clones of independent unions, just as it did with human rights associations. The tactic used was to send several individuals to join an independent union and create a conflict. Numerous associations split because of such internal conflicts. Sometimes, splits were not engineered by agents of the regime, but the latter nevertheless succeeded in capitalizing on them by supporting breakaway factions against the mother organization. The authorities could better control their activities by co-opting former dissidents and supporting their new organizations. A few examples illustrate this technique. To counter the autonomous unions of workers of education and training, or SATEF, led by Mohand-Salem Sadali, the authorities created the SATEF-bis, led by Abdelmadjid Basti. To counter the National Council of Higher Education Teachers (CNES), led by Abdelmalek Azzi, they created the CNES-bis, led by Abdelhafid Milat. To neutralize the CNAPEST, they created the SNAPEST (National Autonomous Union of Secondary and Technical Teachers), led by Mériane Meziane. They did the same with the SNAPAP. Shaken by a severe crisis due to severe ideological differences, personal conflicts, struggles for leadership, and lack of consensus, the SNAPAP witnessed several defections of its members, including cadres. In 2002, the authorities used the SNAPAP's internal dissensions to back a splinter group and created the SNAPAP-bis.

In addition, when an independent union called for a strike, the regime would instruct its clone to call for its strike the day before; a few hours or days later, the clone would announce that the government had accepted its demands and that, as a result, it would now call off the strike (Author's interviews with several trade unionists between July and September 2021). Another technique the government used consisted of using strike-breakers. Such was the case with the National Union of Officers of the Merchant Navy (SNOMMAR). The government was wary of this independent trade union's ability to mobilize. When SNOMMAR announced a strike in 2004, the authorities hired strike-breakers from a transport company to replace them for three months. Strikers were administratively sanctioned with a salary freeze, eight SNOMMAR officers were suspended, and four others were dismissed (Comité National des libertés syndicales, 2005: 15).

CSOs: Mirror Image of the Regime

While it is beyond dispute that the authorities have done much to fragment and co-opt the CSOs, it is also true that the latter share in the responsibility for their fragmentation. In Algeria, CSOs tend to suffer from several intrinsic weaknesses. For instance, there is a severe democratic deficit. Most associations are very hierarchical, with a president who wields immense power. There are also clear organizational weaknesses (lack of training, management skills, and leadership capacities), internal disputes, a frequent lack of consensus, and an absence of mechanisms for conflict resolution through debate and majority voting (author's interviews with several activists between September and October 2021). The CSOs themselves are often responsible for such shortcomings.

This was particularly clear during the 2019 *Hirak*. Initiatives were numerous and creative, but the *Hirak* achieved very little partly because the associational sector could not help the movement organize, structure, and achieve more concrete goals. A few examples are worth citing. The Coordination of Autonomous Trade Unions attempted to coordinate and combine forces with political leaders (Karim Tabbou, Abdelaziz

Rahabi, Mustapha Bouchachi) and political parties (FLN, RND, MPA, MSP, FJD). They succeeded in bringing together some of these stakeholders for a consultation meeting on August 24, 2019. However, this turned out to be the organization's first and final achievement.

It should be noted that from the first weeks of the *Hirak*, ideas began to germinate, with concrete proposals and plans to end the crisis. One of the first organizational frameworks to emerge was the Civil Society Dynamics Collective for a Democratic Transition, which campaigned for a new constituent process including thirty associations, such as RAJ, LADDH, *Mouwatana*, *Tharwa Fadhma n'Soumer*, SOS Disparus, *Djazairouna*, Wassila Network, SOS Culture Bab El Oued, the CNDDC, the Collective of committed young people, Agir pour le Changement et la Démocratie en Algérie (ACDA), CNES, and even SNAPAP. On March 18, 2019, they released a document, a detailed roadmap in which they recommended the organization of "national consensus meetings bringing together all the sensitivities of society" with the task of agreeing on the "practical modalities of setting up the Constituent." The dialogue launched by CSOs extended to the autonomous unions grouped within the Confederation of Algerian Trade Unions (CSA) and extended to the Civil Forum for Change, which from the outset said it was in favor of an early return to elections. Despite differences, the three poles succeeded in holding a national conference on June 15, 2019. They made public a joint declaration proposing a transition period of six months to one year, a presidential body or a consensus personality, and a government by competent technocrats. The Forum initiated the "Aïn Benian Conference" initiative for a National Dialogue. They held a meeting on July 6, 2019, at the Aïn Benian Higher School of Hospitality, under the chairmanship of Abdelaziz Rahabi. Some 80 participants, including Ali Benflis, Abdallah Djaballah, Abderrazak Makri, Soufiane Djilali, Fatiha Benabbou, Ali Fawzi Rebaïne, and Kamel Guemazi participated in the conclave. The dominant option that emerged was to move quickly to a presidential election.

On August 24, 2019, signatories of the June 15 platform met again at Safex, in the presence of several other influential personalities, including Mostefa Bouchachi, Abdelaziz Rahabi, and even sociologist Nacer Djabi. Many party leaders also took part in this conference. Among them were Karim Tabbou, Soufiane Djilali, and Abdallah Djaballah. This conference aimed to "bring together points of view" for a joint initiative to end the crisis (Benfodil, 2021).

94   D. GHANEM

In the same spirit of seeking a framework for consultation and collective reflection, arenas of debate and public discussions were launched all over the city. These agoras were opportunities for brainstorming between citizens who were eager to inhabit the public space after twenty years of silence. Monday debates were organized in the Algerian National Theater space, while Saturday debates, called "Les Rencontres d'Audin" and organized by think tank *Nabni*, took place at the Liberty Park, in Algiers.

Also, there were discussions, conferences, and citizens' workshops agitated the college campuses. Add to this the extraordinary "*Hiraki* literature," which abounded in the columns of newspapers, electronic sites, social networks, blogs, numerous university publications, and Books. This literary efflorescence injected reflection, sociology, and critical distance into the movement. Unfortunately, these efforts have been spoiled, on the one hand, by the inability of people to reach a consensus on how to move forward, and on the other by the repression of the authorities that surveilled the *Hirak* closely and cracked down on activists in the middle of the confinement in 2020.

Taking advantage of the Covid-19 global pandemic, the authorities cracked down on CSOs, activists, and even academics to stifle the last voices of dissent. Arrests and detentions continued in the second year of the *Hirak*, when marches resumed after a one-year halt for pandemic reasons. Some CSOs, including the LADDH and its twin, LADH, did little more than vacillate between shy denunciations and total silence. These two institutions, in particular, were so weak and internally fragmented that they were unable to fight for human rights and the rights of detainees. The LADDH was "atomized," in the words of many interviewees. The LADDH experienced serious dissension starting in 2007, and the crisis reached its apex in 2015 when the LADDH split into three groups. The first was led by Hocine Zehouane, the second by Mustapha Bouchachi before being taken over by Noureddine Benissad, and the third by Salah Dabouz (*El Watan*, 2015).

The Bouchachi/Benissad wing asserted that it was the only genuine LADDH. It was affiliated with the International Federation for Human Rights (Fidh) and the Euro-Mediterranean Human Rights Network (*Liberté*, 2010). The LADH, on the other hand, had very few members, and its leaders were inexperienced and with little background in human rights. During the *Hirak* and the repression that followed, both the LADDH and the LADH did not do much for human rights. Their efforts were either ineffective or non-existent. Not only that, but it seemed that these two institutions were afraid of being associated with those human rights defenders that the authorities deemed "too threatening" (Author's interviews with several activists between July and September 2021).

The LADDH has been described as a "travel agency" due to the fact that members could easily obtain overseas training and education (author's interviews with former LADDH and other human rights activists). Most of the trainees picked were "incompetent," and their sole goal was to spend a few days abroad. As explained by one former member of the organization:

> The LADDH is divided on these issues because its members are human rights activists first and foremost, and we are not angels [smiles]. Identifying and training a more significant number of human rights defenders requires more thorough screening and better selection of those who will serve as multipliers in disseminating knowledge and training.... With time, the league became a travel agency, offering trips to those who would not make any problem back home and remaining silent. (Author's interview with a former member of the LADDH living in Montreal, June 16, 2021)

Many activists agree that the two significant difficulties with their work on human rights were the lack of coordination among different actors, due to a highly fragmented field and repression. Indeed, according to several an activist, even the genuine human rights groups were unable to agree on basic principles. The regime capitalized on this vulnerability to keep things as they were or splinter the groups further. Issues of "ego" and "personalities" were the most cited. There was a constant battle over who should receive credit for what. Rim, an independent human rights activist formerly with the LADDH and then ACDA, explained:

> Whenever a new effort or idea emerges, there is an intense backlash from those who want a larger say in the outcome. There are not enough words to describe how internal struggle, this self-sabotage, is killing the *milieu*. I do not believe the regime or Algeria's security agencies are to blame for this. We are to blame for our self-inflicted wounds. [...] It all turned into a popularity battle to see who could get the most attention and who would become the media's star. (Author's interview with Rim, June 16, 2021)

Another well-known independent human rights activist, one experienced in fighting for the rights of minorities, explained:

> At a certain point with the *Hirak*, many human rights defenders and lawyers wanted to represent the most famous political detainees, forgetting about those arrested and put in jail in the middle of nowhere somewhere in Algeria. They wanted the "selfie"; this is why I call the trials of prominent personalities the "selfie trials." I refuse. I only defend those who have no voice to be heard. I hear them. (Author's interview, July 17, 2021)

Truth be told, organizations such as the LADDH had little interest in improving Algeria's human rights policies. The regime had co-opted the LADDH, and people working there did not want to lose their advantages. Interviewees referred to it as an "empty shell," a "paper tiger." Some stated that, as long as some human rights are prioritized over others and as long as they are not considered in their entirety, the field will remain "atomized," and the fight will be superficial. The LADDH, according to several respondents, should adopt a policy of "leaving no one behind," which means that all human rights should be addressed immediately, rather than prioritizing some and leaving others for later. Many women's rights activists explained that the LADDH was "completely ineffective." As one such activist put it, "women's issues are not of interest to them because they are not a priority and because they do not want to upset the regime."

On the issue of training, interviewees identified the lack of knowledge of international law as a major problem. Many lawyers, for instance, explained that while some lawyers and activists had been trained for over two decades with all the "money that the EU was pouring in" to be able to use international law in local courts, they did not disseminate such knowledge. According to many, this was a "major mistake," as human rights defenders have to exhaust all domestic remedies before bringing a complaint to the international level, and not that many people do so in Algeria. A lack of understanding of how to properly document cases and the lack of information on detainees was also a problem. As one activist explained:

> We are in dire need of campaign planning and communications training. Communicating is critical, whether you create posters, flyers, or short movies! Algerian activists must be trained to communicate their message to the general public and the international community. There is such a level of mediocrity. It is depressing. (Author's interview, July 18, 2021)

Also, numerous respondents emphasized the importance of training journalists to follow trials, collect information about victims, and most importantly, follow cases through to conclusion and report on them regularly in national newspapers. Numerous times, the importance of serious, well-researched, and well-written court chronicles was underlined. As explained by Siham:

> We have hundreds of people who have been arrested, and we hear about them here and there on social media thanks to the work of a few people like Zaki Hanache, who is doing a great job, by the way [...] but then what? Journalists must be trained to observe trials and report in French and Arabic on the proceedings, including the progression of the cases, the conclusions reached, and any possible appeals. This is how we can bring the case of detainees to the public's attention.[...] We lack this. [...] We are bad at communicating and coordinating but great at fighting each other. It is so discouraging. (Author's interview, July 2, 2021)

Financial constraints were also a concern, even though all interviewees agreed that this was the case for small associations but not for those that were "close to the regime," such as the LADDH, among others. Some respondents remarked that the problem was not necessarily about money, which might be mismanaged even when accessible. There was a widespread perception that the money on hand had become a source of enrichment for specific individuals and groups who engaged in patronage and had electoral ambitions.

Essentially, the Algerian regime has proven skilled at controlling the associative sphere through legal means, bureaucratic practices, co-optation, scapegoating, and repression. The techniques used by the state to steer the growth of the associative field parallel the strategies employed by the state to fragment and control the development of political parties. Co-optation, marginalization, and intimidation are tactics used to obstruct CSOs' efforts, just as is done with political parties. Public funds are critical in keeping associations afloat, yet legal and bureaucratic loopholes allow the government to favor "friendly" groups while prohibiting more independent organizations from operating.

Associations, like political parties, are frequently formed in response to the demands of various factions of the regime, each of which needs social representation in society and sometimes a patronage system. The associative field has evolved into a reservoir from which the state may co-opt individuals and appoint them to public service without relying on increasingly discredited political parties (Liverani, 2008: 123). As a result, rather than altering the state's institutional structure, the associative sphere has come to constitute yet another means of propping it up.

As for the civil society organizations themselves, most are weak and unable to articulate citizens' interests and demands or defend their rights. Consequently, their social reach is limited, and they are incapable of being the interface between the population and its leaders. This has led to a lack of trust by many ordinary people, who have felt for a long time that riots are the only way to express their grievances—as shown by the spontaneous riots and demonstrations that have periodically shaken the country since the beginning of the 2000s. In fact, despite the advent of the *Hirak* in 2019 and its peaceful nature, riots flared in parts of the country in 2021 (Ghanem, 2021).

Ultimately, Algeria's political transformation from outright authoritarianism to competitive authoritarianism demonstrates the regime's skill at using associations to shore up its legitimacy, especially before the international community. Associations, at least formally, contributed to the pluralistic nature of Algeria's political system, especially as the 1980s drew to a close, but went on to become a support system for the state, all the more so in the 2000s. Indeed, beginning with the Chadli years, the instrumental use of the associative realm increased, reaching its zenith during Bouteflika's twenty years in office. Enabling Bouteflika to present himself as above the discredited parties, the associative field also provided him with non-traditional channels to communicate his policy agendas and cultivate ties with various population sectors. If anything, the current toxic political environment, coupled with what looks to be challenging economic years ahead, militates against the empowerment of CSOs. The regime is likely to tighten its grip on civil society.

References

Agence France-Presse (AFP). (2021, August 12). Algérie: la diaspora en première ligne face aux feux et à la crise sanitaire. *AFP*. https://www.lefigaro.fr/international/algerie-la-diaspora-en-premiere-ligne-face-aux-feux-et-a-la-crise-sanitaire-20210812. Accessed January 24, 2022.

4 DIVIDE AND CONQUER: THE ATOMIZATION OF CIVIL SOCIETY   99

Alioui, M. (2019, February 5). Une association menacée de dissolution. *Huffington Post*. http://www.droits-laddh.org/une-association-menacee-de-dissolution-pour-avoir-participe-a-la-cop-23.html?lang=fr. Accessed January 24, 2022.

Amarouche, A. (2012). Régime politique, société civile et économie en Algérie: une analyse institutionnaliste. *Mondes en développement, 159*(3), 45–57.

Amnesty International. (2021, October 13). Algeria: Dissolution of Leading Rights Group RAJ: A Blow for Freedoms. *Amnesty International*. https://www.amnesty.org/fr/latest/press-release/2021/10/algeria-dissolution-of-leading-rights-group-raj-a-blow-for-freedoms/. Accessed January 24, 2022.

Amnesty Internationale, Fédération Internationale des droits de l'homme (fidh), Human Rights Watch, Reporters sans frontières. (1998, February 28). MDE 28/18/98f. https://www.amnesty.org/fr/wp-content/uploads/sites/8/2021/06/mde280181998fr.pdf. Accessed January 24, 2022.

Aubenas, F. (1998, February 12). Alger: L'ombre du FIS sur la visite des européens. Une lettre des islamistes sème le trouble dans un show bien huilé. *Libération*. https://www.liberation.fr/planete/1998/02/12/alger-l-ombre-du-fis-sur-la-visite-des-europeens-une-lettre-des-islamistes-seme-le-trouble-dans-un-s_229622/. Accessed January 24, 2022.

Babadji, R. (1987). L'Etat, les individus et les groupes en Algérie: continuité et rupture. *Annuaire de l'Afrique du Nord* (26), 99–115.

Babadji, R. (1989). Le phénomène associatif en Algérie: genèse et perspectives. *Annuaire de l'Afrique du Nord* (28), 229–242.

Benali, A. (2020, September 9). Ould Abbès lors de son procès: 'je n'ai même pas bénéficié d'un logement'. *AlgérieEco*. https://www.algerie-eco.com/2020/09/09/ould-abbes-lors-de-son-proces-je-nai-meme-pas-beneficie-dun-logement/. Accessed January 24, 2022.

Benasseur, R. (2015, April 26). Conseil supérieur de la jeunesse: pourquoi faire? *Algérie1*. https://www.algerie1.com/focus/conseil-superieur-de-la-jeunesse-pourquoi-faire. Accessed January 24, 2022.

Benfodil, M. (2021, February 22). Un formidable laboratoire de réinvention du politique: Les agoras libres du Hirak. *El Watan*. https://www.elwatan.com/edition/actualite/les-agoras-libres-du-hirak-22-02-2021. Accessed January 24, 2022.

Benramdane, D. (2015). Les associations Algériennes des acteurs émergents en quête de reconnaissance. *CISP and the European Union*.

Boukarine, A. (2019, January 6). Association Barik 21 de Skikda: Le processus de dissolution engagé. *Liberté*.

Carlier, O. (1995). *Entre nation et djihad. Histoire sociale des radicalismes algériens*. Presses de sciences Po.

Chagnollaud, J. P. (2002). Interview avec Ali Haroun. *Confluences Méditerranée* (40), 213–238. https://www.cairn.info/revue-confluences-mediterra nee-2002-1-page-213.htm. Accessed January 24, 2022.

Chaker, S. (1989). La revendication Berbère entre culture et politique. *Annuaire de l'Afrique du Nord* (28): 281–296.

Comité National des libertés Syndicales. (2005). Rapport préliminaire du CNLS sur les libertés syndicales en Algérie (1), 1–19. https://algeria-watch.org/ pdf/pdf_fr/cnls_rapport_libertes_syndicales.pdf. Accessed January 24, 2022.

Cox, R. (1999). Civil Society at the Turn of the Millennium: Prospects for an Alternative World Order. *Review of International Studies, 25*(1), 3–19.

Dahak, B. (1982). Pour une approche théorique du phénomène associatif. *RASJEP, 26*, 509–534.

Djilali, B. (2009, July 30). Les Comités de soutien à Bouteflika se transforment en ONG. *Liberté*. https://algeria-watch.org/?p=39070. Accessed January 24, 2022.

Dris-Ait Hamadouche, L. (2017). La société civile vue à l'aune de la résilience du système politique algérien. *L'Année du Maghreb* (16): 289–306. https://jou rnals.openedition.org/anneemaghreb/3093#bodyftn8. Accessed January 24, 2022.

El Watan. (2015, June 2). Plusieurs ailes se disputent le sigle: LADDH, la difficile union. *El Watan*. https://www.elwatan.com/edition/actualite/plu sieurs-ailes-se-disputent-le-sigle-laddh-la-difficile-union-02-06-2015. Accessed January 24, 2022.

Europe Direct Info. (1998, February 10). Algérie: un vent nouveau. *Europa*. https://www.europarl.europa.eu/press/sdp/dirinf/fr/1998/d980211.htm. Accessed January 24, 2022.

Europe Note de synthèse. (1998, March 2). Rapport délégation du PE en Algérie. *Europa*. https://www.europarl.europa.eu/press/sdp/synt/fr/1998/ s980302.htm. Accessed January 24, 2022.

Fatès, F. (1994). Les Associations de femmes Algériennes face à la menace islamiste. *Nouvelles questions féministes, 2*(15), 51–65.

Gadant, M. (1995). *Le nationalisme Algérien et les femmes*. L'Harmattan.

Ghanem, D. (2021, March 24). Algeria's Achilles' Heel? Resource Regionalism in Ouargla. *Carnegie Middle East Center*. https://carnegie-mec.org/2021/ 03/24/algeria-s-achilles-heel-resource-regionalism-in-ouargla-pub-84157. Accessed January 24, 2022.

Hamdi, R. (2021, April 29). Algérie: SOS Bab El Oued a-t-elle vraiment bénéficié d'un financement étranger? *Jeune Afrique*. https://www.jeuneafri que.com/1163192/politique/algerie-sos-bab-el-oued-a-t-elle-vraiment-ben eficie-dun-financement-etranger/. Accessed January 24, 2022.

Hearn, J. (2001). The 'Uses and Abuses' of Civil Society in Africa. *Review of African Political Economy* (87), 43–53. https://www.liberte-algerie.com/actualite/le-processus-judiciaire-de-dissolution-engage-308929. Accessed January 24, 2022.

Human Rights Watch (HRW). (2014, March 30). Bureaucratic Ploys Used to Stifle Associations. *HRW*. https://www.hrw.org/news/2014/03/30/algeria-bureaucratic-ploys-used-stifle-associations. Accessed January 24, 2022.

Izarouken, A. (2004). Le mouvement associatif en Algérie: état des lieux, état des savoirs. *Crasc*. https://ouvrages.crasc.dz/pdfs/2008_algrie_50ans_apres_fr_arab_izarouken.pdf. Accessed January 24, 2022.

Kantar Public for the European Union. (2017). EU neighbours/south: Algeria. *Kantar Survey*. http://www.euneighbours.eu/sites/default/files/publications/2017-12/Factsheet%20Algeria%20ENG.pdf. Accessed January 24, 2022.

Kharoum, O. (2003, July 14). L'argent de Bouteflika. *El Watan*. https://algeria-watch.org/?p=39727. Accessed January 24, 2022.

Lalami, F. (2014). Algérie, pause dans les mobilisations féministes. Nouvelles questions féministes. *Antipodes* (33), 34–42.

Lamchichi, A. (1992). *L'islamisme en Algérie*. L'Harmattan.

Latrous, N. (2014, September 8). Le patronat Algérien règle ses comptes. *L'Opinion*. https://www.lopinion.fr/international/le-patronat-algerien-regle-ses-comptes. Accessed January 24, 2022.

Leca, J. (1990). Etat et société en Algérie., In B. Kodmani & M. Chartouni (Eds.), *Maghreb: les année de transition*. Masson.

Leca, J., & Vatin, C. (1975). *L'Algérie politique. Institutions et régime*. Presses de la fondation nationale de Sciences politiques.

Le Monde. (1987, September 1). Algérie Le pétrole vert au lieu de l'or noir. *Le Monde* (archives). https://www.lemonde.fr/archives/article/1987/09/01/algerie-le-petrole-vert-au-lieu-de-l-or-noir_4046269_1819218.html. Accessed January 24, 2022.

Le Monde. (1998, January 20). En Algérie, l'Europe veut amorcer un dialogue politique. *Le Monde* (archives). https://www.lemonde.fr/archives/article/1998/01/20/en-algerie-l-europe-veut-amorcer-un-dialogue-politique_362 3317_1819218.html. Accessed January 24, 2022.

Libération. (1996, December 3). Algérie: 900 millions de francs de l'union Européenne. *Libération*. https://www.liberation.fr/planete/1996/12/03/algerie-900-millions-de-francs-de-l-ue_192007/. Accessed January 24, 2022.

Liberté. (2003, July 12). Un émissaire de Bouteflika à Béjaïa. *Liberté*. https://www.liberte-algerie.com/radar/un-emissaire-de-bouteflika-a-bejaia-6770. Accessed January 24, 2022.

Liberté. (2010, March 27). L'aile Bouchachi a tenu le 3e congrès de la LADDH. *Liberté*. https://www.liberte-algerie.com/actualite/laile-bouchachi-a-tenu-le-3e-congres-de-la-laddh-76852/. Accessed January 24, 2022.

Liverani, A. (2008). *Civil Society in Algeria: The Political Functions of Associational Life*. Routledge.

M, H. (2003, November 22). Vers la mise en place d'un comité de soutien à Benflis. *Liberté*. https://www.liberte-algerie.com/actualite/vers-la-mise-en-place-dun-comite-de-soutien-a-benflis-9412. Accessed January 24, 2022.

N, D. (2003, July 12). FLN: manoeuvre à l'Est. *Liberté*. https://www.liberte-algerie.com/actualite/fln-manoeuvres-a-lest-6788. Accessed January 24, 2022.

N, M. (2003, April 24). Bouteflika réactive ses comités de soutien. *Liberté*. https://www.liberte-algerie.com/actualite/bouteflika-reactive-ses-comites-de-soutien-4918. Accessed January 24, 2022.

Naïli, M. (2001, October 23). Pas de subventions aux associations qui nous critiquent. *Le jeune indépendant*.

Remaoun, M. (1997). Les mouvements de femmes pour leurs droits en Algérie: quelque éléments d'approche. *Crasc*.

Rouadjia, A. (2006). La lutte des femmes laïques en Algérie. *Confluences Méditerranée* (59), 125–132.

Saliha. (2015, June 8). Oran, 346 associations dissoutes depuis janvier 2015. *Algérie360*. https://www.algerie360.com/oran-346-associations-dissoutes-depuis-janvier-2015/. Accessed January 24, 2022.

Stora, B. (2001). *La guerre invisible. Algérie, années 90*. Presses de Sciences Po.

Sutour, S. (2017). Rapport d'information fait au nom de la commission des affaires européennes sur le volet méditerranéen de la politique de voisinage: Le cas de l'Algérie. *Rapport d'information du Sénat* (689), 3–43. https://www.senat.fr/rap/r16-689/r16-6891.pdf. Accessed January 24, 2022.

Thieux L. (2009). Le secteur associatif en Algérie: la difficile émergence d'un espace de contestation politique. *L'Année du Maghreb*, 129–144. http://journals.openedition.org/anneemaghreb/545. Accessed January 24, 2022.

Tuquoi, J. P. (1998a, January 17). Ayant obtenu gain de cause, Alger accepte la venue de la troïka européenne. *Le Monde* (archives). https://www.lemonde.fr/archives/article/1998/01/17/ayant-obtenu-gain-de-cause-alger-accepte-la-venue-de-la-troika-europeenne_3631074_1819218.html. Accessed January 24, 2022.

Tuquoi, J. P. (1998b). Mission à portée limitée pour la troïka européenne en Algérie. *Le Monde* (archives).

Youngs, R. (2005). *The European Union and the Promotion of Democracy: Europe's Mediterranean and Asians policies*. Oxford University Press.

CHAPTER 5

A Controlled Economic Liberalization

The fifth pillar sustaining the Algerian regime's longevity is the distribution of rent resources, which is closely bound up with patronage and corruption. In a country where the share of hydrocarbons in exports represents 97%, rent was and remains the means by which the regime satisfies its appetite, the hunger of its *ayant droits* and loyal clients, and the population's needs. Resources are concentrated in state hands, and the politico-military elite has enjoyed substantial discretionary power since the country's independence in allocating those resources.

Algeria's rulers have routinely used the tax system, credit, licensing concessions, government contracts, and other economic policy levers to reward allies, punish opponents, and maintain the system. Rent has been a formidable instrument to force compliance and penalize those who oppose the regime. It has also enabled the regime to keep the population in check and buy social peace through the use of major subsidies.

As the government has had a significant and decisive impact on the livelihoods, careers, and business opportunities of a large proportion of the population, opposition in all its forms has become a high-risk venture. Government credit, licenses, contracts, funds, subventions, and even property rights may be denied to political opponents, but also to activists of various kinds and businesses perceived as threatening or associated with a threatening actor. Such people may be denied access to

© The Author(s), under exclusive license to Springer Nature
Switzerland AG 2022
D. Ghanem, *Understanding the Persistence of Competitive Authoritarianism in Algeria*, Middle East Today,
https://doi.org/10.1007/978-3-031-05102-9_5

103

newsprint or advertising; CSOs may be denied funds; public employees, unionists, and critics may be fired or denied access to essential goods and services; and independent media may be shut down. Unless the state distributes resources equitably, resources for independent ventures must come from the private sector and civil society. However, as the state has the vast majority of the means of production and monopolizes the primary sources of wealth, it has kept CSOs weakened and poor, and made sure to hinder and limit the private sector's capacities. Hence, there is no feasible financial foundation for meaningful opposition.

During the first two decades following independence, the Algerian regime pursued a statist socialist economic model based on large State-Owned Enterprises (SOEs), which controlled no less than 80% of all economic activity and served as the principal economic development engine. Massive redistribution was possible due to oil revenues. The government spent formidable resources on education, housing, subsidies for food, and employment opportunities. This method was effective until the mid-1980s. A growing population coupled with the oil shock of 1986 resulted in a 50% decline in budgetary revenues and a severe economic slump. Algeria found itself on the verge of defaulting on its international debt. Furthermore, the balance of payment deficit resulted in a significant decrease in imports, which resulted in an upsurge in social unrest throughout the country. With the riots of October 1988, the *Infitah* [liberalization] was announced, but it was a well-controlled liberalization to avoid jeopardizing the state's monopoly, prevent elite defection, and block opposition challenges (Tlemçani, 1999).

Moreover, during the widespread violence of the Black Decade (1991–2001), the state asserted itself as a provider of security. It took advantage of the long-lasting climate of fear and extreme violence to reformulate the social contract and implement draconian economic policies imposed by the International Monetary Fund (IMF). During the 2000s, state economic power was so extensive under Bouteflika, who benefited from the financial cushion Algeria got due to high oil prices, that he made it very costly for elites to defect, difficult for opposition forces to mobilize resources, and unimaginable for citizens to turn their daily protests into revolutionary ones. Bouteflika remained largely unchallenged for four mandates.

Furthermore, during his 20 years in office, Bouteflika granted control of much of the economy to a group of businessmen who had become wealthy through their access to public contracts. He thereby brought more money into the ruling system and established a support base. This momentarily undermined the military's hold on power. It also fueled widespread corruption: due to economic clientelism, access to Algeria's hydrocarbon wealth became more dependent on devotion to the regime. Bouteflika's exit in 2019 and the jailing of his coterie, including several businessmen, restored the lost equilibrium in which the military got back their full grip on power.

Today, political neutralization through redistribution and co-optation is still a key pillar of the regime. Political actors (parties, unions, CSOs) as well as economic ones have been co-opted. The leeway left to private actors is conditioned on their allegiance. As for the general population, the regime buys (when possible and needed) social peace. In 2011, amid the "Arab Spring," not only did the state pursue its policy of subsidization, but also consolidated it to meet social demands and prevent the politicization of economic demands. It raised wages and pensions and provided jobs, housing, and generous handouts—through loans, tax exemption, and debt cancelation.

Oil rent remains the means by which the regime buys the social peace, especially in the form of political allegiance, that helps the system perpetuate itself. People from the politico-military establishment, the bureaucracy, prominent politically connected people in business, and small-scale manufacturers, traders, and retailers all benefit. This sociological and political configuration, linked to the desire of the ruling elites to remain in power and keep their positions, maintains a fundamental confusion between public and private, and hence increases the opportunities for nepotism, favoritism, and corruption. The cohesion of the ruling groups is maintained through a fair and equitable distribution of the rent money at the top, or at least one that is negotiated between members of different groups. The benefits of such redistribution can be observed from the top state positions and on down. This "neopatriarchal management" of the state, this confusion between public goods and private goods, continues today (Jolly, 2001: 115).

1962–1988: The Monopolization of the Hydrocarbon Industry

After independence, Algeria was thrown into unprecedented economic, social, and political disarray. The war of independence claimed over one million lives and left at least 400,000 orphans. Half a million peasants were relocated, and their villages, crops, and stocks destroyed or abandoned. Over four months, just before and immediately after Algeria declared independence, 90% of the European population, the colons, around one million individuals, abandoned their homes and places of employment and fled the country. They accounted for the vast majority of private capital and professional, technical, and managerial expertise in the country at the time.

Algeria lacked a highly skilled workforce, a thriving entrepreneurial class, and cutting-edge technological expertise. And it showed. For instance, many schools were closed due to a lack of teachers. Doctors had decreased from about 3,000 at the start of 1962 to 600 following independence later that year (Clegg, 1971: 44). There were almost two million jobless agricultural, industrial, and commercial employees. The colons abandoned over a million hectares of the best land, and the time for harvesting and plowing was rapidly coming. The owners sabotaged much of the agricultural and industrial machinery prior to their departure.

Most importantly, the new governmental authorities could not resolve pressing social and economic issues. The economy was in a state of disarray. In this situation, in the summer and early autumn of 1962, while various factions were struggling for control and power, landless laborers occupied farms where they used to work and kept them in production. The *autogestion* [self-management] was born in agriculture.

Ben Bella and Autogestion

Workers and peasants' "spontaneous" and "anarchic" actions overpowered the *Exécutif Provisoire* [Provisional Executive]. The workers' first concern was to ensure their economic survival; the revolutionary effort to capture the means of production for the nation came second. The seizure of factories and farms as an explicit aspect of the battle against colonialism was significantly more prevalent among national groups like the *Union Générale des Travailleurs Algériens* [General Union of Algerian Workers] or UGTA, the FLN, and the Army, notwithstanding their ideological differences. The UGTA was instrumental in establishing the *comités de gestion*, formed of workers, as the ideal form of revolutionary organization dedicated to seizing the means of production, particularly in bigger cities and in the *Mitidja* plain (Chaulet, 1971). The Army took the most valuable estates, and was followed by the bureaucratic elite and their cronies. In western Algeria, the Army redistributed the lands to ex-combatants and placed major estates under the direct supervision of Army units. In many instances, spontaneously created management committees were forcibly disbanded, the original permanent employees were expelled, and the Army assumed control. The Army needed to do so because it wanted to establish a political base through land distribution to ex-combatants whose loyalty was to the Army rather than to other organizations or groups. The army was also, like the UGTA, keen on making the return of the colons impossible and preventing the emerging national bourgeoisie from establishing a foothold in the economy (Clegg, 1971: 51).

Additionally, the Army's ideology, influenced by Mao and Castro, led it to think that the state should control the means of production. Thus, the Army believed in peasant cooperatives and state farms rather than *autogestion*. Simultaneously, several leaders of *wilaya*s (provinces) attempted to place their supporters on European farms in their territories to lay the groundwork for future political and, if necessary, military assistance. They could always rely on their local fiefs' support if a disagreement with the central authorities occurred. The FLN, on the other hand, did not begin establishing *comités de gestion* in agriculture or industry until late October, even though some of its militants had worked alongside the UGTA from the start.

By September, Ben Bella was firmly established as the newly elected Assembly's prime minister. He reorganized the movement of *autogestion*, formalized it through legislation, and wrapped it in socialist rhetoric to gain the working class' support (Ruedy, 1992). The *autogestion* was sold to Algerians as the first step of agrarian reform. Under the *autogestion* system, thousands of agricultural operations and industrial enterprises were codified by several decrees between 1962 and 1965. First, on October 22, Ben Bella's administration published a decree establishing *comités de gestion* of unoccupied agricultural properties. Then, on November 23, this approach was extended to industry and mining. Simultaneously, another order prohibited any transaction in abandoned European property, the *biens vacants* [unoccupied estates], and empowered prefects to nullify any such transactions made since independence (Dumont 1962). In addition to over one million hectares of land, there were thousands of abandoned industrial enterprises, small businesses, and vacant housing units—in Algiers alone, there were no fewer than 200,000 (Clegg, 1971: 58). These houses were given to individuals with whom the leadership wanted to enhance its political and economic ties.

The October 22 and November 23 decrees established *comités de gestion* in agriculture, mining, and industry in those cases in which the enterprise employed more than ten people. The establishment of *autogestion* as a distinct economic management system and the official foundation of Algerian socialism did not occur until March, with the *décrets de mars* (March 18 and March 22, 1963). Ben Bella and the majority of the FLN's leaders, who had been taken aback by the seizure of colonial farms and lands by laborers, publicly embraced the *comités de gestion* as an intrinsic element of Algeria's economic structure and described its practice as the bedrock of Algerian socialism in the March decrees (Clegg, 1971: 51–53). The decrees appeared to give the government official approval for the summer's events.

Yet the workers' and UGTA's efforts compelled Ben Bella and his allies to take a decisive step toward social control of the means of production. The *décrets de mars* made it apparent that the monitoring of *autogestion* would be delegated to the state and that the state bureaucracy would have complete power over the economic operations of the *comités de gestion*. It also provided them with the opportunity to engage in broad manipulation and interference in the makeup of the *comités* and their day-to-day operations. Starting from this point, the system evolved under the supervision of the state, not just in agriculture but also, even if more slowly, in industry and services. SOEs in industry and services began around the same time, in 1963. In theory, the Charter of Algiers, ratified by the FLN in April 1964, marked the culmination of the *autogestion* movement and formalized self-management as the central ideological pillar of Algerian socialism, but in reality self-management was already coming under the tutelage of the state, which was supposed to incarnate the general interests of the community.

One mechanism for maintaining strict central supervision over self-managed farms was establishing a supervisory agency for the self-managed agricultural sector: the *Office National de la Réforme Agraire* [National Office for the Agrarian Revolution] or ONRA. The ONRA exercised complete authority over all agencies dealing with ex-colonial farms and agricultural reform. Then *comités de gestion* also fell under central control. A *comité's* three members were selected by the local prefect or elected by party officials. They were made subject to the *Bureau National de la Protection et de la Gestion des Biens-Vacants* [National Office for the Protection and Management of Vacant Properties], which exercised its authority through the local prefect's office. The local government's

5 A CONTROLLED ECONOMIC LIBERALIZATION   109

comités de gestion were generally appointed, rather than elected, by the workforce. The central authorities requested that all prefects give ex-combatants preference in future appointments to *comités*. Eventually, the UGTA, which was never an autonomous body vis-à-vis the FLN and the state, was subordinated to the party-state. The *comités* fell under even more central supervision, to the point that the administration started to manage every aspect of the *comités'* economic activities, rendering the idea of *autogestion* meaningless. Very quickly, *autogestion* was eliminated in industry and services. In agriculture, it was transformed into a state sector.

Members of the *comités* were chosen based on their relationships with the local government, the FLN, the army, and other supervisory organs. Not only were many *comités* members dependent on these actors for their positions, but they also drew authority and status from them. They adopted the appearance and behavior of past *Caïds*. These were local leaders who worked hand-in-hand with the French as part of France's system of colonial administration. The *Caïds* were chosen and rewarded for their devotion to colonialism; they dispensed patronage, adjudicated conflicts, and briefed the colonial power on potentially subversive elements. Many fled the nation to avoid vengeance or were assassinated during the war or the transition to independence. The newly independent state did not change the local government system or the social structures. Therefore, the presidents of the *comités de gestion* became the new *Caïds*, and they followed the established standards of traditional society, which included nepotism (Clegg, 1971: 191–192). State-appointed *comités* presidents would bring their friends and family to work in the estate's self-management as a permanent labor force and eventually constitute the majority of this force. *Autogestion* was incorporated into the new national mythology, which asserted that class conflict had ceased to exist; the revolution had already occurred and unified all Algerians.

In the years after independence, Algeria experienced a continual fight for power between its emerging national bourgeoisie and the working class. The majority of farmers and the jobless became more disillusioned and impoverished. The fast-receding *autogestion* stood at the heart of this conflict. For its supporters, it represented significant gains in independence and a novel approach to addressing Algeria's economic issues, directly engaging the majority of workers in the country's destiny by giving them total economic and political control. As we have seen, initially, the FLN and the state accepted this notion while emphasizing the

110 D. GHANEM

need for leadership. Over time, however, *autogestion* became a danger to their expanding hegemony. The *comités* started to be perceived as an anarchic obstacle, with the leadership pushing toward political management from the center. The original *comités* were cognizant of the bourgeois nature of the state and considered the FLN, which was closely bound up with the state, incapable of representing the interests of the workers. Yet they were unable to stave off state interference.

Boumediene's Policies and the Rise of Opportunities to "Cash In"

In the context of a class struggle that was already underway, the 1965 coup that brought Boumediene to power helped to consolidate the state and the bourgeoisie. Under Ben Bella, the emerging middle class had already established itself as a powerful force inside the state and the FLN's machinery. The accomplishments of the workers in 1962 had already been considerably eroded. The removal of Ben Bella accelerated this process.

The ideological orientation of the new administration was made clear in 1966, with a series of nationalizations that resulted in a state monopoly over iron, zinc, lead, and marble mines, transportation, banking, insurance, oil distribution, textile production, steel, chemicals, the vast majority of the export–import trade, and a significant share of oil and natural gas production. As the country's primary resource, the government placed a premium on hydrocarbons (Ainas et al., 2012). Thus, the responsibilities of the *Société Nationale pour la Recherche, la Production, le Transport, la Transformation, et la Commercialisation des Hydrocarbures,* or Sonatrach, a state-owned firm founded on December 31, 1963 and initially responsible for transportation and marketing, were expanded to include hydrocarbon exploration, production, and processing (Malti, 2012). Oil output increased dramatically, particularly after 1966, growing from 20.5 million metric tons in 1962 to 26 million metric tons in 1965, reaching 39 million metric tons in 1967, and topping 42 million metric tons in 1968. Similarly, gas output increased from 0.8 billion cubic feet in 1964 to 2.9 billion cubic feet in 1966 (Abdoun, 1990: 20). The nationalized or newly founded state enterprises were organized into *Sociétés Nationales*, modeled after French nationalized enterprises such as Renault. Although the general directors were appointed by the ministry and the *sociétés* were sponsored by the state (through the *Caisse Algérienne de Développement),* they retained legal autonomy and were allowed to pursue their investment production and marketing strategies. Workers' engagement in management was limited to solely consultative *comités des travailleurs* in each manufacturing unit and, in certain cases, a central *Conseil des travailleurs*. State capitalism supplanted state socialism, in the process eliminating the majority of orthodox socialists from the government and stifling the voices of dissent in the UGTA. Large enterprises under self-management, such as the *Huileries Modernes d'Alger*, were turned into *société nationales*, those in the construction industry were incorporated into *Société Nationale Des Travaux d'Infrastructures et des Bâtiments* (SONATIBA), those in transport were taken over by the *Société Nationale Des Transports Routiers* (SNTR), and so on (Clegg, 1971: 149).

The rising middle class, and specifically a bureaucratic elite, had prevailed over the revolution's early radical successes. This elite held a solid grip over the means of production and the party and state machinery. The working class, the jobless, and the peasants were the losers. The working class was weakened, culturally and economically isolated, and compelled to adopt a purely defensive posture against the bureaucracy and the army's overwhelming power.

After putting an end to *autogestion* as a development model, industrial development became a priority. State capitalist strategy was centered on central economic planning, the nationalization of foreign capital, and the state sector's development. Economic development was emphasized for the purpose of acquiring the technological know-how to produce goods for internal consumption. While this model promised an agrarian revolution, it gave priority to heavy industries. The *industries industrialisantes* was the promotion of big, capital-incentivizing industries (i.e., hydrocarbons, petrochemicals, steel) that were supposed to make Algeria "the Japan of the Mediterranean" (Junqua, 1981).

During the first phase, 1967–1973, the Algerian economy implemented a model centered on local production. This translated into nationalizations (1971), the creation of large industrial complexes, and state management of enterprises. Steel-making developed with the creation of the *El Hadjar* complex (Annaba), petrochemicals in Skikda, Annaba, and Arzew, electrolysis in Ghazaouat, building materials with the creation of cement-making plants, engineering with the machine tools complex in Constantine, industrial vehicles in Rouiba and Algiers, handling equipment in Algiers, and so on and so forth (Belghenou, 1992). These industries developed in the framework of companies owned and controlled by the state. The state's economic approach gave importance to essential

112 D. GHANEM

goods and capital industries to create an industry conducive to employment. There were 70 State-Owned Enterprises (SOEs), and Boumediene considered them the "backbone" of the Algerian economy. SOEs became big businesses with large numbers of employees, managed by some 50,000 executives, half technicians, and half engineers, and employed more than 500,000 workers (El-Kenz, 1997: 270).

The second phase (1974–1979) saw a rise in oil prices, an increase in Algeria's financial capacity, and a sharp acceleration in industrial investments, which led to a growing need for technical assistance as well as an accumulation of external debt. During this period, the state injected massive capital into the industrial sector, representing 57.3% of the GDP for the first plan (1970–1973) and 61.1% for the second plan (1974–1977) (Ouchene & al., 2018: 5). Investments peaked at 62.1% in 1978, making Algeria the country with the highest investment rate that year. Beginning in 1979, the investment rate declined because the projected growth was too great for existing absorption capacities. The government decided to pause investments and focus on completing overdue projects (Talahite, 2010: 70–71).

Boumediene had consolidated his power beyond the Army, and although he repressed most of his opponents, he appointed some of them to positions in the public sector and national companies to weaken their potential nuisance. His ruling coterie was made up of individuals from the Army's ranks who were promoted to civilian office and formed the elite of the new bourgeoisie. He oversaw the return of private industrialists, considered under Ben Bella as a bourgeoisie favorable to the capitalist economic system and therefore contrary to the building of a socialist nation. Under Boumediene, the regime let a new social class, composed of public works entrepreneurs, construction entrepreneurs, big traders, and captains of industry, develop. The investment code of 1966, which revised those aspects of its 1963 predecessor that were unfavorable to private capital, allowed this bourgeoisie to benefit from state-financed infrastructure development and contracting, particularly in construction and public works.

The regime continued gaining support from the small capitalist class as it protected the interests of the small yet expanding private sector. While under Ben Bella, Algeria counted only 245 private enterprises, under Boumediene, specifically between 1966 and 1971, 930 private enterprises were in existence. Between 1966 and 1977, the size of the private sector, which had stakes in the downstream industry, light industrial establishments, and internal trade, expanded by 50% (Chhibber, 1996: 134). Because downstream industries relied on the activity of larger state enterprises, the capitalist class' economic interests were linked to the state sector, introducing a political element into the relationship between the owners of light industrial establishments and the larger state-run enterprises.

As for rent, it was used to enhance state-led development programs. This was the time of the magnanimous state that financed colossal social and economic programs and put in place a generous welfare system. The distribution, although supposedly egalitarian, was hierarchical: first, the *famille révolutionnaire* [revolutionary family], meaning the veterans of the war of independence and their *ayant droits*; then their allies, those close to the regime and their clients; and at the bottom of the ladder, ordinary people. The redistribution system exacerbated clientelism, which cemented the already strong collegial, familial, and regional relationships that carried over from the colonial period (Lowi, 2009: 154–155). Indeed, *Asabiyah* [tribalism] was still quite strong, and alliances were made and dismantled through the links of brotherhood, kinship, region, ethnicity, tribe, or *zaouia* [religious community]. Co-opting one important person from any of the above often meant co-opting his family members, kin, tribe, and region. This created the possibility of securing the loyalty and allegiance of thousands of people who were connected in one way or another to this person (Werenfels, 2007: 149).

Also, the regime co-opted specific socio-professional cohorts such as engineers. Engineers played an important role in the Algerian state's development projects, especially under Boumediene, and their commitment to the regime and the attachment of their fate to that of the regime were both facilitated by rent distribution. The financial oil resources under Boumediene allowed the country to send students to study engineering in the most reputable training centers and universities abroad, especially in Europe and the USSR. Algeria also built efficient local training institutions and technical universities. Studies in the country or abroad were paid entirely by the state, and abroad, students were given generous scholarships. Once back in Algeria, the freshly graduated engineers were systematically integrated into authority structures in management positions. They were *Al Itarat* [the cadres, the executives], the "agents of the state," the "activists of development and socialism," with a special status and high salaries (El-Kenz, 1995: 568). Unlike teachers, doctors, and lawyers, they had special status and loyalty that, for instance, the major retailers did not show to the regime. Their professional integration presupposed a minimum of political loyalty, sometimes even an active political engagement. They had a special status in leading party-aligned groups at the company level and municipalities, provinces, and even central administration. Many joined the FLN and became cadres, ministers, or senior army officers.

In most cases, such people remained disinclined to join autonomous and independent-minded organizations, which might jeopardize their relationship with the authorities, who would have perceived their involvement as a sign of ingratitude and even a betrayal worthy of punishment. Besides, they were well looked after by the FLN/state (El-Kenz, 1995: 570). Indeed, engineers were the "spoiled children" of the new Algerian state because they were the "vectors of modernity" and played a crucial role in the political legitimation of a regime that used development to justify disregarding political liberties (El-Kenz, 1995: 570–571).

Development was a state ideology to which all Algerians were required to subscribe, despite austerity measures, since it promised stability and a better life. The money from the sale of hydrocarbons helped the country's government reach a social compromise with competing groups. It could pursue state-led industrialization, let private businesses grow in downstream industries, subsidize consumer goods, and provide jobs by hiring people in the public sector. In other words, for the leaders, oil revenues financed development and subsidies, and as long as people enjoyed, even if marginally, improved living standards, they would refrain from placing demands on their leadership concerning their fundamental rights.

The state's monopoly on foreign trade and the regulation of prices (through subsidies) led to an *économie de pénurie* [economy of scarcity] (Talahite, 2010). Investments were all public and without any control mechanism: hence embezzlement, overcharging, and bribes were the rule. From 1962 to 1988, the state was the main contributor to economic and industrial development. From 1963 to 1986, the state contributed a 40% share in capital accumulation and nearly 25% in the distribution of household wage income. The state's crucial role in financing economic development and capital accumulation generated budget deficits due to the faster growth of spending in comparison with the generating of revenues. For two decades following independence, deficits were persistent, with occasional periods of surplus. Transfer expenditures fluctuated between 14 and 20% of total expenditure: they covered household consumption subsidies, allowances, pensions, and operating subsidies for public enterprises.

These expenses played a fundamental role in the shares of the budget allocated to support the financing of public enterprises. They became part of an economic model where the state played a significant role as an economic and social regulator. SOEs became so powerful that it became increasingly difficult to compete against them. They possessed enormous projects and significant monopolies and benefited from substantial subsidies from the government and their directors. Due to their political connections, they possessed considerable autonomy in their domain of operations. They got increasingly involved in the trade of favors and other forms of social accommodation as they grew more deeply embedded in patron–client networks of state administration.

For instance, the state-owned hydrocarbons company, Sonatrach, had a privileged position because of the crucial importance of hydrocarbons in state revenues (Aïssaoui, 2001: 63). By 1980, Sonatrach had no fewer than 100,000 employees (Abdoun, 1990: 24). The petroleum industry served as the backbone and primary tool of state authority. Indeed, Sonatrach became the key vehicle for channeling rents and the primary source of wealth for members of the ruling class and their relatives. To this day, it has remained beyond the reach of government oversight, regulation, and accountability mechanisms.

Sonatrach also came to symbolize two central features of the disjuncture between state and society: the state's deliberate neglect of the rural sector, which was home to the vast majority of people until the late 1980s; and the state's preference for a francophone, Europeanized elite to assume senior positions in the economy and bureaucracy. As rightly described by Lowi, Sonatrach became "something of a sacred cow in the Algerian political economy, and those who managed it were allowed to become (or at least to behave) virtually untouchable" (Lowi, 2009: 90).

However, Boumediene's economic policies were a failure. The *Industries industrialisantes* failed for two main reasons. First, large sums were invested in heavy industry without a corresponding investment in infrastructure. Such inept planning resulted, for example, in many factories being too large, difficult to manage, and operating at 30 or 50% of their capacity (Balta, 1982). Second, the commercial monopolies associated with the SOEs resulted in inefficiencies and shortages that aided in the proliferation of corruption and contraband activity. As for the agrarian reform initiative, it failed miserably because, rather than dismantling vast

116   D. GHANEM

landholdings and allocating plots evenly among the peasants, the latter were coerced into forming cooperatives, while war veterans individually took ownership of the most attractive plots. Because there was little motivation to create sustainable farms and living standards were low, migration to the cities continued unabated, increasing the number of people living in poverty in metropolitan areas (Fontaine, 1992).

Indeed, agricultural productivity failed to keep up with population expansion, and the requirement for food imports grew considerably. In 1980, Algeria covered barely 30% of its food needs against 70% directly after independence (Junqua, 1980a). It had to increase its food imports year after year. In 1974, food products represented 16% of total imports. This increased to 18.5% in 1979 and reached 25.8% in 1989 (Djenane, 2012). The authorities preferred imports to the detriment of local production, itself hampered by the decline in investment.

The enormous expansion in the size and number of cities, a natural population increase of 3.2% annually, and the drying up of the *biens vacants* led to an acute housing crisis and exacerbated social tensions (Lesbet, 1994). Nevertheless, the leadership chose to overlook the housing issue, the increasing demography, and youth problems and demands. Together with the impact of leadership choices, these problems led to the politicization of socioeconomic cleavages (Aouragh, 1996). Under the guise of socialism, which was really comprador capitalism, some executives and high-ranking officials amassed colossal fortunes in broad daylight. As cited earlier, in a 1973 speech in Constantine, Boumediene himself called on "the billionaires to leave the bodies of the state if they want to continue to make billions, and to leave the revolution to the revolutionaries" (Yefsah, 1992: 84). Yet Boumediene could not upset the balance of power, especially since his coterie, firmly anchored in the Army, was part of the bourgeoisie. He could not very well alienate his power base. Instead, Boumediene let things rot and became more resented by his people, even if discreetly. Some CR members criticized his policies, while others criticized his authoritarianism, describing him as another Ben Bella, a "Ben Bella bis" (Yefsah, 1992: 84). In the mid-1970s, the Oujda clan broke apart while the CR crumbled. The country was beginning to fray.

Despite these conditions, Boumediene chose quick fixes as his solution. With the backing of an influential faction of the Army and the unanimous support of government-beholden mass organizations, Boumediene traded his revolutionary legitimacy for a constitutional one with the 1976

Charter. The Charter was intended to legitimize the regime by calling Algerians to the ballots and hence allowing for their political participation. Under the auspices of a resurgent and "new" FLN, and coming as no surprise, the Charter was approved on June 27, 1976. To soothe a discontented population amid an economic downturn, Boumediene, through this new constitution, reaffirmed the regime's commitment to social justice. Throughout Algeria, there was a sense that President Boumediene had a social mission and that he was truly devoted to constructing a "new Algeria." The new constitution reaffirmed the old clichés about popular will, the myth of the homogeneous, unanimous Algerian people, without particularism, without class and conflicts, and spoke of their will to continue their revolution to fight under-development. The Charter was a continuous incantatory repetition of words to demonstrate the regime's achievements. For instance, the word "revolution" was cited 268 times, "socialism" 117, and "socialist" 169 (Parti de la révolution socialiste (PRS), 1976: 3).

However, the Charter, its phrasing, and its incantations could not hide realities: political power in Algeria represented the interests of a class, that minority of the bourgeoisie that plundered the country's wealth to enrich themselves and their coterie. More and more, this ruling class was seen as corrupt and contemptuous of the people. Economically, investments had sacrificed the collective and social sectors to benefit the oil and gas sector, creating Algeria's commercial, technical, financial, and food dependency on the international market (Swearingen, 1992). Socially, workers and peasants were exploited for low wages; they had no rights or social protections, even as executives within the economic sector, and the Army officers had high salaries. Social differences became more evident as a minority was living in opulence while more and more Algerians suffered from unemployment and sank into poverty. Algerians soon understood that the new Algeria was the same as the old one. It was only a question of time before their disgust for the state, and its FLN leadership, turned into a rage that would be hard for the regime to ignore, much less control (Entelis & Arone, 1992; Mortimer, 1991).

118   D. GHANEM

1978–1992: Chadlism, Infitah, and *Affairisme*

With Boumediene's death in 1978, Colonel Chadli Bendjedid, former head of the military region of Oran, was chosen by the military as the only candidate in a presidential election that he ended up winning. Bendjedid tasked his government with evaluating the two five-year plans of 1969–1973 and 1974–1977. Though he personally avoided criticizing Boumediene's policies, which he declared had positive results, such as creating some 700,000 jobs, Bendjedid's new team highlighted the gaps, inadequacies, and disparities those very policies had created (Junqua, 1980a). The heavy industrialist strategy of the former ruling team was frozen.

For a Better Life?

A new economic plan was announced, one that was meant to respond to the needs and "fundamental social aspirations" of people lacking food, houses, running water, and economic infrastructures. No less than 40% of lands were fallow, and industrialization had devoured some 250,000 hectares of agricultural land, widening regional disparities, especially between the narrow northern coastal fringe and the rest of the country (Junqua, 1980b). The *wilaya* of Algiers alone concentrated within it 14% of the country's total employment. Some two million new housing units were needed for Algeria to return to a situation qualitatively comparable to that of 1966, and the deficit in drinking and industrial water reached 40% (Junqua, 1980b).

Helped by the second oil boom in 1979/1980 and with an increase of 130% in the price of a barrel caused by the suspension of oil production in Iran due to the Islamic Revolution, Bendjedid had significant oil rents at his disposal. With the price of a barrel going from $14 in 1978 to $37 in 1980, he dubbed his economic plan, which was scheduled to last from 1980 until 1984, "For a better life" (Balta, 1983). With his easygoing nature and reputation as a man sensitive to ordinary people's everyday problems, the successor of the Spartan Boumediene gave rise to immense hope among Algerians. He established the *Plan Anti-Pénuries* (PAP) [anti-shortage program] in 1980 and endowed it with six billion francs. The plan put several basic products on the market, which were cyclically lacking under Boumediene, but also more "exotic" products such as bananas (Junqua, 1980b). The increasingly contested regime used the "banana and the stick" to quell social dissent and buy some time and some degree of social peace (Yefsah, 1992: 86). In this "new Algeria," austerity seemed to be a thing of the past.

Bendjedid, whom everyone, including national and international media, called by his first name, "Chadli," was seen and presented as the man of change, the one who would in "less than a year, move Algeria from tension to relaxation," in the words of Paul Balta, Algeria expert and *Le Monde* correspondent (Balta, 1983). His economic plan aimed to improve state management by completing ongoing projects and opening new investment programs in priority sectors such as agriculture and hydraulics. In agriculture, the authorities ordered the restructuring of inefficient self-managed farms and agrarian revolution cooperatives by March 1981. Some 3,429 state farms, called *domaines agricoles socialistes* (DASs), were created, and agrarian lands were privatized and distributed to their former owners or individual cooperative members (Swearingen, 1992: 128). However, industry retained its preeminent position. It was allocated 38.6% of government expenditures, a slight dip from 43% in the 1974–1977 plan. As in the past, hydrocarbons took the lion's share of industrial investment, with 40% and 15.7% of total expenditure. As for agriculture, even though the authorities proclaimed their intention to favor agriculture and hydraulics, they were granted only 11.7% of loans, as against more than 15% in the previous plan. Agriculture remained the poor cousin of all sectors, receiving only 6% of government expenditures (Junqua, 1980b).

Also, the new industrial policy was meant to restructure the management of public enterprises, which had experienced a chronic deficit and a heavy debt. The authorities dismantled the 70 State-Owned Enterprises (SOEs) and parceled them out into 404 smaller companies, called *Enterprise Publiques Economiques*, or EPEs (El-Kenz, 1997: 270). The 19 state-owned industrial enterprises became 115 new enterprises after restructuring (Abdoun, 1990: 40). Whenever possible, headquarters were decentralized, and offices established in production areas where the factories were located (Mira, 2017: 9). The restructuring into a large network of small and medium-sized EPEs was meant, on the one hand, to improve the management of previously large industrial complexes and improve the management of public enterprises, which were too expensive, bureaucratic, and unproductive. It was also meant to increase the state's control and enable it to oversee the use of credit granted by the public treasury. Restructuring led to a severe reduction in the average number of employees in each enterprise. On average, the number of employees of a state-owned industrial enterprise before restructuring was over 19,000, whereas it was around 3,200 after restructuring (Abdoun, 1990: 40).

However, there was no big shift in the system. In reality, the EPEs were led by the clients of the new administration, and despite Bendjedid's "cleanup campaigns," clientelism, mismanagement, waste, and corruption flourished (Junqua, 1980d). Bendjedid's policies and the available oil revenues helped strengthen the junction of the civilian and military bureaucracies in which interests were intertwined. In fact, the involvement of various actors from these two worlds in state structures was strengthened by alliances (interpersonal, family, tribal, political marriages) and allowed an explosion of corruption. The bourgeoisie (state bourgeoisie, petty bureaucratic bourgeoisie, private bourgeoisie, landowners) that was born under Boumediene became more parasitic than productive under Bendjedid. The enrichment of individual members of the state bourgeoisie came from their position as exclusive intermediaries between the world market and Algeria. Bribes, commissions, and percentages on international tenders were means by which they accumulated wealth. For instance, the anti-shortage program (PAP) reinforced personalism, patrimonialism, and clientelism. The PAP proved to be a scandalous source of profit for those associated with the bureaucracy; although import limits had been relaxed, distribution rights remained restricted to the people connected to the regime.

In the name of socialism, the state took several monopolies: much of real estate, transportation, industry, domestic trade, agriculture, and all foreign trade. Public and private capital was monopolistic, but the former served the latter. A large part of real estate fell under the monopoly of the state, which placed draconian conditions on ownership and activity, reserving such privileges for its clientele. Besides, the freezing of commercial real estate and the fact that there was virtually no construction of new business premises for several years exacerbated the problem of access to trade activity (Bencherif, 1982: 209–210).

Consequently, there were obstacles to entering into business. Whoever occupied commercial premises was certain not to have a competitor, given the lack of premises. Therefore, the public monopoly on commercial premises entailed a monopoly on private capital already installed on these premises and, *ipso facto*, a monopoly on the activity carried out there. The door was thus closed to competition.

There was also a monopoly on activity since this was reinforced by the system of authorizations/agreements given by the state for commercial activities and the importation of equipment. When an individual obtained permission/agreement to import a piece of equipment, he enjoyed a monopoly because permissions were hard to obtain and needed strong backing from an insider in the system. Once again, the capital already in place was favored when it came to issuing authorizations. Similarly, the distribution of products was governed by a double monopoly: state enterprises and already installed private capital. Only approved traders could buy supplies from state enterprises and resell them to individuals. While they bought these products at a fixed price, they were free to sell at any price and hence make large profits.

Businessmen, almost all of whom were affiliated with the regime, quickly amassed fortunes. This allowed private capital to enlarge itself and reinforce its monopolies. Due to the means it possessed, private capital forged alliances within the administration and obtained the exemptions or authorizations necessary to pursue its activities. It was the only category that could also launch new activities, as the door to newcomers was practically impossible to open. Thriving thanks to state authorizations, private capital under Bendjedid was one of the most ardent supporters of the regime and its stability.

Due to its monopolistic nature, private capital enjoyed over-profits and rents. In addition to the land rent, a situational rent was linked to the real estate monopoly and a stock rent as frequent breaks in distribution generated capital gains on stock. Besides, there was no lifestyle tax, as the bourgeoisie's villas multiplied while the country's housing crisis was raging. And there was a consumption rent, as the owners of capital enjoyed, as consumers, the same subsidized prices as the other categories of the population.

Money made it possible for the bourgeoisie to forge alliances with the individuals, senior or not, responsible for ensuring these regulations' application. Such individuals were called *Khobzists* [Litt. Bread eaters], were in the administration, the FLN, or the UGTA, and were all the more sensitive to the advancement of private capital because their salaries were low (a tax inspector hardly reached 3,000 dinars per month in 1982) (Bencherif, 1982: 209–213). This created huge social inequalities. In 1980, it was estimated that no fewer than one million employees received an average salary of 40,000 dinars per year, while 12,000 employers had an income of over one million dinars each (Bencherif, 1982: 209).

122   D. GHANEM

The bourgeoisie not only benefited from generous commissions for services provided, but they also took advantage of their privileged positions to exchange state-sector goods between themselves. Among these goods was real estate, particularly agricultural land in the Mitidja. Additional activities included the establishment of underground supply networks and the establishment of a fairly broad parallel economy by the state bourgeoisie to ameliorate the shortcomings of both the public and private sectors.

This so-called liberalization of the economy aided in the proliferation of rent-seeking opportunities, the institutionalization of patronage, and the consolidation of bureaucratic authoritarianism. The liberalization of the economy also adversely affected the state's administrative apparatus. Bureaucratic red tape grew so suffocating that it became nearly impossible for the public and private sectors to function smoothly; corruption and nepotism became state-sponsored mechanisms that drove private investors to connect with high-ranking officials from the party and the army (Bennoune, 1989: 271).

Several officials, high in the hierarchy of the state, the army, and the FLN, built villas at great expense, bought luxury cars, opened foreign bank accounts, offered bribes, and were involved in currency trafficking. The phenomenon was such that many parliamentarians denounced corruption during the FLN congress of June 19, 1980, and state television reported their comments (Junqua, 1980c).

Moreover, Abdelhamid Brahimi, minister of planning and regional development from 1979 to 1984, and prime minister from 1984 to 1988, publicly stated in March 1990 that over the previous twenty years, Algerian economic operators had received some $26bn in bribes in public contracts signed with foreign countries; this was the equivalent of Algeria's external debt at the time (*Le Monde*, 1990). As a result, inequalities within society increased and became hard to hide with populist discourse. Indeed, in the mid-1980s, 5% of the population held 45% of the national income, while 50% of the population had barely 22% of the national income (Chikhi, 1995: 502).

The regime soon faced the emergence of two major social opposition movements: the Mouvement Culturel Berbère [Cultural Berber Movement], or MCB, and the Islamist movement. Both were determined to resist the practices of the exclusionary, anti-democratic state; nonetheless, the second would establish itself as a distinctive player on the social and political scene, becoming increasingly impossible to satisfy, contain, or suppress. In a few years, Chadlism had laid the groundwork for the Islamist movement to grow and channel Algerians' economic frustrations and politico-ideological disillusionment. The wave of Islamism, which would grow stronger and eventually overwhelm the regime in the 1990s, was partly a reaction against corruption and a gentrified leadership that grew more and more detached from the population.

"Work and Rigor," a Difficult Serenity

In 1985–1986, when crude oil prices fell to about $12 a barrel, Algeria was a mono-exporting country. Oil export revenues collapsed by 36% between 1985 and 1986, then by 31% between 1986 and 1987, and reached a decline of 42% between 1987 and 1988 (Mira, 2017: 10). The country was in a deep crisis; its export earnings plummeted from $12.5bn in 1985 to less than $8bn in 1986 (*Le Monde*, 1987). The national debt at the end of 1986 was estimated at around $21bn. Foreign exchange reserves estimated at $600 million gave the regime some leeway, but its hope of containing inflation to 8.5% in 1986 did not materialize. Inflation was close to 18%, prices exploded, and poor households paid a hefty price.

The job market was saturated and unable to absorb the yearly 400,000 young people entering it on an annual basis (Bouklia & Talahite, 2008). No more than 150,000 could be absorbed in the best of years. Official unemployment figures stood at 16% in 1983, rose to 19.2% in 1987, and reached 23.6% in 1989 (Chikhi, 1995: 506). The drastic reduction in imports negatively affected the supply of agricultural material, which stopped being imported. This included fertilizers and chemicals, seeds and planting materials, machinery, and equipment, all of which affected the production of consumer goods. While the agricultural production index increased by 6% in 1986, and Algeria did not import potatoes or eggs for the first time in 25 years, it was still too little relative to demographic growth and food demands (*Le Monde*, 1987). The average annual rate of growth in national production, all sectors combined, was negative, standing at −1.2% between 1985 and 1988, due to the reduction in imports of goods necessary for production. Both public and private enterprises experienced difficulties. SOEs, which were still in a restructuring process, experienced growing deficits. This weighed on the state budget, whose deficit rose from 12.9bn dinars in 1986 to 20.7bn dinars in 1988.

124   D. GHANEM

Bendjedid, like his predecessor, used the political subterfuge of change without change by adopting a new national charter by referendum on January 16, 1986. About 11.5 million voters were called to the polls to vote "yes" or "no" on the new charter. In this new charter, the word "socialist" did not punctuate each paragraph, despite remaining a fundamental means of "banishing injustice and exploitation." This socialism was based more on religion, specifically the "social justice" advocated by Islam. Finally, the role of the Army was de-emphasized (Fritscher, 1986).

However, Bendjedid's Algeria did not have the same institutional resilience the country had enjoyed under his predecessor in the face of acute social conflict. The political system was unable to absorb the internal and external shocks that it was facing. The FLN was losing ground, something that would become all too clear in 1991, when it not only lost power but did so to a radical Islamist party.

The government raised a new slogan, "Work and Rigor," and reoriented its economic policy toward more austerity. Unable to borrow from international institutions, it reduced investment programs and imports. The latter were cut by 15% in 1985 and 28% in 1987. Food subsidies, which had increased to about $500 million by 1988, had progressively driven up food costs. Furthermore, drought and the country's worst locust invasion in three decades had caused significant crop losses, resulting in food shortages and rising food costs. Widespread hoarding and ineffective supply networks exacerbated shortages dramatically (Swearingen, 1992: 117). Algerians had, after a period of consumption frenzy, to go back to spending long hours in endless queues to enter *Souk El Fellah* [Litt. Peasant's markets] to acquire basic products such as sugar, eggs, or flour.

Youth nurtured on Bendjedid's now infamous "for a better life" slogan faced these shortages, as well as a saturated job market, social marginalization, and political exclusion. Meanwhile, among the engineers, the "spoiled children" of the system under Boumediene, the younger cohorts would be attracted, under Bendjedid, to the Islamist movement. The older group, composed of the pioneers of the Algerian development experience, remained faithful to the regime. At the heart of this divide was a conflict between those who had benefited from the state and expected to do so again on the one hand, and, on the other, those too young to have benefited then, unable to do so now, and despairing of the future. Similarly, workers in the public sector split into the upper-level public-sector managers who supported the regime and the lower level of poorly paid public employees who no longer saw the FLN state as a protector of their interests and defected to support the FIS (Richards & Waterbury, 1990).

Anti-regime riots in Algiers, Oran, and Constantine erupted in November 1986. Four people were killed, and 186 were arrested (Duran 1986). Less than two years later, between March and July 1988, the government introduced economic reforms. In July 1988, there was a reform regarding opening capital to the local private sector, aiming to encourage investment by Algerian holders of capital. Law 88-25 of July 12, 1988, on the orientation of national private economic investments, aimed to set up an incentive framework for national private investment in three "sectors of priority": industries, services, and construction/public works. However, private investors could not access strategic sectors such as banking and insurance, mining, hydrocarbons, steel, air, rail, and maritime transport (Dahmani, 1999).

Owners of private companies were allowed to join the Association for Creation and Business Promotion (ACPE). According to the Chamber of Commerce and Industry (CNC), which was responsible for implementing the provisions of this law, nearly 2,210 investment projects were given authorization in 1988, as against 1,666 in 1989. The private sector was increasingly being considered the state's economic partner.

Nevertheless, state control was tight. The CNC was directed by the state, which employed CNC officials, and any project involving economic investment required approval by a high-ranking official. Even during this era of ostensible liberalization, all private investments were monitored by a government agency, the Office for the National Coordination of Private Investment (OSCIP), established in 1983 under the Ministry of Planning (Lamchichi, 1991: 223). As such, the private sector was hindered, forced as it was to operate in an environment of burdensome bureaucracy and state corporations and alliances (Dillman, 1992: 48–49). Reforms also targeted the liberalization of foreign trade, repealing previous regulatory provisions to grant exclusivity to public enterprises or the state. This step was more symbolic than real because state monopoly continued, and only the Trade and Finance Ministry could grant import and export concessions/licenses. Maintaining state control over foreign trade resulted from the struggle between the reformist wing of the governing coalition and the conservative wing hostile to economic reforms.

The reforms were not enough. While an increasingly prominent minority—strongly aligned with the regime and protected by the military—accumulated extraordinary fortunes and skillfully managed the

126   D. GHANEM

Infitah of supply and distribution networks during Bendjedid's first term, the majority was thrown into disarray. In factories, workers developed several forms of resistance, such as absenteeism and strikes, which were met with administrative harassment, intimidation, jail sentences, and physical violence. In 1980, no fewer than 922 strikes were recorded, as against 648 in 1987 (Chikhi, 1995: 505). Because the regime did not allow any form of expression and used violence against whoever wanted to mobilize against it, because it was no longer able to continue with the welfare state, and because the urban masses did not have any autonomous organizations, all that remained for them was to revolt.

On October 5, 1988, riots erupted in Algiers and spread to other towns. While the reasons behind the riots are numerous, it is instructive that when they erupted, food prices had already risen by 40% since the beginning of that same year. In a country where people struggled to survive, such an increase exacerbated social tensions. Rioters waved empty couscous boxes in the streets, and an empty wheat bag replaced the Algerian flag on top of a famous government building (Swearingen, 1992).

Unable to buy social peace, Bendjedid used the stick against young demonstrators, thus intensifying opposition. No fewer than 500 people are believed to have been killed by the security forces between October 5 and 9, several hundred injured, and as many as 3,500 arrested (Rummel, 1992: 53). The riots of October 1988 were a moment of rupture in the national consensus between the population and the Army, between the people and their leadership, in which authority and legitimacy were openly, violently, and nationally contested for the first time since Algeria's independence. The political consequences of October 1988 were significant, as the riots were a shock to the system that would culminate in the cancelation of elections in December 1991 and the rise of political violence in 1992.

Impossible Reforms

In an attempt to placate the people, the government, backed by the military, adopted a new constitution on February 23, 1989, the major political impact of which was the establishment of political pluralism. The multiparty system promulgated by the law of July 5, 1989, which was supposed to open the political field to a democratic transition, also allowed economic reforms by abolishing political constraints and burdens related to the one-party system and socialism. The economic program aimed to stabilize the crisis-hit economy, control inflation and external debt as a prerequisite for monetary reform, and reorganize the commercial circuits as a prerequisite for the reform, competition, and liberalization of national and foreign trade.

With the blessing of Bendjedid and the Army, the government, with newly appointed Prime Minister Mouloud Hamrouche at its head, decided to renegotiate the national debt with the main creditors on a voluntary basis, without cessation of payment or a moratorium. The IMF approved this approach, and a series of negotiations was launched with a consortium of banks, the Italian government, and the Japanese financial leasing companies. At the end of May 1990, negotiations with the IMF led to the release of a loan and a reprofiling (voluntary rescheduling outside the Paris and London Clubs) of $4bn of debt due in 1991–1992. The government undertook to move toward further privatization of the public sector, the promotion of private capital, the ending of subsidies, and the establishment of a free market.

With these developments, many products invaded the market, and a new business class appeared. The state monopoly on foreign trade was replaced by private monopolies in which well-connected people benefited from the protection of individuals in leadership positions who also granted them access to credit (Jolly, 2001: 114). One's closeness to the leadership became the primary route to social advancement and access to resources (Roberts, 1984: 28).

Prime Minister Hamrouche faced a serious challenge with the rise of the Islamic Salvation Front (FIS), and on June 5, 1991, Bendjedid, with the support of the military, dismissed him. He was replaced by Sid Ahmed Ghozali, who would face a greater challenge with the FIS victory in the first round of the legislative elections on December 26, 1991. The rise of the FIS pushed the new government to stop the reforms, and the state pledged to financially assist dozens of companies in great economic difficulty. Public spending increased, and the budget deficit rose.

Reforms quickly stalled because the military and the different client networks linked with the regime could not adjust to norms of governance that did not entail the maintenance of their hegemonic grip on power and society. As soon as changes began to jeopardize the hidden interests of power holders, they opposed them and forced their abandonment. Meanwhile, the FIS could not gain entry into power since it would have excluded the military politically and economically. Indeed, the FIS

128   D. GHANEM

was advocating economic liberalization, including less state intervention in the economy, no more state socialism, privatization of all sectors, lower taxes and incentives for private sector development, as well as reductions in public-sector privileges and restrictions on state intervention in the industrial sector. All of this would have jeopardized the interests of the politico-military elite and those associated with it (Al-Ahnaf et al., 1991; Benderra, 2002; Henry & Springborg, 2001).

1992–1999: War Economy and the Structural Adjustment

The regime had few economic or political resources with which to wean increasingly disaffected youth off the FIS, which was growing in popularity (Aït Aoudia, 2006; Bekkar, 1992; Ben Mansour, 2002; Boudjenoun, 2000; Carlier, 1992). In 1992, the Army dismissed Bendjedid, called off the second round of the legislative elections to avoid a crushing victory by the FIS, and took effective control of the country. It turned out that violence was the only answer the regime had for its political and economic deficit. It was how it would seek to preserve itself and its system, meaning that the country's descent into the abyss became inevitable. As for the militants, the violence they decided to engage in had its source in the *jihad* of their fathers and grandfathers against colonial France. The new *jihad* was, to the FIS generation, in some ways a continuation of the old one, given that they directed it against a state that marginalized, discriminated against, and humiliated them.

The economic situation was catastrophic, especially during 1992–1993. Algeria's foreign debt in 1992 stood at $26bn. During the same year, the country repaid $9.42bn, or 75%, of its export earnings, representing a tangible danger for the balance of payments (Cesari, 1992: 632). This led to a fall in investments, generalized shortages, a strong surge in inflation, and an overvaluation of the exchange rate. The authorities' response was to restrict foreign trade flows. Between 1994 and 1995, the situation improved. In total, two debt rescheduling agreements, signed in 1994 and 1995, provided the state with over $20bn in financing, comprising deferred payments, IMF credits, and European Union and European Investment Bank credits (Cavatorta, 2012).

Indeed, IMF Managing Director Michel Camdessus called on the international community to help Algeria get its economy out of the doldrums. On June 1, 1994, the country entered into a rescheduling agreement with the Paris Club. In June 1994, Algeria's creditors agreed to restructure a total of about $5.4 million in sovereign debt accumulated up to September 1993, with repayments rescheduled over a fifteen-year period following a four-year grace period. On July 22, the World Bank made a loan of $175 million available to Algiers, attached to another loan from Japan (Eximbank) of $150 million. Finally, a bilateral agreement between Algeria and the United States was concluded at the end of 1994 to reschedule approximately $1bn of the Algerian public debt (Rouzeik, 1994). The IMF approved, in February 1995, a $1.8 million three-year extended fund facility for Algeria, and in May of the same year, the EU agreed to lend Algeria $268 million on conditions similar to those of the IMF.

Algeria had to comply with the conditions set by the IMF, such as limitation of short-term borrowing, suspension of the subsidy given to basic goods, devaluation of the national currency, and the restructuring of public-sector enterprises. To meet the debt deadlines, the authorities increased supplies to the productive system by giving priority to capital goods and intermediate goods, reducing imports of consumer goods (except for drugs and food), and rationing the use of short-term borrowing for the benefit of government and multilateral credit.

To increase the country's financial resources, the authorities turned to the south, the economic heartland of Algeria. The regime turned oil/gas-rich regions such as Hassi Messaoud, Hassi R'mel, Ain Amenas into heavily fortified exclusion zones. Despite the violence in the country, it convinced international oil companies that it was safe to invest in southern Algeria's hydrocarbon sector (Volpi, 2003: 114). The government sold the right to access production from the oil and gas fields. This right allowed several types of involvement of foreign companies, among them the purchase of all or part of a field or the sharing of production with Sonatrach and advance payment on the next production. The government also levied new taxes, such as the value-added tax (VAT), the Tax on Personal Income (IRG), and a law transforming tax evasion from a misdemeanor to a crime, all of which contributed to improving state revenues and overall fiscal health (Cesari, 1992).

In following the IMF's Structural Adjustment Plan (SAP), Algeria entered a period of austerity. Prices rose, purchasing power fell, and unemployment increased. The middle class' fortunes declined, and the poor became poorer. The Algerian dinar went through a series of devaluations over the years, which caused a big drop in the purchasing power of

130 D. GHANEM

people on fixed incomes, which was about two-thirds of the population at the time. Employees' purchasing power dropped by 20% on average, against 41% for executives. This made the middle class poorer. In addition, inefficient public companies whose deficit cost €700 million were restructured (Mounir, 1994: 34). This led to layoffs of between 400,000 and 500,000 people and increased unemployment, especially for young people and women.

The National Assembly voted to privatize the public sector, but the government did not want to go too far with these reforms. It preferred to alter distribution parameters in response to political-administrative decision-making (Rouzeik, 1994). In a nutshell, the regime convinced foreign actors that Islamism was terrorism and secured funds from Western governments afraid of the green threat and from international institutions. The IMF averted Algeria's insolvency.

The debt rescheduling enabled the regime financially and militarily. On the financial front, amid widespread violence, the regime successfully diverted attention away from its questionable economic operations, in which high-ranking generals held personal monopolies on the import of basic supplies while calming social tensions. The authorities prioritized the social question to appease social tensions and frustrations. The authorities came to understand that the "all-security" approach was counterproductive and began to employ, in parallel, a soft approach to combat jihadism and neutralize the domestic challenges by distributing resources (Ghanem, 2019).

Because of concerns that Islamists had infiltrated the political system, as evidenced by the close ties that many *walis* [provincial governors] had with armed groups, and in order to re-establish a monopoly on the country's governing structures, the government fired a large number of officials who had previously worked in customs or public administration. The newly appointed *walis* were tasked with putting in place a national program meant to assist jobless young people in finding employment. The *walis* set up "private multiservice cooperatives," which brought together unemployed young people and gave them jobs (as security guards, parking guards, plumbers, etc.) supported by local communities (Martinez, 1998: 268–275). In addition, agreements with public companies such as SOTROUJ (road works) or DHW (hydraulics) were signed to benefit young university graduates. Some 150,000 jobs were created between 1994 and 1996. Other youth, particularly those from small and medium-sized towns in the country's interior, joined the Army, even though some, especially in big cities, continued to join armed Islamist groups during the same period (Vergès, 1994). The Army's public relations campaigns significantly improved the image of the army, which was depicted as providing recruits with excellent professional opportunities and favorable benefits, as well as the opportunity to leave their small towns for a better life, participate in the fight against terrorism, and protect their country. The authorities thereby restored confidence in the Army and deprived local jihadist groups of human resources.

The authorities also established the Agency for the Promotion, Support, and Monitoring of Investments (APSI), which created the Local Assistance and Investment Promotion Committees (CALPI) in December 1994 to study investment projects. According to official figures, eight months after the start of the APSI, some 900 registered economic projects worth €1550 million, creating 70,000 to 100,000 jobs, were in operation (Abdelmoumene, 1995: 9). *Wilayas* such as Aïn Timouchent, El Bayyedh, and Khenchla set up facilities for investors, granting concessions for a symbolic dinar. This encouraged the emergence of new cities that would help reduce the congestion of the capital and its outskirts, rebalance development plans, and give support and hope to a population long felt abandoned by the state.

In addition to this employment policy, the authorities took a special interest in the housing question, a major problem in Algeria. As of 1994, the new *walis* were tasked with resolving local disputes related to property rights and building permits. From May 1995, the Minister of Housing, Mohamed Maghlaoui, delivered some 160,000 units and oversaw the completion of 30,000 participatory social housing and rural housing (self-construction). The state devoted €530 million to the housing sector, including the removal of slums and real estate development (Algérie-actualité, 1995a).

The state also established an assistance policy to help Internally Displaced People (IDPs) return to their region of origin when these were freed from armed groups and reverted to state control. By doing so, the authorities aimed to reduce the capital's congestion after massive displacement during the first years of the civil war. Regional planning policies were also put in place in order to address spatial disparities and encourage citizens to leave the overcrowded northern regions (Mouhoub, 1995). In addition, in 1995, the government set aside $2.2bn for food and medicine and another $2.2bn for capital goods (Algérie-actualité, 1995b: 5).

The authorities also opened up the field of investment by putting in place, from the end of 1993, legislation favorable to investment. Commercial and trade monopolies moved from the public to the private sectors and gave birth to oligopolies directly linked to the main political actors, mainly high-ranking military and state officials. During the civil war, the import market, which represented between $10bn and $11bn, fell under the control of businesspeople linked to the military and the civilian elite (Dillman, 2000). Political figures, business tycoons, and high-ranking officials in the Army were tightly linked and mutually involved in the public and private, formal, and informal sectors (Werenfels, 2007: 50). Market liberalization did not result in a shift in power structures or access to resources; rather, it only further blurred the existing permeable borders between the public and the private, the formal and the informal, the economic, political, and military (ICG, 2001). The selective liberalization undergone since the 1980s was highly beneficial to the core elite and its clients.

Besides, whereas previously, the regime did not allow the association between foreign capital and national capital (public and private), which restricted foreign participation to 40% and prohibited direct investment at 100%, the new law of October 5, 1993, decree 93/12, allowed investment by residents and non-residents. Contracts with foreign countries were signed and joint ventures established. As a result, on January 17, 1995, four Algerian pharmaceutical companies, with 40% of the capital, and seven foreign laboratories, with 60%, announced the creation of a mixed company named SOREPAL, creating 300 jobs (Bariki, 1995: 551). On May 13 of the same year, Sonatrach signed with the Italian subsidiary of ENI, AGIP, a contract for the exploration and exploitation of hydrocarbons in the eastern erg in southern Algeria, worth $25 million, for three years (Marchés tropicaux et méditerranéens, 1995).

On May 30, an Algerian-Belgian company, Mondial Associated Shipping Companies, was created after an agreement between the Algerian company International Shipping and the Belgian company Decker et Witz. In June, EKCO, a regional cement company, signed a $3 million contract with the Portuguese group SECIL to manage cement plants in western Algeria (Bariki, 1995: 551). The Algerian company SONELGAZ signed a two-year energy supply contract with the Moroccan electricity company ONE that was worth $25 million (Marchés tropicaux et méditerranéens 1995). SONATRACH also announced the doubling of the trans-Mediterranean gas pipeline, connecting Hassi R'mel to Italy, (Marchés tropicaux et méditerranéens, 1995).

The IMF debt rescheduling, the investments combined with the privatization of the hydrocarbon sector, and the opening of mixed companies, all helped the regime to maintain itself–providing it with funds that went into the modernization of its repressive apparatuses for its "total war on terror." Besides, the fragmentation of jihadist groups, their internal infighting, and their use of extreme violence, including against civilians who previously sympathized with their cause, contributed to their failure. A unilateral ceasefire was signed by the Islamic Salvation Army (AIS) in 1997. The group laid down its arms, and its *emir*, Madani Mezrag, persuaded approximately 800 fighters to return to civilian life (Ashour, 2009: 59). Also, a government-backed amnesty, the co-optation of former insurgents, and the skillful infiltration of what remained of jihadist groups all helped the military-backed regime to regain control of the country (Ghanem, 2017). By 2000, the authorities had mostly brought the insurgency under control.

The military emerged from the nearly decade-long conflict in good shape. The patrimonial system of clan politics, established by the politico-military establishment and from which clients and allies of the regime derived rent benefits, remained intact. Then, in the wake of 9/11, the Algerian regime successfully presented itself to Western countries as experienced in fighting "terrorism," and possibly even worthy of emulation.

1999–2019: Bouteflika and the Rise of the Algerian Oligarchy

Bouteflika, like his predecessors, utilized oil rents to strengthen alliances and build new coalitions, co-opt rivals, and crush intransigent opponents. Through selective distribution and repression, he was able to dominate politics uncontested for twenty years and increase the regime's maneuverability. For the first two terms (1999–2009), the army's top echelon remained the regime's centerpiece, while during the last two terms (2009–2019), the private sector had special access to the government and was, with the acquiescence of the army's top echelon, the main recipient of state largesse.

The Creation of Custom-Made Monopolies

Toward the end of the civil war, oil prices rose considerably. The cost of a barrel of oil went from $13 in 1998 to $28 in 2000. This resulted in a doubling of state revenue. The deficit of −1.9% of GDP in 1998 became a surplus of 16.8% in 2000. Foreign exchange reserves increased from $6.8bn to $17.9bn, while the overall debt proportion of GDP decreased from 64% to roughly 40%. While economic growth remained sluggish overall, averaging between 2.4% and 3.4% annually between 1999 and 2001, Algeria had never been in such a strong financial position (Lowi, 2009: 141).

By the time Bouteflika started his campaign for his second term in 2004, the cost of the barrel had reached $40, Algeria's oil revenues had reached $24bn, and its foreign reserves exceeded $32bn. In 2008, at the end of his second term, the barrel reached $140, Algeria's oil revenues stood at $81bn, and exchange reserves were $143bn. While his repeated re-election could not have been possible without the backing of the military (or at least its most powerful faction), oil revenues helped Bouteflika tremendously.

Indeed, Bouteflika consolidated the practice of purchasing much of the population's loyalty or acquiescence. Some forms of rent distribution, such as social welfare programs, were open to all citizens, while others, like lucrative contracts and employment in high-ranking positions, were restricted to a select few. Inadequate institutional frameworks hampered the equitable distribution of rents, which disproportionately benefited the well-connected, those called *shab el chkara* [Litt. Bag's owners. Figuratively: those who have bags of money]. Such discriminatory distribution of rents deepened class and social divisions. Indeed, access to oil wealth was unequal. Disparities became glaring, reflecting the country's major sociological and regional divisions: urban businesspeople and high-ranking officials close to the Bouteflika family or the military were favored and received substantial material rewards, and repentant jihadists were pampered, but many Algerians received only basic services. Indeed, on the eve of Bouteflika's third term, 39% of the population lived under the poverty line (Tardrew & Piot, 2013).

Essentially, the Algerian regime stabilized but did not modernize the economy. Personal and family ties, clan and tribal connections, and political marriages continued to intertwine the politico-military establishment with a business elite. These two groups together furthered the

5   A CONTROLLED ECONOMIC LIBERALIZATION   135

oligopolization of the economy (Werenfels, 2007: 49–50). The pharmaceutical market is one among several that illustrate this dynamic. The pharmaceutical industry was dominated by public companies until 1995, then liberalized for the benefit of a few, and eventually, 85% of the market was dominated by a dozen people close to the politico-military elite under Bouteflika (Hachemaoui, 2011: 130). Mustapha Ait Adjedjou, head of the Algerian Pharmaceutical Laboratory (LPA), held 20% of the Algerian market share in the pharmaceutical industry and was known for his friendship with the late Mohamed Lamari, who was the Army's chief-of-staff from July 1993 until August 2004. Mustapha's son had a surveillance company called *Errahma*, that provided electronic surveillance equipment to Sonatrach. General Mohamed Ghenim, former secretary-general of the Ministry of Defense, owned the pharmaceutical company Apotex. The daughter of the former chief of counter-espionage Smaïn Lamari (who died in 2009) was the owner of Pharmalliance (Hachemaoui, 2011: 129–130).

The son of Major-General Ahmed Boustila, former head of the *Gendarmerie Nationale*, was believed, according to local media, to have had a dozen companies in the food industry, the handling and storage of goods, and machinery for major construction works. The son of General Nezzar, one of the most well-known and powerful generals of the 1990s, had a private telecommunications company, SLC (Hachemaoui, 2011: 130). Opening an import–export company often serves as a means of accessing credit in return for overvalued/overpriced imports of consumer goods. Overbilling, false invoices, damaged products, non-standard products, and the registering of fictitious imports are all practices that exploded in the past two decades in Algeria. Such trafficking cannot occur without the complicity of state agents in customs, banks, regulatory compliance control services, etc. (Talahite, 2000).

The Kouninef brothers were the symbol of patronage and clientelism under Bouteflika. The Kouninef brothers are the sons of Ahmed Kouninef, a longtime friend of Bouteflika and his younger brother Saïd, and the head of KouGC, a firm specializing in construction in the 1970s. Shortly after Bouteflika became president in 1999, he welcomed Kouninef into his circle with open arms and showed his willingness to help him grow his business, which Kouninef's three grown sons, Rhéda, Noah, and Karim, had joined. In 2004, 2009, and 2014, the Kouninefs loaned out their villa to serve as campaign headquarters for the presidential elections and contributed financially to Bouteflika's re-election. KouGC, which employed more than 5,000 people at its peak, amassed contracts in construction, public works, hydraulics, mobile telephones, and agribusiness, to the point that it became one of the most successful companies in the country. According to a non-exhaustive count, the Kouninefs obtained no fewer than 11 public contracts worth €891 million between 2002 and 2018 (Alilat, 2021).

Another example of patronage and clientelistic relations is CEVITAL, a family group that includes around twenty subsidiaries created in the 1990s by Issaad Rebrab, a Kabyle businessman. Rebrab, worth $4.8bn, benefited from generous public contracts and tailor-made tax favors, thanks to the support of General Toufik Médiène of the Department of Intelligence and Security (DRS). Rebrab came to occupy a dominant position in the economic sectors of agro-food, car dealerships, and household appliances, and made a fortune. After a decade of favors and patronage, CEVITAL's market shares were estimated in 2011 at nearly 70% for refined sugar and 65% for oil. The remaining third of the oil market shares were shared for the most part by three private individuals close to the "presidential clan," including the Kouninef brothers (Hachemaoui, 2011: 131–132). This monopolistic situation violates the law, which caps the "concentration" of sales of goods and services made on the domestic market at 40%.

Another prominent business figure under Bouteflika was Ali Haddad. The latter was the head of the largest private company in construction and public works, road and railway equipment, *Enterprise des Travaux Routiers, Hydrauliques et Bâtiments* (ETRHB). Haddad carried out an intense campaign to rally as many members of the *Forum des Chefs d'Entreprises* (FCE) as possible to support President Bouteflika, especially during his presidential campaigns. Besides Haddad, many businessmen, such as Ahmed Mazouz, Hassan Arbaoui, Mahiedine Tahkout, and Mohamed Bairi, among others, gave millions of dollars to Bouteflika's campaigns and were rewarded in return (Amir, 2021). Haddad's rewards included his nomination in November 2014 to head the FCE, and an $18bn loan plan between 2000–2015 under the successive infrastructure programs initiated by Bouteflika (Algérie-info, 2020). Like the UGTA, the FCE became the ally of the government, another mass organization in the service of the pouvoir.

In short, the politico-military hierarchy, with the cooperation of the business elite, controlled every economic sector. According to a 2001 ICG assessment, individuals privileged by their connection to the regime—whether as members of the business elite or as beneficiaries of extensive patronage—numbered 600,000 to 800,000 (ICG, 2001: 10). Solidarity at the top cuts across the political spectrum, and is oiled by the rentier state (Werenfels, 2007: 151).

The Mechanics of Corruption

Corruption is a major problem in Algeria. The Corruption Perception Index published by Transparency International (TI) ranks Algeria as one of the most corrupt countries in the MENA region. In 2016, Algeria ranked 108 out of 176 countries. In 2020, it ranked 104 out of 180 countries. Corruption in Algeria is neither sectorial nor accidental; it is a system of governance (Hachemaoui, 2011: 114). According to former vice-president of Sonatrach Hocine Malti, at least $5bn to $6bn, and maybe even $10bn, go into the pockets of members of the politico-military establishment annually (Malti, 2014). In Algeria, the weakness of the bureaucracy is not a result of rent-seeking; rather, it is an objective sought by the system. Corruption is a method of conflict resolution (Hachemaoui, 2011: 127).

Indeed, corruption is used to pay for people's loyalty to the regime, compromise competitors, and weaken the opposition. Alliances are fragile and fluid, so the system is forced to diversify its connections. This tactic helps it mitigate the danger of this or that co-opted individual or group reverting to opposition, but also allows the system to cover its bases should it decide to rid itself of allies. The arrest of high-ranking people in public companies accused of embezzlement and corruption following Bouteflika's fall from power in 2019 is proof of what can happen when alliances are broken or reversed.

The story of Abd Al Mumen Rafiq Khalifa is another such case. Young businessman Khalifa, son of former Minister of Energy and Industrialization Laroussi Khalifa, started his career in the 1990s in pharmaceutical operations before establishing an import firm for pharmaceutical goods. To restore the regime's image, tarnished by ten years of violence, and sell the image of a "new Algeria under reconstruction," open to a world in which capitalists can prosper thanks to the peace and the liberalization of the economy, the regime co-opted the young businessman. Two key figures would introduce him to the corridors of power and help him build his networks: General Larbi Belkheir, then Director of the Presidency's Cabinet, and the brother of the president, Abdelghani Bouteflika.

When the Algerian government decided to relinquish its monopoly on external trade on March 25, 1998, Khalifa established El-Khalifa Bank. The Bank was established with the approval of the financial authorities, notably the Money and Credit Council (MCC), and the treasurer of the Bank of Algeria. Not only was El-Khalifa Bank granted a license and permission to commence operations, but it also became the first private Bank in Algeria to be awarded the distinction of being allowed to accept deposits and create private accounts.

El-Khalifa Bank established 130 subsidiary banking offices in the country with approximately $1.5bn in primary bank assets and 1.5 million clients (Belhimer, 2007). El-Khalifa Bank soon became the favored front for governmental organizations in which to deposit their funds. These included the National Social Insurance Fund for Salaried Workers (CNAS), the National Unemployment Insurance Fund (CNAC), the National Equalization Fund for Social Work (FNPOS), and the Office for Real Estate Development and Management (OPGI). In response to several government agencies withdrawing their funds from public banks and depositing them in El-Khalifa Bank, the latter's reserves swelled.

The money funded all Abd Al Mumen's undertakings. The "Algerian golden boy" built a €1.3bn corporate empire spanning banking, building, aviation, media, and sports. Khalifa Bank, Khalifa Airways, the France-based Khalifa TV network, and a high-profile sponsorship of the French football team *Olympique de Marseille* were his businesses (Alilat, 2020). Sons, daughters, and wives of high-ranking military and state officials and well-connected people worked in this conglomerate, thereby demonstrating the intricate links between the leadership circle and the shady corporation. Between 1999 and 2003, El-Khalifa Bank, which tampered with its balance sheets, is believed to have irregularly transferred some €689 million out of the country, of which a little less than half wound up in France. No investigation was opened during that period. Khalifa, the golden boy, remained untouchable.

In fact, despite a 2002 report by French *Direction Générale de la Sécurité Extérieure* [General Directorate for External Security] that pointed to a lack of corporate transparency, the opacity of El-Khalifa Bank, and the insolvency of Khalifa Airlines company, the Algerian authorities remained silent until 2003, when the affair surfaced in the French media and could no longer be hidden. In March 2003, the Algerian authorities decided to revoke El-Khalifa Bank's license, engage an expert to assess the size of losses and scope of embezzlements, and launch a judicial investigation into El-Khalifa Group. The investigations concluded in 2006 and revealed various findings, including those made by the person assigned to the Group's liquidation, who stated that while El-Khalifa Group did not exist legally, it did exist materially. He referred to it as an "empty shell."

The trial was the biggest scandal in Algeria's post-independence history because it exposed the reality of corruption to the general public and the role and responsibility of the authorities in political and financial wrongdoing. Among those who gave testimony at the trial were Mourad Medelci, then-Minister of Finance; Abdelmadjid Tebboune, then-Minister of Housing; Aboudjerra Soltani, then-Minister of Labor and Social Security; Mohamed Terbache, then-Minister of Finance; and Karim Djoudi, Director of the Treasury.

In 2007, the court charged Abd Al Mumen Khalifa with 123 counts of various crimes, including organizing a fraudulent organization, grand larceny, fraud, betrayal of public trust, bribery, exploitation of influence, and forging official documents. The court sentenced him to life in prison in absentia. He was detained in the United Kingdom in 2007 based on a European arrest warrant issued by a French court. Although a British court approved his extradition in June 2009, he was granted four extensions; it took until 2010 for him to be extradited to Algeria (Jacinto, 2010).

Abd Al Mumen had always been a pawn in the hands of those in political power and special-interest organizations, which were willing to grant him political protection in exchange for his providing them with cover for their shady financial dealings. The bankruptcy of the El-Khalifa Group in 2003 caused damage estimated between 1.5 and five billion dollars to the Algerian state.

The El-Khalifah case revealed that corruption is a system unto itself, one essential to the regime's continuity, in that it uses resources and decision-making authority to purchase, sell, and siphon off public funds via networks involving the regime's most senior political and military figures. The El-Khalifa case sent a strong message to the regime's clientele: beyond the fluidity of bonds and connections, corporate leaders are tied to the system and have no interest in organizing against the reigning structures. Of course, the system is not monolithic, and solidarity among thieves sometimes fissures, revealing embarrassing details to the public. At such a point, the system might have to sacrifice those who constitute the weakest link in order to save itself.

Since El-Khalifagate, numerous major scandals have blown open in Algeria. The most significant was the Sonatrach scandal, which involved the national petroleum company and then-Minister of Energy Chakib Khalil, and the East–West Highway scandal, which involved the construction of a six-lane highway across the country.

The Sonatrach scandal occurred in 2013. A preliminary investigation conducted by the DRS in 2009 revealed that the level of corruption extended to state institutions and that foreign lobbies—with the assistance of high-ranking officials of the state—could act as agents of the Algerian market. Businessman Farid Bedjaoui obtained some €197 million in commissions, which is believed to have facilitated the conclusion of seven contracts of €8bn between the Italian firm Saipem and Sonatrach. Minister Khalil—a childhood friend of then-President Bouteflika—and his relatives were suspected of receiving bribes from Bedjaoui (Alilat, 2019a). The latter, also called the "Algerian Madoff," was also involved in another case involving contracts obtained by the Canadian firm SNC Lavalin from the Department of Energy. Bedjaoui collected millions of dollars in commissions (Alilat, 2015).

The East–West Highway project was to run 1,200 km between Algeria's western border with Morocco and its eastern frontier with Tunisia. In 2006, China International & Investment Company (Citic) and the Japanese Consortium for the Algerian Highway (Cojaal) won the tender for a six-lane highway ahead of candidates, such as French Bouygues and American Bechtel, who filed a complaint against the Algerian authorities over "favoritism." The megaproject, which was supposed to be completed by July 2010 and cost $13bn, suffered continuous delays and swallowed some $20bn. In 2008, the DRS initiated an investigation. The corruption scandal erupted in 2015. Fourteen Algerians, including former officials and businessmen, and seven foreign firms involved in the construction project were accused of murky management and graft. The investigation incriminated former Islamist Minister of Transport (2013 and 2015) Amar Ghoul, and former Minister of Foreign Affairs (2005 and 2007) Mohamed Bedjaoui, both close to Bouteflika. After five years and 160 pages of indictments, the two ministers and other state officials were spared while only two businessmen were incriminated. Chani Medjoub, owner of consulting company ADC, advisor to the Chinese company Citic, and Mohamed Khelladi, civil servant at the Ministry of Public Works, were each sentenced to ten years in prison (Sereni, 2019).

In theory, the Algerian Court of Audit is responsible for inspecting the government's budget and the financial statements of state-owned firms and delivering an annual report to the president. However, audits are rarely performed, and the results are rarely made public. The court does not audit hydrocarbon taxes to begin with, and Sonatrach does not disclose audited financial statements. Algeria was placed 22nd in the 2010 edition of the Revenue Watch Index, which measures earnings transparency in 41 resource-rich nations, defining it as a country with limited to no disclosure on its oil and gas revenue. Along with Kuwait and Saudi Arabia, Algeria ranks toward the bottom in all areas of revenue transparency (Revenue Watch Index, 2010: 17).

Each time a corruption case has been investigated thus far, those implicated have included ministers, military leaders, and others in their inner circles. Corruption is deeply ingrained in the political system and the judicial system. According to a World Economic Forum report on global competitiveness, the Algerian judicial system is susceptible to manipulation and influence by executive branch members and influential individuals and businesses. In 2017–2018, Algeria ranked 86th out of 137 countries in judicial independence. Algeria also received poor marks when it came to diverting public funds, as it ranked 83rd; on irregular payments and bribes, where it ranked 92nd; and on transparency of government policymaking, and the strength of auditing and reporting standards, ranking 121st and 129th, respectively (The Global Competitiveness Index, 2017–2018).

In addition to the big scandals that made the headlines, there have been constant smaller scandals of mayors and political representatives being charged with embezzlement, squandering public funds, corruption, and professional misconduct at the local or provincial level. In 2015, 65 presidents of the communal assembly (mayors) were imprisoned, and 532 elected local officials were convicted on charges ranging from mismanagement to embezzlement, squandering of public funds, and professional misconduct (Mouhamed, 2015). In 2017, 250 mayors were arrested and charged with corruption.

There is a high level of interconnectedness between the different circles of power, but this also means that arbitrating and solving issues is complex. Any attempt at reform is risky, as any decision could harm one group while favoring another. The dismissal of former Prime Minister Abdelmadjid Tebboune was one of the proofs of these delicate balances.

142   D. GHANEM

As soon as he took office, Tebboune questioned the previous government's actions, such as the free allocation of 15,140 plots for investment, but not exploited (Remouche, 2017). In addition, the new minister called off the creation of 40 industrial zones and the privatization of state farms. Tebboune's approach to "separate money from power" was seen by Bouteflika's coterie, Ali Haddad, and his friends as a real danger to their business. As a result, after less than three months in office, Tebboune was dismissed by the President and replaced by Ahmed Ouyahia, who made his umpteenth return and who is above all a pure product of the system, a man who understood that upsetting the prime decision-makers is a mistake, and that real reforms could undermine the system and its very existence (Werenfels, 2007: 162–163).

2019: Yet Another Reset?

By the time the *Hirak* erupted in February 2019, Bouteflika was ailing, and could not respond effectively to the challenges of the situation. The army forced him to resign in March 2019. His coterie unraveled as soon as the military sacrificed him. Some twenty prominent figures—former politicians, powerful entrepreneurs, and senior officials—were prosecuted for "hidden" financing of Bouteflika's electoral campaigns, as well as for "nepotism" and "favoritism" in various industries. These tycoons had benefited from significant subsidies and substantial tax advantages, despite rarely meeting their stated obligations. High-ranking military and civil servants were also jailed or dismissed (Alilat, 2019b).

Ali Haddad, head of the FCE, was one of the first to fall; he was arrested in early April at a border post with Tunisia, tried, and sentenced to 18 years in prison for "obtaining public contracts in violation of the law," "squandering public funds," "abuse of power," "conflict of interest," and "corruption in the conclusion of public contracts" (*Le Monde*/AFP, 2020). His four brothers, Omar, Meziane, Sofiane, and Mohamed, were sentenced to four years each while their assets were seized and their bank accounts frozen. Rhéda, Noah, and Karim Kouninef were arrested and sentenced to 16, 15, and 12 years, respectively, for "influence peddling," "money laundering," "undue advantages," and "hidden financing of electoral campaigns." The owner of Global Motors Industries (GMI), Hassen Arbaoui, and former FCE vice-president Mohamed Bairi, were sentenced to four and three years, respectively. Seven former ministers were sentenced to prison terms of between two to five years, while another one, Abdeslam Bouchouareb, ex-Minister of Industry and Mines, who fled the country, was sentenced to 20 years in absentia.

Arguably the most spectacular fall from grace was that of the aforementioned product of the system Ahmed Ouyahia, a four-time prime minister who was prosecuted and sentenced to fifteen years in prison for "granting undue privileges," "malfeasance in office," "conflicts of interest," and "money laundering" (Zerrouky, 2019). During his trial in January 2021, which also addressed the case of the secret financing of Bouteflika's ultimately aborted electoral campaign for a fifth term as president, Ouyahia made an astounding revelation regarding the origin of his private wealth, which amounted to €4.3 million. Ouyahia admitted that, over a period of nearly two decades, he, Bouteflika, former head of the executive Abdelmalek Sellal, and several ministers, senior army officials, and other high-ranking officials, had received gold bars from Gulf emirs who would visit Algeria to hunt protected species such as bustard and gazelle in the Algerian desert. Between 2014 and 2018, Ouyahia alone received sixty gold bars that he resold on the black market via intermediaries, before depositing the money in his Algerian bank accounts without ever declaring anything to the tax authorities. Ouyahia subsequently suffered the wrath of Algerians, who nicknamed him "Or-Yahia" [gold-Yahia] on social media (Meddi, 2021).

From the perspective of the politico-military establishment, this was necessary. Indeed, partly as a sop to the *Hirak*, the establishment offered up individuals who had become too greedy and constituted the system's weak link. Sacrificing them was vital to protect the system and the regime's stability. The "clean hands" operation, initiated following Bouteflika's departure from the scene, was meant to restore the regime's image and give people the impression that a new Algeria was coming into being. The theatrical arrests of members of the highest echelons of the state, and their trial and conviction, were what the regime used to try to calm a population that kept demonstrating every Friday, chanting "klitou lebled ya saraqin" [Litt. You ate the country, you thieves]. The Algerian authorities expected that the trial of some officials would calm the population, put an end to the *Hirak* and its demands for transparency and democracy, and help the regime polish its image nationally and abroad. Yet for many Algerians, while the guilt of these officials was clear, they were seen as scapegoats.

The current president, Abdelmadjid Tebboune, a former prime minister who took office in December 2019, inherited a dismal political and socioeconomic situation. As a result, his capacity to maneuver was limited to begin with, as was his capacity to pacify the opposition. Moreover, Algeria's economy, which was already suffering from lackluster performance, took an additional hit with the March 2020 fall in oil prices and the outbreak of the coronavirus pandemic. Under Tebboune, Algeria began undertaking cuts in this increasingly challenging economic situation, but without calling them "cuts." They were instead termed a "rationalization of spending" aimed at "preserving the social character of the state" (APS, 2021).

In May 2020, the government announced a 50% budget decrease, which affected salaries in all sectors but health and education. Sonatrach was required to slash its operational and capital expenditures by 50%. As in 2016 and 2019, the government opted to reduce spending by restricting its import bill—bringing it down to $31 bn in 2020, as opposed to $41 bn the previous year. Algeria's GDP contracted by 4.9% in 2020, and in the first six months of 2021, the GDP and non-oil real GDP growth rate stood at 3.1 and 3.9%, respectively, which was below their pre-pandemic levels. And the government took to relying on the country's foreign reserves to finance public investments. Of course, this is not a long-term solution. Between 2013 and 2021, the country's reserves decreased by $150 bn, going from $194 bn to barely $44 bn (Titouche, 2022).

In November 2021, the authorities declared the end of generalized subsidies for essential goods. According to the Ministry of Finance, the state has been spending around $17bn per year on funding essential food supplies (semolina, oil, bread, milk, etc.), electricity, water, gas, and gasoline (Ayache, 2021). The authorities chose to discontinue these broad-based subsidies and refocus aid programs on poor and middle-income households. How this new policy would be implemented remained undetermined at the time of writing.

Yet while these lines are being written, Algeria is experiencing a brief period of respite, as hydrocarbon prices reached new highs in January 2022 and the COVID-19 epidemic seemed to ease. Following Russia's invasion of Ukraine in February 2022, the Algerian leadership saw its fortunes turning once again as energy prices rose further. As a result, Tebboune canceled most of the tax increases and subsidy reforms, and then unveiled a new unemployment stipend for jobless youth between the ages of 19 to 40. Increased income from hydrocarbon exports will lead to a significant drop in external financing needs and a short-term stabilization of domestic financing needs. Meanwhile, the economic recovery in non-energy sectors has stalled, staying essentially incomplete, and inflationary threats have materialized. The economic forecast indicates a modest rebound and medium-term deterioration of fiscal and external balances (World Bank, 2021).

What is certain, however, is that the ongoing dramatic slowdown in economic development will result in a rise in the already-high unemployment rate and a drop in earnings. The relevance of the social question will only grow as social and economic conditions worsen. The government no longer has the financial resources to restructure Algeria's economy, diversify its producing sectors, and improve its competitiveness. Algeria's decision-makers appear unable to deal with the impending disaster. Indeed, despite constant discussion about diversifying the economy to reduce dependency on hydrocarbons, weed out corruption, and enhance the business climate, the authorities have done precious little to bring any of this about. If anything, the authorities seem likely to face further social dissent, whether in the form of the *Hirak* or something else.

REFERENCES

Abdelmoumene, K. (1995). Terrain défriché … en attendant le boom. *Algérie-Actualité* (1550).

Abdoun, R. (1990). *Algeria: The problem of Nation-building* (M. Azzam, Ed., pp. 14–48).

Ainas, Y, Ouarem, N., & Souam, S. (2012). Les hydrocarbures: atout ou frein pour le développement de l'Algérie? *Revue Tiers Monde, 210*, 69–88. https://www.jstor.org/stable/23593881. Accessed January 25, 2022.

Aïssaoui A. (2001). *Algeria: The Political Economy of Oil and Gas* (pp. 63, 71). Oxford University Press.

Aït-Aoudia, M. (2006). La naissance du Front Islamique du Salut: une politisation conflictuelle (1988–1989). *Critique International, 30*, 129–144.

Al-Ahnaf, M., Botiveau, B., & Frégosi, F. (1991). *L'Algérie par ses islamistes*. Karthala.

Algérie info. (2020, October 16). Ali Haddad avoue avoir bénéficié de l'équivalent de 18 milliards de dollars de crédits. *Algérie info*. https://www.algerieinfos.com/corruption-ali-haddad-avoue-avoir-benefi cie-de-lequivalent-de-18-milliards-de-dollars-de-credits/. Accessed January 25, 2022.

Algérie Press Service (APS). (2021, November 23). PLF 2022: la préservation du caractère social de l'Etat mise en avant. *APS*. https://www.aps.dz/economie/131282-plf-2022-la-preservation-du-caractere-social-de-l-etat-mise-en-avant. Accessed January 25, 2022.

Algérie-actualité. (1995a). Habitat: 160 000 logements en 1995? *Algérie-Actualité* (1541).

Algérie-actualité. (1995b). M. Sifi devant le CNT. L'exposé en quelques chiffres. *Algérie-Actualité* (1526).

Alilat, F. (2015, November 12). Affaire Saipem-Sonatrach: la justice italienne ordonne la saisie de 250 millions d'euros de biens. *Jeune Afrique*. https://www.jeuneafrique.com/278647/societe/affaire-saipem-sonatrach-la-justice-italienne-ordonne-la-saisie-de-250-millions-deuros-de-biens. Accessed January 25, 2022.

Alilat, F. (2019a, April 24). Corruption en Algérie: ces hommes d'affaires au cœur de scandales financiers. *Jeune Afrique*. https://www.jeuneafrique.com/mag/765064/economie/corruption-en-algerie-ces-hommes-daffaires-au-coeur-de-scandales-financiers/. Accessed January 25, 2022.

Alilat, F. (2019b, April 21). En Algérie, la grande purge dans les milieux d'affaires proches de Bouteflika. *Jeune Afrique*. https://www.jeuneafrique.com/mag/765041/politique/en-algerie-la-grande-purge-dans-les-milieux-daffaires-proches-de-bouteflika/. Accessed January 25, 2022.

Alilat, F. (2020, November). Rafik Khalifa: des milliards à la prison d'El Harrach, la déchéance d'un golden boy algérien. *Jeune Afrique*. https://www.jeuneafrique.com/1080566/politique/serie-rafik-khalifa-des-milliards-a-la-prison-del-harrach-la-decheance-dun-golden-boy-algerien/. Accessed January 25, 2022.

Alilat, F. (2021, June 4). Algérie: les frères Kouninef, la saga des milliardaires qui ont fini à la prison de Koléa. *Jeune Afrique*. https://www.jeuneafrique.com/1182892/politique/algerie-les-freres-kouninef-la-saga-des-milliardaires-qui-ont-fini-a-la-prison-de-kolea/. Accessed January 25, 2022.

Amir, N. (2021, January 12). La générosité des hommes d'affaires envers Bouteflika. *El Watan*. https://www.elwatan.com/edition/actualite/la-generosite-des-hommes-daffaires-envers-bouteflika-12-01-2021. Accessed January 24, 2022.

Aouragh, L. (1996). *L'économie algérienne à l'épreuve de la démographie*. France: Centre français sur la population et le développement.

Ashour, O. (2009). *The De-Radicalization of Jihadists: Transforming Armed Islamist Movements*. Routledge.

Ayache, S. (2021, November 17). En Algérie, le gouvernement tente de réguler la crise de la patate. *Le Monde*. https://www.lemonde.fr/afrique/article/2021/11/17/en-algerie-le-gouvernement-tente-de-reguler-la-crise-de-la-patate_6102464_3212.html. Accessed January 25, 2022.

Balta, P. (1982, July 6). Succès et échecs d'une révolution. *Le Monde* https://www.lemonde.fr/archives/article/1982/07/06/succes-et-echecs-d-une-revolution_2890978_1819218.html

Balta, P. (1983, November 4). Pour une vie meilleure. *Le Monde* (archives). https://www.lemonde.fr/archives/article/1983/11/04/i-pour-une-vie-meilleure_2847179_1819218.html

Bariki, S. (1995). Algérie. Chronique intérieure. *Annuaire de l'Afrique du Nord* (34).

Beau, N. (1989, September 5). Algérie: Les jokers de Chadli. *L'Express*. https://www.lexpress.fr/informations/algerie-les-jokers-de-chadli_591208.html. Accessed January 25, 2022.

Bekkar, R. (1992). Taking Up Space in Tlemcen: The Islamist Occupation of Urban Algeria. *Middle East Report, 179,* 11–15.

Belghenou, A. (1992). La gestion socialiste des entreprises en Algérie: Participation et conflit. *Relations Industrielles, 47*(2), 300–324. https://www.jstor.org/stable/23073836. Accessed January 25, 2022.

Belhimer, M. (2007). *Imbaraturiyet al-Sarab: Qissat Ihtiyaal al-Qarn* [Illusion empire: fraud story of the century]. Manshū rāt al-Khabar, Dār al-Hikmah.

Ben Mansour, L. (2002). *Frères musulmans, frères féroces. Voyage dans l'enfer du discours islamiste.* Ramsay

Bencherif, O. (1982). Algérie 1982: Monopoles d'Etat et monopolistes privés. *Esprit, 66*(6), 209–210. https://www.jstor.org/stable/24272421. Accessed January 25, 2022.

Benderra, O. (2002). Economie Algérienne 1986–1998: Les réseaux aux commandes de l'Etat., In J. Cesari (Ed.), *Marchands, entrepreneurs et migrants entre l'Europe et le Maghreb.*

Bennoune, M. (1989). *The Making of Contemporary Algeria, 1830–1987: Colonial Upheavals and Post-Independence Development.* Cambridge University Press.

Boudjenoun, M. (2000). *Les années fastes et néfastes de l'islamisme algérien.* autoédition.

Bouklia, R., & Talahite, F. (2008). Marché du travail, régulation et croissance économique en Algérie. *Revue Tiers Monde, 49*(194), 413–437. https://www.jstor.org/stable/23593290. Accessed January 25, 2022.

Carlier, O. (1992). De l'islahisme à l'islamisme: la thérapie politico-religieuse du FIS. *Cahiers d'études africaines,32* (126), 185–219.

Cavatorta, F. (2012). La reconfiguration des structures de pouvoir en Algérie: Entre le national et l'international. *Revue Tiers Monde, 210,* 13–29. https://www.jstor.org/stable/23593878. Accessed January 25, 2022.

Cesari, J. (1992). Algérie. Chronique intérieure. L'année des incertitudes. *Annuaire De L'afrique Du Nord, 31,* 615–683.

Chaulet, C. (1971). *La Mitidja autogérée: enquête sur les exploitations autogérées agricoles d'une région d'Algérie (1968–1970).* SNED.

Chhibber, P. K. (1996). State Policy, Rent Seeking, and the Electoral Success of a Religious Party in Algeria. *The Journal of Politics, 58*(1), 126–148. https://www.jstor.org/stable/2960352. Accessed January 25, 2022.

Chikhi, S. (1995). Question ouvrière et rapports sociaux en Algérie. *Review Fernand Braudel Center, 18*(3), 487–529. https://www.jstor.org/stable/402 41337. Accessed January 25, 2022.

Clegg, I. (1971). *Workers' Self-Management in Algeria.* Monthly Review Press.

Dahmani, A. (1999). *L'Algérie à l'épreuve: économie politique des réformes, 1980– 1997.* L'Harmattan.

Dillman, B. (1992). Transition to Democracy in Algeria. In P. Entelis & P. Naylor (Eds.), *State and Society in Algeria.* Westview Press.

Dillman, B. (2000). *State and Private Sector in Algeria: The Politics of Rent-Seeking and Failed Development.* Westview Press.

Djenane, A. (2012). La dépendance alimentaire: un essai d'analyse. *Confluences Méditerranée, 81*(2), 117–131.

Dumont, R. (1963). Des conditions de la réussite de la réforme agraire en Algérie. *Revue Tiers Monde, 4,* 79–123.

Duran, K. (1989). The Second Battle of Algiers. *Orbis, 33,* 403–421.

El-Kenz, A. (1995). Les ingénieurs et le pouvoir. *Revue Tiers Monde, 36*(143), 565–579.

El-Kenz, A. (1997). Prometheus and hermes. In T. Shinn & J. Spaapen et al. (Eds.), *Science and Technology in a Developing World.* https://docplayer.fr/61837380-Promethee-et-hermes-ali-el-kenz.html

Entelis, J., & Arone, L. (1992). Algeria in Turmoil: Islam: Democracy and the State. *Middle East Policy, 1*(2), 23–35.

Fontaine, J. (1992). Quartiers défavorisés et vote islamiste à Alger. *Revue Des Mondes Musulmans Et De La Méditerranée, 65,* 141–164.

Fritscher, F (1986, January 11). Soumise à référendum le 16 janvier: la nouvelle charte nationale reste dans un certain flou idéologique. *Le Monde* (archives). https://www.lemonde.fr/archives/article/1986/01/11/soumise-a-refere ndum-le-16-janvier-la-nouvelle-charte-nationale-reste-dans-un-certain-flou-ide ologique_3117824_1819218.html. Accessed January 25, 2022.

Ghanem, D. (2017, November 17). A Life After Jihadism. *Carnegie Middle East Center.* https://carnegie-mec.org/diwan/74708. Accessed January 25, 2022.

Ghanem, D. (2019, May 3). The Shifting Foundations of Political Islam in Algeria. *Carnegie Middle East Center.* https://carnegie-mec.org/2019/05/03/shifting-foundations-of-political-islam-in-algeria-pub-79047. Accessed January 25, 2022.

Global Competitiveness Index. (2017–2018). *Algeria profile*. https://www3.wef orum.org/docs/GCR2017-2018/03CountryProfiles/Standalone2-pagerprof iles/WEF_GCI_2017_2018_Profile_Algeria.pdf. Accessed January 25, 2022.

Hachemaoui, M. (2011). La corruption politique en Algérie: l'envers de l'autoritarisme. Esprit, *375*(6), 111–135.

Henry, C., & Springborg, R. (2001). *Globalization and the Politics of Development in the Middle East*. Cambridge University Press.

https://www.france24.com/en/20100428-rafik-khalifa-rise-fall-algeria-golden-boy-uk-fraud. Accessed January 25, 2022.

International Crisis Group (ICG). (2001). Algeria's Economy: The Vicious Cycle of Oil and Violence. *ICG*. http://bit.ly/2gx61X0. Accessed January 25, 2022.

Jacinto, L. (2010, April 28). The Rise and Fall of Rafik Khalifa, Algeria's Golden Boy. *France 24*.

Jolly, C. (2001). Les cercles vicieux de la corruption en Algérie. *Revue internationale et stratégique*, *43*, 112–119.

Junqua, D. (1980a, February 12). Le réalisme du président Chadli Bendjedid. *Le Monde* (archives). https://www.lemonde.fr/archives/article/1980a/02/12/le-realisme-du-president-chadli-bendjedid_2814325_1819218.html. Accessed January 25, 2022.

Junqua, D. (1980b, June 17). Le nouveau plan quinquennal prévoit une forte augmentation des dépenses à caractère social. *Le Monde* (archives). https://www.lemonde.fr/archives/article/1980b/06/17/examine-par-le-congres-du-f-l-n-le-nouveau-plan-quinquennal-prevoit-une-forte-augmentation-des-depenses-a-caractere-social_3071723_1819218.html. Accessed January 25, 2022.

Junqua, D. (1980c, June 20). Algérie: au congrès du FLN. La corruption de certains dirigeants a été violemment dénoncée par de nombreux orateurs. *Le Monde* (archives). https://www.lemonde.fr/archives/article/1980c/06/20/algerie-au-congres-du-f-l-n-la-corruption-de-certains-dirigeants-a-ete-violemment-denoncee-par-de-nombreux-orateurs_3072085_1819218.html. Accessed January 25, 2022.

Junqua, D. (1980d, December 20). Le président Chadli Bendjedid paraît décidé à mettre fin à la corruption et au laxisme à tous les niveaux. *Le Monde* (archives). https://www.lemonde.fr/archives/article/1980d/12/20/le-president-chadli-bendjedid-parait-decide-a-mettre-fin-a-la-corruption-et-au-laxisme-a-tous-les-niveaux_2807759_1819218.html. Accessed January 25, 2022.

Junqua, D. (1981, December 1). Les changements intervenus depuis la mort de Boumédiène ont été conduits avec prudence et habileté. *Le Monde* (archives).

https://www.lemonde.fr/archives/article/1981/12/01/les-changements-intervenus-depuis-la-mort-de-boumediene-ont-ete-conduits-avec-prudence-et-habilete_2725889_1819218.html

Lamchichi, A. (1991). *L'Algérie en crise; crise économique et changements politiques*. L'Harmattan.

Le Monde with AFP. (2020, July 1). Algérie: des caciques de l'ère Bouteflika lourdement punis pour corruption. *Le Monde*. https://www.lemonde.fr/afrique/article/2020/07/01/algerie-des-caciques-de-l-ere-bouteflika-lourde ment-punis-pour-corruption_6044881_3212.html. Accessed January 25, 2022.

Le Monde. (1987, September 1). Algérie Le pétrole vert au lieu de l'or noir. *Le Monde* (archives). https://www.lemonde.fr/archives/article/1987/09/01/algerie-le-petrole-vert-au-lieu-de-l-or-noir_4046269_1819218.html. Accessed January 25, 2022.

Le Monde. (1990, October 24). Algérie: L'affaire des 26 milliards de dollars de pots-de-vin Un ancien premier ministre accuse le pouvoir de ne pas combattre la corruption. *Le Monde* (archives). https://www.lemonde.fr/arc hives/article/1990/10/24/algerie-l-affaire-des-26-milliards-de-dollars-de-pots-de-vin-un-ancien-premier-ministre-accuse-le-pouvoir-de-ne-pas-combat tre-la-corruption_3981273_1819218.html. Accessed January 25, 2022.

Lesbet, D. (1994). Effets de la crise du logement en Algérie. Des cités d'urgence à l'état d'exception. *Maghreb-Machrek* (Special issue), 212–221.

Lowi, M. R. (2009). *Oil Wealth and the Poverty of Politics, Algeria Compared*. Cambridge University Press.

Malti, H. (2012). *Histoire secrète du pétrole algérien*. La Découverte.

Malti, H. (2014, April 2). L'Algérie est-elle encore une république démocra-tique et populaire? *Algeria-Watch*. https://www.algeria-watch.org/fr/article/analyse/malti_montreal.htm. Accessed January 25, 2022.

Marchés tropicaux et méditerranéens. (1995a). April 28. N°2581.

Martinez, L. (1998). *La guerre civile en Algérie*. Karthala.

Meddi, A. (2021, January 12). Braconnage, marché noir et lingots d'or: le scandale qui secoue l'Algérie. *Le Point*. https://www.lepoint.fr/afrique/bra connage-marche-noir-et-lingots-d-or-le-scandale-qui-secoue-l-algerie-12-01-2021-2409169_3826.php. Accessed January 25, 2022.

Mira, R. (2017). Institutions et ordre politique dans le modèle économique algérien. *CEPN, 7234*, 1–22.

Mortimer, R. (1991). Islam and Multiparty Politics in Algeria. *Middle East Journal, 45*, 575–593.

Mouhamed, M. (2015, May 3). 65 mayors in prison for corruption. *El Khabar*. https://www.djazairess.com/elkhabar/514848. Accessed January 25, 2022.

Mouhoub. (1995). Interview with Cherif Rahmani. *Algérie-Actualité, 1533*.

5 A CONTROLLED ECONOMIC LIBERALIZATION 151

Mounir, R. (1994). Les faucons rentrent dans le rang. *Le nouvel Afrique Asie*, 56.

Ouchene, B., et al. (2018). De l'économie socialiste à l'économie de marché : l'Algérie face à ses problèmes écologiques. *VertigO*, *18*(2), 1–22.

Parti de la révolution socialiste (PRS). 1976. Remarques critiques à propos de la « charte nationale. *Collection Ei Jerida*, 1–32. https://www.ahmeddahm ani.net/PDF/Experiences/El%20Jarida/RC-PRS.pdf. Accessed January 25, 2022.

Remouche. K. (2017, July 13). Foncier industriel: 18 000 hectares à l'abandon. *El Watan*. https://www.liberte-algerie.com/actualite/foncier-industriel-18-000-hectares-a-labandon-273492. Accessed January 25, 2022.

Revenue Watch Index. (2010). *Transparency: Government and the Oil, Gas and Mining Industries*.

Richards, A., & Waterbury, J. (1990). *A Political Economy of the Middle East: State, Class, and Economic Development*. Westview Press.

Roberts, H. (1984). The Politics of Algerian Socialism. In R. Lawless & A. Findlay (Eds.), *North Africa: Contemporary Politics and Political Development*. Croom Helm.

Rouzeik, F. (1994). Algérie. Chronique intérieure. *Annuaire de l'Afrique du Nord, 33*.

Ruedy, J. (1992). *Modern Algeria: The Origins and Development of a Nation*. Indiana University Press.

Rummel, L. (1992). Privatization and Democratization in Algeria. In P. Entelis & P. Naylor (Eds.), *State and Society in Algeria*. Westview Press.

Sereni, J. P. (2019, October 29). Algérie. Le scandale de l'autoroute Est-Ouest refait surface. *Orient XXI*. https://orientxxi.info/magazine/algerie-le-scandale-de-l-autoroute-est-ouest-refait-surface,3365. Accessed January 25, 2022.

Swearingen, W. (1992). Agricultural Policies and the Growing Food Security Crisis. In *State and Society in Algeria* (pp. 118–265). Routledge.

Talahite, F. (2000). Economie administrée, corruption et engrenage de la violence en Algérie. *Revue Tiers Monde*, *41*(161), 49–74.

Talahite, F. (2010). Réformes et transformations économiques en Algérie. *Economies et finances*. Université Paris-Nord - Paris XIII. https://tel.archives-ouvertes.fr/tel-00684329/document. Accessed January 25, 2022.

Tardrew, C., & Piot, O. (2013, June 4). Algérie: les 7 défis de l'après-Bouteflika. *Le Parisien*. https://www.leparisien.fr/week-end/algerie-les-7-defis-de-l-apres-bouteflika-04-06-2013-2865111.php. Accessed January 25, 2022.

Titouche, A. (2022, July 28). L'Algérie engloutit son épargne en devises. *Liberté*. https://www.liberte-algerie.com/economie/lalgerie-englou tit-son-epargne-en-devises-362535. Accessed January 25, 2022.

Tlemçani, R. (1999). *État, Bazar et Globalisation. L'aventure de l'Infitah en Algérie*. Éditions El Hikma.

Vergès, M. (1994). La Casbah d'Alger: chronique de la survie dans un quartier en sursis. *Naqd, 6,* 36–43.

Volpi, F. (2003). *Islam and Democracy: The Failure of Dialogue in Algeria*. Pluto Presses.

Werenfels, I. (2007). *Managing Instability in Algeria: Elite and Political Change Since 1995*. Routledge.

World Bank Report. (2021). Algeria: Economic Monitor: Restoring the Algerian Economy After the Pandemic. *World Bank* (Fall). https://www.worldb ank.org/en/country/algeria/publication/algeria-economic-update-fall-2021. Accessed January 25, 2022.

Yefsah, A. (1992). L'armée et le pouvoir en Algérie 1962–1992. *Revue Des Mondes Musulmans Et De La Méditerranée, 65,* 77–95.

Zerrouky, M. (2019, June 12). En Algérie, la chute brutale d'Ahmed Ouyahia. *Le Monde*. https://www.lemonde.fr/international/article/2019/06/12/ algerie-l-ex-premier-ministre-ouyahia-ecroue_5475392_3210.html. Accessed January 25, 2022.

CHAPTER 6

The Policies of Violence and Repression

The ability of a non-democratic regime to impose coercion is crucial to its success. Authoritarian regimes succumb to revolution when their coercive apparatus is weakened (often by war) (Skocpol, 1979) or when they lack the will or capacity to crush dissent (Bellin, 2012). Competitive authoritarian stability requires coercive capabilities. The more a government can avoid or suppress opposition protests, the better its chances of survival (Levitsky & Way, 2010).

In Algeria, the regime has maintained itself in part by suppressing resistance. The security forces, intelligence services, and local *Walis* provide the regime with the tools to monitor, co-opt, intimidate, and repress real and potential opponents. Precisely because these state institutions frequently engage in illiberal and even illegal activities, they remain effective and valuable for the regime's stability.

The Algerian regime has employed different types of coercion throughout its history. In the 1960s and 1970s, it was outright authoritarian, and hence the scope and intensity of violence were high. Besides hunting down well-known opponents and torturing or assassinating dissidents, the regime also used symbolic violence against society by imposing on it a fictional history and a homogeneous identity. This would come at a significant cost; in 1981, the regime had to face the first spontaneous mass mobilization in the Berber hinterland. During these protests,

© The Author(s), under exclusive license to Springer Nature   153
Switzerland AG 2022
D. Ghanem, *Understanding the Persistence of Competitive Authoritarianism in Algeria*, Middle East Today,
https://doi.org/10.1007/978-3-031-05102-9_6

which came to be called the "Berber Spring", the Berbers of Kabylia demanded the recognition of their language, culture, and identity. The regime's answer was straightforward: the security forces cracked down on protesters, injuring and arresting hundreds of people.

The regime would face other protests in Oran and Saïda (1982), Constantine and Sétif (1986), and Algiers (1988). As we have seen, this last episode was a watershed. On October 5, 1988, the regime dispatched troops that fired on unarmed youth protesting rising costs of goods and the high unemployment rate. According to official figures, 159 people were killed, although unofficial reports put the number at 500 (Comité National Contre La Torture, 1988). The army, the real locus of power, introduced a controlled multiparty system in 1989 but put in place electoral engineering to avoid any victory by the opposition. For this reason, it did not expect the most prominent opposition party, the Islamic Salvation Front (FIS), to emerge as popular enough to win local elections followed by the first round of parliamentary elections.

The regime's decision in 1992 to shut down legal and peaceful means for the FIS to challenge political power tragically pushed the more radical elements of the party to jihadism against state institutions, employees, and eventually civilians. The state fought the violence of the jihadist insurgency with a range of repressive practices, including the opening of detention camps in the south of the country. Thousands affiliated and unaffiliated with the Islamist movement were jailed in these camps; they included politicians and notable journalists convicted of defaming government officials. The regime's security forces used arbitrary detention without charge, torture against detainees under interrogation, summary executions, and disappearances throughout the decade-long civil war.

Repression continued following the end of the civil war, albeit generally in far less violent ways. Hafnaoui Ghoul and Mohammed Benchicou are only two examples of dozens of people against whom the regime used a selective application of legal tools to silence their opposition. Ghoul, a journalist, was subjected to judicial harassment by the authorities in order to muzzle him. On May 24, 2004, he was arrested by plainclothes police officers and placed in preventive detention; this came following the filing by the Wali [prefect] of Djelfa of two complaints, one regarding "defamation" and the other concerning "insulting a state constituent body." In the newspaper *Le Soir d'Algérie* on May 17, 2004, Ghoul had denounced the suspicious deaths of sixteen newborns at the Djelfa public hospital and criticized the *Wali* for his misuse of public funds. He had also denounced the poor situation of human rights, particularly for journalists, and castigated the authorities for irregularities during the 2004 presidential election and the pressure exerted on opposition candidates. The *Wali* and his coterie (chief-of-staff, chief of protocol, executive directors, and the mayor) filed fourteen complaints against Ghoul. This judicial saga continued for months, and each time he was brought up on a charge, Ghoul was sentenced to several months in prison (OMCT, 2004).

Benchicou, director of the daily *Le Matin*, was suspended in July 2004. Benchicou was an opponent of President Bouteflika. On the eve of the 2004 presidential election, Benchicou published a vitriolic book entitled *Bouteflika, une imposture algérienne* [Bouteflika, an Algerian sham], in which he ridiculed the head of state, his family, and his supporters. A few weeks later, Benchicou, returning from a trip to France, was arrested at Algiers airport in possession of treasury bills. He was prosecuted for violating capital controls and sentenced to two years in prison (Le Figaro, 2006).

The regime calibrated its repression when needed. For instance, when what came to be called the "Arab Spring", which had broken out in neighboring Tunisia in 2011, reached Algeria, the regime swiftly contained protests without resorting to the military. It used the memory of the civil war to scare people and generous handouts to mollify them. To dissuade those who persisted in demonstrating (in smaller protests), the regime dispatched its well-trained, well-equipped, and well-paid police force to mete out forceful repression.

As for the 2019 *Hirak*, the regime did not stick to a single response mode to protests. It switched between attrition (waiting it out), tolerance (*Hirak*ists' demands were mainly ignored, but the government let them demonstrate every Friday all over the country), concessions (engineering the departure of Bouteflika and arresting his coterie), and low-intensity repression (arresting and detaining people for several hours, surveilling them, and subjecting them to physical harassment). The regime combined these different tactical responses and adapted its strategy to avoid bloodshed but, more importantly, to avoid genuine change even as it maintained itself.

1962–1988: The Years of Lead

The lessons associated with the violence of colonization (1830–1954) and the War of Independence (1954–1962) were duly noted by the FLN and then applied once it took control of Algeria in 1962. The newly independent state would use the same methods used by the French colonizer: killing opponents, silencing intellectuals, and depriving the people of their freedoms. Indeed, at the heart of the creation of the Algerian state was intense violence. Within the FLN, which would take control of the state, relations were governed by force, as were the state's relations with society. The power of the rifle was all that counted, even after independence (Moussaoui, 2000).

Violence Against Opponents

Long repressed, muzzled, and infantilized by the colonizer, ordinary Algerians would be deprived of representation under the newly independent state. The FLN established itself as the only party, the "vanguard" that had given birth to the revolution and led the people to independence. After being excluded for 132 years, Algerians had to face exclusion by their elites. The latter, having control of the state's politico-economic-security apparatus, were detached from the people (Nair, 1995: 38).

The regime used the powerful Military Security (SM) to silence opponents, including former FLN/ALN fighters, executives, and political activists. It infiltrated congresses, public debates, dissident FLN subgroups, and the police (Harbi, 1992: 187). This started with Ben Bella, who, out of fear, ousted or eliminated all those who had backed him in his successful bid to become Algeria's first president. In August 1963, Ben Bella outlawed the Socialist Revolution Party (PRS). The party's president, Mohamed Boudiaf, was kidnapped and sequestered for more than five months in Tsabit camp in the south before being sent into exile, where he would remain for twenty-eight years before he was allowed to return. In November, Ben Bella banned the Algerian Communist Party, its newspaper *El Huriya* [Liberty], and arrested its leader, Bachir Hadj Ali.

Abderrahmane Farés, former president of the provisional executive, was arrested in July 1964. Farés was released one year later, when Boumediene came to power. Ferhat Abbas, GPRA's former president, was arrested in

6 THE POLICIES OF VIOLENCE AND REPRESSION   157

August 1964 and imprisoned for ten months. The violence of Ben Bella's rule went further when he condemned to death Mohamed Chaabani, in charge of the fourth military region of Biskra, for mutiny and conspiring against the FLN. Chaabani was executed in September 1964. Hocine Aït Ahmed, who, along with the soldiers under his command, had joined Chaabani's mutiny in Kabylia, was also sentenced to death, in April 1965, before being pardoned (Haroun, 2005: 311–313). It should be said that during this revolt, Kabylia had as many insurgents against the regime of Ben Bella as there were supporters.

Under Boumediene, things were not different. To start with, he put Ben Bella under house arrest for sixteen years, to be released only in 1981 by Chadli Bendjedid. People who criticized the regime were systematically discredited as "counter-revolutionaries" and "saboteurs of socialism" and were exiled or died in mysterious circumstances. Mohamed Khider, a major figure in the War of independence who left Algeria in 1963 to join the opposition after disagreements with Ben Bella, was killed by unidentified men on January 4, 1967, in Madrid (Herreman, 1967). Mohamed Harbi, director of the weekly *Révolution Africaine*, was arrested and imprisoned for five years without trial. Bachir Hadj Ali, the founder of the Party of the Socialist Avant-garde (PAGS), was jailed and tortured. FLN Political Bureau member Hocine Zahouane was placed under house arrest for six years.

The most striking crisis was undoubtedly the one between Colonel Zbiri and Boumediene. Zbiri attempted a coup in December 1967. Boumediene bombed armed columns of Zbiri's insurgents in the region of El Affroun (Blida) and stopped the coup in its tracks. Zbiri fled to Tunisia and then took up residence in France. Later, in 1969, Krim Belkacem, who led the Algerian Democratic Movement for Renewal (MDRA) abroad, was sentenced to death in absentia. Belkacem was found strangled with his tie in a hotel room in Frankfurt in October 1970. Important actors from the War of independence, such as Ferhat Abbas, Benyoucef Ben Khedda, Hocine Lahouel, and Mohamed Kheireddine, were placed under house arrest in March 1976. Their crime? They had criticized Boumediene in a manifesto calling for the establishment of an elected Constituent Assembly. Finally, Ahmed Medeghri, Minister of Interior, died in mysterious circumstances in December 1974.

With Bendjedid, intimidation of opponents continued, though often in a more subtle way. As soon as he came to power, he ousted those close to Boumediene but did so by using the Court of Auditors. To cite a

158 D. GHANEM

few cases, Ahmed Bencherif, Minister of Hydraulic and Environment, and Tayebi Larbi, Minister of Agriculture, were indicted for mismanagement and corruption. At the same time, Abdelaziz Bouteflika, then-Minister Advisor to the president, was accused of embezzlement of public funds. As early as April 1983, around 100 magistrates and clerks were accused of fraud, misappropriation, and abuse of power. This ostensibly anti-corruption drive opened a window of opportunity for Bendjedid to sideline his opponents and appear virtuous (Junqua, 1981). At the same time, his circle and relatives were enriching themselves. Indeed, corruption would be one of the reasons that pushed thousands of Algerians to take to the streets on October 5, 1988.

Violence Against Society

Under the pretense of preserving national unity, society was closely monitored and repressed. Violence against society, beyond the physical type, took other, symbolic forms: the imposition of a fictional history and a unique identity. At the time of independence, the regime wiped out every single story that did not conform to the image it wanted to give of *el thawra el majida* [the Glorious Revolution]. Entire swathes of history were erased, and the Algerian authorities would highlight only the fight against the French, which would itself be sublimated and idealized. The regime propagated a fictional history based on three founding myths: no history to speak of before 1954, a homogeneous people united behind the FLN/ALN with the famous slogan "One hero, the people," and a revolution against the French undertaken by the peasants (Harbi, 1998: 20; Remaoun, 1993).

The political struggles within the FLN and between the FLN and those who had long questioned its particular version of Algerian nationalism (PPA of Messali El Hadj and the reformists of Ferhat Abbas) were hidden (Carlier, 1991). By concealing these episodes and highlighting only the ALN's armed struggle, the state reinforced the idea that only force and violence can secure demands and maintain positions. This manufactured vision of the war, in which fighting prowess overshadowed political principles, would eventually backfire. Indeed, this overflow of manufactured memory generated dangerous attitudes among the younger generations (Stora, 1995: 261). Youth in the 1990s would take up arms, as their fathers and grandfathers had done, but this time to fight for the establishment of an Islamic state. The Algerian state's answer, like the colonizer's, was the use of lethal force to maintain itself.

In the aftermath of independence, the iconography of historical figures was diverted, readjusted, and readapted to better conform to the norms of Algerian nationalism. Consider, for instance, the controversial figure of the Emir Abdel Kader, seen by some as a "traitor" (because of his surrender to the French) and by others as a national hero. To celebrate him, official portraits of him were commissioned from Mohamed Racim and Hocine Ziani, but the decorations given to him by Napoleon III were not painted in. The regime controlled all research on history via the National Center for Historical Studies (CNEH). The work of historians such as Mohammed Harbi and Ferhat Abbas, to name a few, was systematically dismissed (Stora, 2004: 70–72). Algerian authors who picked apart this unified vision of history were not published in Algeria. The regime's monopoly on foreign trade reinforced this stance as books' import was controlled, and censorship was systematic. Any work at variance with the ideological, political, economic, or cultural boundaries designed by the regime was prohibited. In all its forms, the conveying of information to the public was but a sounding board for manipulative and partisan "official" truth. Freedom of expression was prohibited in books, on the screen, and on the streets, and Algerians were encouraged to self-censor and even muzzle themselves.

The Repression of Identity and Its Culmination: The Berber Spring

Algerians who experienced profound suppression of their identity during colonization would experience another form of this phenomenon under the independent state: Arabization-Islamization. While Algerian cultural identity—with its Berber, Arab, Turkish, and French dimensions—is rich and complex, the Algerian leadership rode roughshod over this diversity in the name of homogeneity.

In the aftermath of independence, the regime formalized the Arab-Muslim character of the Algerian nation in the 1963 constitution. Article 2 stipulated that "Algeria is an integral part of the Arab Maghreb, of the Arab world." Article 4 stated: "Islam is the religion of the state." Article 5 stated: "The Arabic language is the national and official language of the state." And according to Article 76, "the effective realization of Arabization must take place as soon as possible on the territory of the Republic."

160   D. GHANEM

This revival of Islamic culture and Arabic language was to allow an alliance between tradition and political, economic, and scientific modernity. It was also a way for the young Algerian nation to join other Arab states and thus be attached to the *Umma* they supposedly formed (Mengedoht, 1997: 78).

With the help of the *Ulema* [Muslim religious scholars], the state imposed on Algerians a fabricated and homogeneous Arab-Muslim identity. This imposition would pass through language purification. The Arabic literacy campaign started, and the state leaned on mosques for this campaign. The national television broadcast 30% of its five hours of programming in Arabic. *Derija* [colloquial Algerian] was excluded from official speeches, and Berber was dismissed as a mere dialect. Even use of the French language was systematically weeded out (Benrabah, 1998: 69). However, it remained the language of the elite and was considered a tool of upward social mobility. Between 1965 and 1967, the Arabization of education was a priority: the first year of primary school was Arabized in 1964, and Arabic teaching hours increased. Foreign teachers were called upon because the country suffered from a significant shortage of teachers and professors (Remaoun, 1995: 88). Nearly 10,961 Arabic-speaking teachers from the Middle East came to teach in Algerian schools. School books, which were sorely lacking, were imported from neighboring countries, and the country's first Arabic Language Institute was established at the University of Algiers (Souriau, 1976: 368).

In line with the Arabization of the administration, the ordinance of April 24, 1968, required civil servants to master the national language. This policy intensified in the 1970s with the ministerial decree of February 12, which stipulated that promoting civil servants and accepting new candidates would depend partly on their ability to pass a written and oral examination in Arabic (Souriau, 1976: 371). Meanwhile, Arabized baccalaureate graduates benefited from the creation of multiple Arabized departments (History, Geography, Philosophy, Sociology, and Trade). No less than 54% of teachers at the Institutes of Education were Arabic speakers (Blanchet, 2006).

Arabization continued throughout the decade, and the French language was no longer taught within primary education but rather as a foreign language. The number of Arabic-educated baccalaureate graduates increased considerably. The problem of job openings appeared and, with it, job creation. Paradoxically, positions in the public services and national companies were still given to French-educated people. As a

6 THE POLICIES OF VIOLENCE AND REPRESSION 161

result, Arabic-speaking students demonstrated in November 1979 and went on a strike that was observed by some 3,000 of their number (Junqua, 1979). They asked for the extension of Arabization to universities, the public sector, and national companies. The Arabic speakers, called *arabisants*, and the French speakers, *francisants*, clashed in May 1980 in Algiers and Constantine, as the first felt wronged in relation to the second when it came to educational and job opportunities.

A more significant outbreak of protests was the Berber Spring of March–April 1980. It happened in Berber-majority Kabylia, the region where some had taken up arms against Ben Bella between 1963 and 1964 to oppose his authoritarianism. Three years after its inauguration, the University of Tizi-Ouzou had earned a reputation as a hotbed of political protest and unrest. The central authorities were apprehensive about the region in general and this university in particular. As a result, when anthropologist Mouloud Mammeri, champion of the defense of Berber language, identity, and culture, was scheduled to headline a March 10, 1980 a conference at the university to discuss Berber poetry, the authorities feared that a demonstration would take place afterward and called it off. Mammeri was also instructed not to go to the university.

The day after the cancelation of Mammeri's conference, students and teachers organized a protest in Tizi-Ouzou. Breaking down the wall of fear, what started as a student protest morphed into a mass movement backed by the local population. It demanded the recognition of Berber identity and Berber heritage. Protests reached other towns and villages in Kabylia, and the authorities decided to receive a delegation of protesters at El-Muradia Palace on March 15. A few days later, the authorities delivered their response to the delegation and its demands through an editorial in the state's official newspaper, *El Moudjahid*. The editor, Kamel Belkacem, wrote a piece entitled "The Lesson-Givers," in which he attacked Mammeri, insisted that the values of Algerians were Arab-Muslim, and asserted that their only language was Arabic (Alilat, 2020).

The protests spread to Algiers, home to thousands of students from Kabylia. On April 7, no fewer than 500 people demonstrated in the capital demanding freedom of expression, democracy, and cultural and linguistic pluralism. The regime saw this as a humiliating provocation and answered with repression. Protesters were arrested, beaten, and tortured. A general strike was declared in Kabylia on April 16 and adhered to by schools, universities, and factories across the region. In a speech delivered on April

162   D. GHANEM

17, Bendjedid stated that Algeria was an Arab-Muslim country and that any attempt to undermine national unity would be fought by all means. On April 20, the security forces launched the "Mizrana operation"—named after a mountain in Kabylia—to evacuate Tizi-Ouzou University. More than 450 people were injured and hundreds arrested. The rumors of security forces raping and killing students set the region ablaze, and riots and strikes broke out anew and lasted three days.

The Berber Spring was Algeria's first spontaneous popular movement since its independence in 1962. Algerians voiced their concerns and questioned the Algerian regime publicly. The Berber Spring foreshadowed the riots of Constantine in 1986 and Algiers in 1988. Above all, the Berber Spring questioned the symbolic violence of the regime against Algeria's identity and culture and its intensive Arabization policy. It lifted the linguistic and cultural taboo and raised awareness about the importance of cultural, language, and identity rights. The Berber Spring demonstrations allowed the Kabyle movement to organize itself into associations and political parties—illegal at the time—to better structure and organize their demands. Constituted around the *thajmaath [traditional village assemblies or councils]*, pre-independence bodies that managed villages, the activists tried to give meaning to a culture that the regime thought it had largely erased through its Arabization program, and left a lasting impression on opposition movements in Algeria.

October 1988, the Grapes of Wrath

At independence, inequalities existed within society but were eclipsed by state aid and nationalistic discourse. Nevertheless, the inequalities would become glaring under Bendjedid. The 1980–1984 plan, with the infamous slogan "For a better life," put in place by the government to overcome socioeconomic difficulties, austerity, and high levels of unemployment, and boost sluggish productivity, was a failure. At the heart of these issues were population growth and distribution—owing to an annual growth rate of 3%, urbanization that reached nearly 50% in 1988, a rural exodus, and the failure of Boumediene's industrialization policy. Housing, water, and even food staples were lacking. Algerians had to wait in long lines early in the morning to get oil, sugar, flour, and eggs, among other items.

The country suffered from a two-fold dependency. First, there was food dependency caused by listless crop yields and an increase in food demand. The latter could not be met because Boumediene's industrialization policy gave priority to heavy industry, to the disadvantage of agriculture and the production of consumable goods. This put the country in a situation of dependency on food product imports. Second, there was financial dependency: the external debt went from $1.9bn in 1970 to $17.2bn in 1985 and reached $21.5bn in 1987 (Aouragh, 1996: 97–100).

The financial capacities of the Algerian state, the economy of which relied mainly on oil and gas exports, was considerably eroded between 1980, when the price of an oil barrel was $40, and 1986, by which time it had fallen to $10. The welfare state was declining, the poor were getting poorer, and the middle class was disappearing—with some of its members entering the bourgeoisie, but most heading down the social ladder.

While prices soared, unemployment skyrocketed, reaching 30%, and living conditions deteriorated dramatically (Stora, 2006: 63–64). Young people were either working in the informal sector or idle, unable to secure a living. Many were dubbed *hittist*, (from the Arabic word "hiit" for "wall"), as they spent their days leaning against the walls of their neighborhood. *Hittism* can be considered an informal mobilization, a form of protest through performative laziness by young people who refused to join an economy that did not give them their due. The gap between the *tchi tchi* [rich kids] and the *zawaliya* [poor and humble kids] was widening. *Hittism* was an act of resistance to the regime responsible for such developments.

On October 2, resentment boiled over, and riots started in Abane Ramdane high school in the El Harrach neighborhood and the suburb of Eucalyptus in Algiers. On the night of the 4th, the riots reached other neighborhoods of the capital, such as the popular area of Bab El Oued, and eventually the cities of Annaba, Oran, Tizi-Ouzou, and Béjaïa. Nevertheless, no city witnessed a level of popular mobilization and state repression similar to that of Algiers. The riots plunged the country into unprecedented chaos that even the Berber Spring, which was highly localized, had not reached. The rioters were mainly youngsters aged between the ages of 12 and 20—in other words, high school and college students, the unemployed, and *hittists*. A majority lived in poor or marginalized neighborhoods of the capital and came from the working classes. They were unaffiliated with political opposition movements and self-organized during the six days of the riots. Their taking to the streets was spontaneous despite the authorities' claim that the Islamists were behind them.

Fed up with *El Hogra*, meaning the leaders' contempt, youths attacked the regime's symbols, including ministries, FLN offices, post offices, national companies, state markets known as *Souk el Fellah*, public transport, and telephone booths. Rioters, who expressed no unified political demands, attacked every symbol representing *edula* [the state] to show their disgust toward their leadership for their *mal-vie* [ill-life], for which the "profiteers of the system" were responsible.

The police force was underequipped, unprepared, and understaffed for such mobilization. The capital, Algiers, had no more than 2,000 police officers for three million inhabitants (Zerrouky, 2002: 151). Bendjedid declared an *état de siège* on October 5 and granted the Army administrative and security prerogatives to deal with the situation. He called on General Khaled Nezzar, the Deputy Chief-of-Staff of the Army and commander of its Land Forces, to protect the capital. Tanks rolled down the streets of Algiers.

The Army took control of the capital's main axes and, along with the police, fired on the crowds. When it was all over, the official toll stood at 159 dead and 154 wounded, while hospital sources and associations claimed 500 deaths and torture of detainees was reported (The Middle East, 1988). Algerians were in shock, and the regime lost what remained of its meager legitimacy and credibility.

Throughout the protests, the state apparatus and the military depicted the rioters as "disruptive elements," "troublemakers," and "people manipulated by Algeria's enemies." Rioters were portrayed as "thugs" whose only interest was destroying "public goods built with the sweat of Algerians." Such depictions were meant to discredit the popular mobilization and its actors and legitimize the violent means used against them. Nevertheless, the social contract was broken. The populist discourse was unable to conceal the authoritarian nature of the regime and the grim social realities of Bendjedid's era. The Algerian state had slipped toward bureaucratism with a burdensome and inefficient administration. As had now become clear, it had also slipped from authoritarianism to dictatorship, one characterized by arbitrariness, privileges, patronage, and generalized corruption (El-Kenz, 1992).

6 THE POLICIES OF VIOLENCE AND REPRESSION   165

During the riots, sympathetic individuals from various social spheres (doctors, lawyers, journalists, academics, and human rights activists) organized collective actions to support rioters—but stopped short of demonstrating in the streets to avoid repression. Meetings and general assemblies were organized in closed spaces such as newsrooms or university amphitheaters, petitions were signed, leaflets were distributed, and open letters to the president were written. Doctors organized general assemblies in their universities to disseminate information on the wounded and denounce the ill-treatment inflicted on young rioters. Bridges between these different groups were built to denounce repression and ask for more democratic freedoms. These people and their actions presented the events of October differently from the way the regime did. For them, October 5 was a social and political revolt led by the young victims of the FLN system. In a nutshell, the riots became an opportunity that various political actors, including the Islamists, seized upon to amplify demands they had made before 1988.

Far from being homogeneous, the reactions within the Islamist movement differed from one leader/imam to another. While denouncing the repression, state-sponsored imams did not go as far in their speeches as those not certified by the state. Depending on their relationship with the authorities and the level of repression in their neighborhood, most state-sponsored imams denounced state repression against rioters but did not criticize the regime.

One imam emerged from this crisis: Ali Belhadj. He presented himself as a capable spokesperson for the rioters, denounced repression, and went as far as questioning the regime's nature and the FLN's system. Belhadj was believed to be behind an anonymous call on October 10 calling for people to demonstrate against state repression and protect Islam. Thousands of people answered the call, a new round of protests took place, and participants were met with state-sanctioned violence. General Nezzar, responsible for maintaining order, and El Hadi Khediri, minister of Interior, used all kinds of repressive measures against demonstrators. The Army's bullets felled no fewer than thirty demonstrators. The Army gave Algerian Islamists their first *shuhada* [martyrs], who came on top of the 500 deaths of October 5.

For his part, Belhadj made a majestic entry onto the religious and political scene, becoming the preacher whom Algerian disenfranchised youth would listen to. On Friday, October 14, during a sermon at the *Sunna* Mosque in Bab El Oued, the 32-year-old preacher issued a sweeping indictment. He accused the regime of failing on the educational, cultural, social, and political levels. He demanded the end of the *état de siège*, amnesty for all political detainees and prisoners of conscience, and the moralization of the political life in the interest of fighting the rampant corruption of the leadership (Charef, 1990: 117–118).

The leadership put together a team of lawyers, academics, civil servants, and Army representatives guided by Mouloud Hamrouche to work on *El Infitah* [the economic opening] and *El ta'adudiya el hizbiya* [the political opening], despite the reservations of a faction of the military, headed by Kasdi Merbah. The new Constitution of February 23, 1989, introduced fundamental changes: on the economic level, all references to socialism were removed, trade union pluralism was recognized, the right to strike was guaranteed and codified, and labor relations were reorganized. Additionally, the right to private property was guaranteed, and the state's monopoly on foreign trade was abolished. On the political level, a law on associations and the multiparty system was promulgated on February 25, 1989. Freedom of expression, association, and assembly were guaranteed to citizens (Art. 39), and the right to create political associations was recognized (Art. 40). Between July 5 and July 31, 1989, the Interior Ministry approved no fewer than 50 parties (Mortimer, 1991). To appease the Islamists, the regime inserted a symbolic gesture into the Constitution's preamble, which described Algeria as "a land of Islam" and allowed the institutionalization of an Islamic High Council (Art. 161).

However, very quickly, contradictions appeared. The FLN had preferential treatment, as it did not have to seek an approval/agreement as a political party while every other party had to do so. Besides, the National Assembly remained the same, dominated by the FLN, and no legislative election was planned. Furthermore, President Bendjedid was re-elected for a third term on December 22, 1988. And the Army, which remained unaccountable to the government, remained the real locus of power. The reforms suffered from a severe deficit: they were marked by the spirit of people who were pure products of the same system they purportedly sought to change. In other words, these so-called reformists had little legitimacy and little credibility to carry out the radical and far-reaching reforms necessary for the Algerian economy, political system, and society (Dahmani, 1999: 159). As a result, Algerians were by and large unimpressed.

1989–1992: THE DESCENT INTO VIOLENCE

The multi-party system greatly benefited the Islamists, who took advantage of the freedom of political expression embodied in the multiparty system to draft a radical project for Algerian society. Leading Islamists formed the Islamic Salvation Front (FIS), which obtained a legal permit from the authorities on October 2, 1989. The FIS leader was Abbassi Madani, although Ali Belhadj was more popular among the youth. The FIS had several bulletins, and its official newspaper, *El Munkid* [The Savior], was printed to the tune of 100,000 copies and sold at mosques (Rouadjia, 1990).

Once the FIS was legalized, it launched its participationist strategy. In June 1990, it established the Islamic Union of Workers (SIT). From then on, Islamists stopped infiltrating the General Union of Algerian Workers (UGTA) and worked to build their own labor base (Christopher, 2000). The announcement of the creation of the SIT coincided with that of the UGTA's congress for the election of new leadership. This allowed the FIS to offer an alternative to union members who disagreed with the UGTA (Chikhi, 1995).

The FIS also set up several associations, such as the Association of Young Muslims, the Islamic Association of the Handicapped, and the Islamic Association of the Children of Shuhada. These associations controlled no fewer than 20,000 cultural, religious, sports, and charitable groups (Al-Ahnaf et al., 1991: 31).

The FIS was able to capture and channel millions of Algerians' anger against the state. It was able to offer an alternative within the framework of strict application of the Sharia. The party offered an ideological horizon, an ethical ideal of political Islam, and a utopic image of society. Its slogans were simple but alluring: "The FIS is the people"; "Islam is the solution"; "You are voting for Allah because you are voting for Islam"; and "Your choice is a loan for which you will be held accountable on Judgment Day." As a result, it attracted some three million voters and as many sympathizers (Rouadjaïa, 1993: 99).

The FIS believed that society was sick and needed a cure, that it was lost and needed guidance, that it was illiterate and needed education, and that it was debased by Western values and needed purification. For all these evils, there was one solution, the Sharia, and one savior, the FIS. To the various dysfunctions that afflicted Algerian society, the FIS provided a theoretical answer, a solution on the ground, and "neighborhood committees" that played a crucial role in conquering social space, which the state had partially abandoned (Ghanem, 2012). For instance, to address economic dysfunction, the FIS set up, through the neighborhood committees, the "Islamic Solidarity Fund," *Asweq Al Rahma* [Lit. Compassion markets], and "popular restaurants" to help the most marginalized. The movement also set up projects to fight unemployment and delinquency in FIS-sympathetic neighborhoods (Boukra, 2002: 136–138).

The Islamists created green spaces in cities, repainted shops and facades, and built football stadiums in disadvantaged neighborhoods. In the June 1990 garbage collectors' strike, the FIS took care of garbage waste in the districts of Belcourt, Bab El Oued, and the Casbah. Armed with brooms and buckets, FIS members and sympathizers cleaned the streets of their neighborhood, showing the population that where the municipality and the state failed, the FIS did not. Through this strategy of occupying public space, the FIS planted its roots in society. Once its foundations were laid, it raised funds for its projects from the petty bourgeoisie, mainly business people who were suffocating due to the FLN's strict trade regulations. They supported the movement because it promised to abolish taxes and allow for a free market.

The FIS created a new subculture. It promoted the sartorial preferences of the Muslim Brotherhood of Egypt. Jeans and athletic shoes gave way to *Kamis*, beards [tinted with henna for the more conservative], and sandals. By advocating a new model of religious adherence that included dress and other readily apparent identifiers, the FIS provided a new set of symbols that young people, who were disillusioned with the state's symbols, keenly took up (Merzouk, 1997).

The FIS was welcomed by many as a godsend through which change would come, followed by order, justice, and equity. FIS discourse appealed to various segments of Algerian society because it transcended social classes and their contradictions. The party managed to bring together neo-urban youth from the under-proletariat, lumpenproletariat, and specific segments of the working class, particularly the young working class, of recent formation (Fontaine, 1992). They were joined by the petty bourgeoisie (i.e., small traders, employees, artisans, small entrepreneurs, etc.) certain factions of the bourgeoisie (large traders, jewelers, businessmen, landowners, etc.), and the Islamist intelligentsia (teachers,

6 THE POLICIES OF VIOLENCE AND REPRESSION   169

doctors, academics, engineers, technicians, executives) (Boukra, 2002: 238).

In the run-up to elections, the FIS disseminated information and commentary across its localities on the nature of authoritarian politics in Algeria, and condemning past successive governments and the military. The FIS became the intermediary that connected millions of dissatisfied people and generated awareness of widespread dissatisfaction with the regime. With its networks and mobilization potential, the party became the first real challenger of the regime.

It is in this atmosphere that made an impressive showing in the municipal and regional elections of June 12, 1990: victory in 853 of the 1551 municipalities, including a majority in big cities (64% in Algiers, 70% in Oran, 72% in Constantine). Control was guaranteed in 31 wilayas out of 48 (Cubertafond, 1999: 8; Kapil, 1990). Despite an unequal arena of electoral competition and the difficulty of collective action, the FIS had succeeded in mobilizing broad sectors of Algerian society and challenging the regime.

The FIS: From Accommodation to Confrontation

Encouraged by the FIS victory, its supporters took control of mosques and neighborhoods in municipalities where a majority had voted for the party. They imposed their vision of Islam, which was based on a strict application of Sharia, on locals. The FIS dispatched "*El Muslihun*" [Litt. Reformers], a repressive morality brigade that surveilled people and punished those who refused to follow FIS rules. Cultural events and concerts were canceled, and pubs, nightclubs, video shops, and all businesses considered "debauched" were forced to close or change their activities. Swimming and wearing shorts in some coastal towns such as Tipaza were prohibited because *la yajuz* [illicit]. Women without a headscarf were called *El a'riyet-kasiyet* [the naked-dressed] and were ordered to "dress decently" and "stay at home" (Kebir, 1998).

Unsettled by the FIS victory, the regime tried to contain its growing power. On April 2, 1991, the authorities promulgated a new electoral law that revised constituencies' division to the detriment of the FIS. This gerrymandering upset Madani and Belhadj, who called for a general and open-ended strike. They gave President Bendjedid a week to repeal the electoral law in view of the parliamentary elections on June 27.

The strike lasted eight days, from May 26 to June 3. FIS members, elected officials, and sympathizers occupied several public spaces in Algiers. Demonstrators chanted *Chadli barra* [Chadli out], *La mitak, la dustur, kala Allah, kala el rasul* [Neither a charter nor a constitution, God said and His Prophet said], *Dawla Islamiyah bla ma n'voté* [Islamic State without a vote]. The military intervened and violently ended the strike on June 3, causing the death of nearly 50 people and the injury of 300.

On June 5, a presidential decree proclaimed an *état de siège* for four months. The decree declared legal house arrest, day and night searches, and prohibited gathering, political rallies, meetings, or publications. The Hamrouche government resigned by the president's order, and the parliamentary elections scheduled for June 27 were postponed (Benchikh, 1992). In response, on June 6, the FIS's *Majlis el-Shura* [Advisory Council] released a statement calling on its followers to "form groups to organize and execute attacks against the enemy's nerve centers, with instructions to withdraw to mountains" (Zerrouky, 2002: 81). This text marked a new stage in the rise of violence. On June 30, the authorities arrested Madani and Belhadj, accusing them of "armed conspiracy against state security."

The first "security centers," which in reality were detention camps, came into existence following the presidential Decree No. 91–201 of June 25, 1991. There were four such centers located in the north of the country (Ouled Fayet, Blida, Oran, and Aïn M'Lila) and two in the south, in Ouargla and El Menia. An Amnesty International report stated that in July 1991, over 1,000 individuals were placed in these security centers for up to two months (Amnesty International, 1993).

While FIS leaders were jailed, the extremist wing of the movement, *El Afghaniyun* [Afghans; Algerians who fought in Afghanistan in 1979] acted on November 28, 1991. Sixty people, led by Aïssa Messaoudi, aka Tayeb El Afghani, attacked a border post in the locality of Guemmar, near the border with Tunisia. During this attack, 25 people were killed, only three of whom were soldiers, yet the militants were able to seize ammunition and machine guns. The Guemmar attack marked the start of jihadism in Algeria.

After three months and three weeks, on September 29, 1991, the *état de siege* was lifted and on December 26, 1991, the parliamentary elections took place. The FIS presented its candidates, and despite losing a million votes compared to the June local elections, the FIS performed very well in the first round, winning 188 of 232 seats. For the 199 remaining seats, the second round of elections was scheduled for January 1992. Fearing that Islamists would attain a majority in parliament, the military obliged Bendjedid to dissolve parliament and then resign on January 11, 1992, thereby interrupting the election process. The Army suspended the constitution and effectively took control of the country, establishing a transitional executive body, the High Committee of State (HCE), to which it entrusted the task of exercising political authority. Another newly established body, the National Consultative Council, would act as parliament. The military appointed Mohamed Boudiaf, exiled in Morocco since 1966, to head the HCE.

At the same time, the army rounded up the remaining FIS leaders, thereby effectively decapitating the party. On January 22, 1992, they arrested Abdelkader Hachani, President of the FIS Provisional Office, who had called on the army to respect the verdict of the ballots. On January 28, they arrested Rabah Kebir, a member of the FIS political leadership, for "inciting rebellion against authority." They also launched vast night arrests of FIS elected officials, party members, and sympathizers. From the end of January 1992, the pace of arrests increased, and tens of thousands of people were arbitrarily rounded up, including 150 FIS deputies who had been elected in the first round, 800 mayors, and 4,000 local councilors (Mellah, 2004). In police stations, gendarmerie, and military barracks, detainees were often mistreated and even tortured. The FIS called on people to defect from state institutions and join them, which further stoked the regime's wrath. Torture was a tool to obtain crucial information and a means of intimidating entire segments of the population. Many detained in these barracks and police stations ended up in "security centers" in the south.

On February 9, 1992, the HCE issued Decree 92–44, which declared an *état d'urgence* [state of emergency] for twelve months; the latter was systematically renewed every year for 19 years until the authorities lifted it during the Arab Spring in 2011. On March 4, the FIS was officially outlawed, its 450 local assemblies were dissolved on March 29, and all its charitable and religious associations were outlawed. Special courts were set up in Algiers, Constantine, and Oran, whose presidents and assessors remained anonymous. No fewer than 10,000 individuals were tried in these courts between February 1993 and June 1994, of whom 1,127 were sentenced to death (Fidh, 1998).

172 D. GHANEM

It is erroneous to date the beginning of armed violence in 1992 to the interruption of the electoral process because, as we have seen, Guemmar attack was perpetrated in 1991. However, it is safe to say that the interruption of the electoral process was the catalyst for mass violence. The regime's scrapping of the elections reinforced the FIS radical wing's conviction that the only possible strategy was armed violence because any peaceful political settlement was doomed to failure. After the interruption of the electoral process, many Islamist groups, among them the Armed Islamic Group (GIA), the Armed Islamic Movement (MIA), and the Salvation Islamic Army (AIS), sprang up all over Algeria to fight what they called *dawlet al-taghut* [the impious state]. Islamist violence was a response to the attacks and deceptions of a political order that no longer honored its promises. Violence was presented by the Islamists as a necessity for the triumph of a new, supreme, absolute, and totalizing order: that of *el dawla el Islamiya* (Ghanem, 2012).

The Islamist insurgency started with attacks on members of the security forces and then proceeded to civilians. On August 26, 1992, a bomb exploded at Algiers airport, killing eight people and injuring 124. This was the first attack against civilians, and it began a long period of indiscriminate violence against them. After all, their lifestyle did not conform to the jihadists' reading of Islam because they were working in/with state institutions or because they did not adhere to the project of an Islamic state. In a nutshell, every person perceived as hostile to establishing an Islamic state had to be killed. The list of targets extended to all strata of Algerian society. For instance, civil servants became a "legitimate" target because they allowed for the sustainability of state production. Schools and teachers were targeted because they kept society running, and voters because they provided the regime with legitimacy. In the eyes of the jihadist groups, especially the GIA, the struggle was against the whole system, not against an individual or a group. It was, therefore, "lawful" to attack any person or institution that served to maintain the system. In its official journal, the GIA quoted the Quran for justification: "And fight against them until there is no fitnah and [until] the religion, all of it, is for Allah. And if they cease—then indeed, Allah is seeing of what they do" [Sura VIII, El Anfal, Verse 39].

With a firm commitment to "eradicate terrorism," the military high command answered with a body of laws. In September 1992, Ali Kafi, the successor of Mohamed Boudiaf as head of the HCE, promulgated a legislative decree relating to the fight against terrorism and subversion, which categorized a range of vaguely defined offenses as terrorist or subversive acts. At the same time, the state security apparatus brought together the special army units responsible for carrying out the fight against terrorism under the Center for Conduct and Coordination of Anti-Subversive Actions (CCLAS), headed by General Lamari.

From 1993 onward, a bloody struggle between armed Islamist groups and the state security forces took place. No segment of society was spared. Armed groups placed bombs in public spaces, killing hundreds. At a later stage, at the end of 1996, armed groups escalated and perpetrated massacres of entire populations in the Mitidja plain and in remote villages, killing people indiscriminately (Ghanem, 2012). The jihadist groups did this because they, especially the GIA, had cut themselves off from their social base and even from the youth (especially urban youth). This is sometimes called the "inversion mechanism" because distance appears and then widens between a social movement and the political actor speaking on its behalf. The relationship with the base disappears, and the political actor need not consult anyone (Wieviorka, 1988: 97–98).

By 1996, the GIA had started losing control of many villages to the security forces or other jihadist groups. This, together with fragmentation, internal dissension, numerous defections, the fear of disintegration, and the FIS/AIS talks with the government impacted the GIA's decision-making. Through a series of massacres that culminated in 1997, the GIA wanted to punish the population, prove its strike capability, and scupper political mediation efforts initiated by the FIS/AIS with the authorities. Extreme violence also had as its aim forcing the state to abandon the use of force as futile (Ghanem, 2012). Similarly, civilians were also victims of state repression because they were considered the rear base of armed Islamist groups. Suspected of supporting the Islamists, working-class neighborhoods and remote and/or poor areas, including those affected by terrorism, were relentlessly targeted by state security forces in their bid to eradicate Islamism.

1992–1998: Repression and the "Total War on Terror"

In the name of the fight against terror, the security forces engaged in forced disappearances, summary executions, and mass arrests in an indiscriminate manner that ultimately was counterproductive. This played a crucial role in radicalizing many people, particularly young men (and women), who responded positively to the FIS radical wing's call to wage jihad against the state. In short, the security forces' repression contributed significantly to violent radicalization and the proliferation of armed groups.

The "Security Centers"

The authorities established ten "security centers" in total, all of which were located in the south. Article 5 of Decree 92–44 allowed the Minister of Interior to confine in these detention camps "any adult whose activity is dangerous to public order, public security, or the proper functioning of public services." Camps were placed under the military's authority, but the Ministry of Interior and the Wali were empowered to place people in them.

Looking back at that era, Ali Yahia Abdennour, honorary president of the Algerian League for the Defense of Human Rights (LADDH), described detention conditions as "inhuman." He spoke of "a world record of human rights violations," explaining that these camps were "worse than the camps during colonialism" (Abdenour, 2007). Indeed, the Algerian authorities were following in French colonial authorities' footsteps, replicating what the French did during the war of independence under article 6 of the 1955 state of emergency law. Under this law, French authorities opened "centers" for individuals "whose activity was dangerous to security and public order" (Thénault, 2003).

Detainees were distributed between Reggane, Aïn Salah, Ouargla, El Homr, Borj Omar Driss, El Menia, In M'Guel, Tsabit, Tiberghamine, and Oued Namous. In 1992, officials reported 6,786 prisoners (Zighem, 1992), while the FIS spoke of 14,000 (Cesari, 1994). According to a former detainee, Noureddine Belmouhoub, the camps were used for "the internment of thousands of people (more than 24,000) [...]. The capacity of the camps varied between 1,500 and 3,500 people. The people there suffered from temperatures of minus 5 degrees [Celsius] at night to over 55 during the day and lived in tents. The water, although available, was provided in small quantities" (Algeria-Watch, 2010).

The camps were opened hastily and closed even more suddenly. In June 1992, El Menia was closed; Aïn Salah and Ouargla's turn came in March 1993. The last camp, In M'guel, was closed at the end of 1995. If anything, this shows the arbitrariness of the decision-makers and the genealogy of repression that dated back to the war of independence. Detainees set up a strict organization with a representative council. Every *wilaya* was represented by one or two detainees who became members of this council, which was an intermediary between the detainees and the military administration in charge of the camp. It also played a mediation role in internal conflicts between inmates via the *Majlis ta'dibi* [Disciplinary Council]. The council was headed by an emir [leader]. Usually, the *emir* was a college-educated FIS cadre. For instance, in Reggane, Messaoud Ouziala, a nephrologist and formerly the FIS mayor of the municipality of Aïn Taya in Algiers, was appointed emir of the camp (Arezki, 2019).

The camps brought together Islamists from different factions and regions, including FIS members and sympathizers, breakaway jihadists, cadres, elected officials from the Popular Assemblies of Wilayas (APW), and the Communal People's Assemblies (APC), under the same roof, which allowed them to discuss strategy. Also, as the security forces' repression was indiscriminate and innocent people were jailed in these camps, this allowed the Islamists to indoctrinate them and enlarge their networks.

Most detainees were not tried and did not know how long their detention would last. The moral and physical pressure in these camps inadvertently cultivated radical opposition to the state and reinforced a sense of revolt against it. Indeed, the camps were places of radicalization where many individuals were indoctrinated, prepared, and trained for the armed struggle. The camps offered FIS militants and supporters the opportunity to consolidate their conviction that the state was "tyrannical" and had to be fought with the rifle (Labat, 1995: 251). Many would join the *maquis* once their sentence was completed.

Revenge was among the most cited motivation of those former detainees to whom the author spoke, many of whom had become jihadists in the camps. While insisting that their first motivation was to raise the banner of Islam in Algeria, their discourse showed a clear desire to retaliate for what had been done to them by zealous members of the security forces. The camps played a crucial role in their choice to follow the jihadist path. In a nutshell, repression and torture strengthened the beliefs of some to take up weapons while forging links between activists (Bennani-Cheraibi & Fillieule, 2002; Combes & Fillieule, 2011). Consider the words of Hanan, who, during a fieldwork visit in Algiers in 2010, spoke about her cousin's fiancé:

> My cousin Hadjira, who was engaged at the time to a nice boy, told me that after his return from the Ain M'Guel camp, the man she had in front of her was not any longer the one she had known. He told her that they were starved [...]. Most of them were released with severe malnutrition and health problems, and some died upon leaving the camps. Others were forced to sit on bottlenecks or were penetrated with broom handles. They burnt their beards with torches and tortured them with electricity. Fouad [...] went into the *maquis* with friends from the camp, and we never saw him again. (Author's interview, Algiers October 2010)

Young people who, at the beginning of the crisis, were not swayed by Islamist discourse despite their hatred for *edula*, would, as a result of intimidation, arrests, and repression, gravitate to this same Islamist discourse after their experiences in the camps. Many would join armed groups to quench their thirst for revenge. It should have been obvious to the regime that its widespread repression was counterproductive because it fueled dissent and radicalized people. However, in the regime's calculus, violence was employed on a large scale because the likelihood of subversive acts against it was high. Also, widespread violence can be explained for practical reasons relating to the lack of information, particularly when it comes to identifying civilians who collaborated with jihadists, something which required complex and expensive infrastructure (Kalyvas, 2006). There was quite a bit of organizational incompetence on the part of the Algerian army, 80% of which was made up of conscripts.

The Total War on Terror and Forced Disappearances

People made to disappear by the security forces were civilians arrested at their homes, at work, or in public spaces. There were several stigmatizing criteria—such as age, district of residence, political opinions, profession, family, and friendships—on which the authorities relied to consider that a certain person or group had Islamist leanings. The district of residence was a particularly stigmatizing criterion. People living in suburbs of Algiers, such as Kouba, Badjarah, el Harrach, Belcourt, and Bab el Oued, to cite a few, were in the eyes of the security services likely to maintain links with the Islamist movement and to provide information to armed groups, and thus were targeted by the security agencies.

From 1992, special anti-terrorist units were created within the Army, then the Gendarmerie and the Police. Under the Coordination of the Intelligence and Security Department (DRS) and the Army, the fight against terrorism involved the various bodies of the state security—Army, Gendarmerie, Police—and the paramilitaries instituted in 1994. The special, mobile units and the ordinary, local units of the security forces cooperated under the coordination of the Army and two DRS directorates: the Directorate of Counter-espionage and the Central Directorate of Army Security.

Active from 1992, the special units to fight terrorism and subversion, the Army's CCLAS para-commandos, the Gendarmerie's Rapid Intervention Group, and the Police's Mobile Brigades of Judicial Police, acted in cooperation with one another within the various coordination structures set up by the DRS and the Army. Their mission was to reduce the scope of action of armed groups in the capital and its outskirts, as well as in rural areas. The security apparatuses were helped from 1994 onward by militias created under the government of Redha Malek. Their central mission was to protect the villagers and towns where they were established. Their activities were meant to disrupt the supply network and even the operations of jihadist groups. This kept the army from over-extending itself.

Three types of militias were formed: the Groups for Legitimate Defense (GLD), the Patriots, and the Communal Guard. The GLD were mainly born in the Berber hinterland and used as armed support for political parties and regional associations. The GLD operated more or less independently because they were not under the authority of any ministry. They are believed to have committed numerous atrocities against civilians. The Patriots—who had the support of the National Mujahidin Organization (ONM)—worked in close collaboration with the National Gendarmerie but were linked to the Ministry of the Interior. Patriots usually operated in towns and villages in the country's interior, and some 4,000 are believed to have died fighting jihadists. The Communal Guard was the result of a joint decision by the Ministry of Interior and the Defense Ministry. It was placed under the mayors of the Communal Executive Delegation (DEC) and the *Walis*. Recruits received a two-month accelerated training course within the Gendarmerie, wore a uniform, and received a monthly salary. Their mission was to prevent the return of jihadist groups to liberated areas (areas no longer under armed groups' control). They also occasionally helped the army in its mopping-up operations in mountainous regions.

The army and the security apparatuses enabled the regime to withstand the challenges of 1992–1995 when it was most at risk of collapsing in the face of the jihadist onslaught. Though the political establishment was divided between "eradicators" and "dialogists," internal cohesion remained high. And the elites' cohesion, rooted in solidarity ties dating back to the war of independence, enhanced the cohesion of the security forces. This was critical to the success of the regime's high-intensity coercion of the 1990s. High-intensity coercion poses a particular threat to the chain of command, increasing the likelihood of internal disobedience. Nevertheless, in 1990s Algeria, even highly controversial and illegal orders such as firing on crowds, indiscriminate violence against civilians, torture, forced disappearances, and extrajudicial killings were carried out by high-level security officials and rank-and-file soldiers and bureaucrats. It is because cohesion was high that coercion was effective. Except for a few exceptions, members of the security forces reliably followed their superiors' commands (author's interviews with military personnel). For instance, when desertions started in 1993, they were likely rooted in soldiers' fear of being killed by armed groups that systematically targeted them rather than a refusal to obey orders (author's interviews with former soldiers met between 2016 and 2018).

State cohesion is also rooted in the state's fiscal health. Unpaid or poorly paid security forces are less likely to follow orders—especially high-risk orders such as violent repression. In the 1990s, Algeria struggled with a severe fiscal crisis that could have eroded discipline within the security forces. Noncompliance of unpaid or poorly paid security forces could have left the regime without the means to crack down on the opposition and conduct its total war on terror. However, from mid-1994 until the beginning of the following year, the Algerian state reached an agreement with the IMF to reschedule its debt. This allowed it to invest in development and soothe social tensions by meeting much of the population's housing and employment needs. It also allowed it to inject important funds into modernizing the army and its repressive apparatuses. Military spending increased substantially, rising from $662 million in 1988, representing 1.7% of the GDP, to $1.5bn in 1995, meaning 2.9% of the GDP; this is an increase of 126%. Throughout the decade, military spending continued to increase: $1.7bn in 1996, $2bn in 1997, $4.5 bn in 2010, and $10bn in 2019, representing 6% of the GDP.

On the ground, 1995 was the year of "the eradication of terrorism." The regime equipped itself with a formidable arsenal of 80,000 counterterrorism army corps supported by more than 200,000 militiamen and nearly 80,000 gendarmes. The military, police, and gendarmerie) undertook increased reconnaissance missions, search and destroy operations to dislodge the *tangos* [this is what the security forces called jihadists], and *ratissage* [security sweeps]. These operations allowed the security forces to considerably reduce the strength of armed groups and recover large stocks of weapons. Captured jihadists were of critical importance in obtaining information.

The army carried out bombardments and security sweeps in rural areas (i.e., Douars Béni Zermane, Douar Béni Aref, Attaba), and mountainous areas (Mont Zbarbar, Mont Chréa). The police were present in urban areas, while the gendarmerie conducted operations on the urban and rural fronts. Special forces were mobilized for special missions. The police and the gendarmerie, helped by the army's aviation, combined their efforts for large-scale missions. Such was the case in March 1995, for "the battle of Aïn Defla." During this mission, the army, the gendarmerie, and the police conducted large-scale search and destroy missions in the Djurdjura mountains and in Zaccar, where they used napalm (Très Très Urgent, 1995b). Nearly 800 combatants were killed, including 300 in Jijel and more than a hundred in Tébessa.

Similarly, on May 17, the air force bombed Mount Babor, 50 km from Sétif. On May 21, in an effort to dislodge armed groups, the army and the gendarmerie napalmed mountains in the region of Sidi Ali Bounab in Kabylia, causing large fires (Zerrouky, 2002: 161–162). The army conducted bombings at the borders to push jihadists to leave the cities and fall back on the interior of the *maquis*. The bombardments were so intense that Tunisian soil was affected (Très Très Urgent, 1995a).

The security forces also confronted the violence of the Islamist insurgency with a range of repressive practices, including arbitrary detention, torture of detainees under interrogation, summary executions, and disappearances. The role of the DRS in these forced disappearances was crucial, according to human rights organizations, including the human rights commissioner appointed by Bouteflika in 2001. Agents of this branch of the army were authorized to operate as a judicial police under Article 19

180   D. GHANEM

of Algeria's Code of penal procedure. Military Security operated with the most impunity out of all the security forces and remained "untouchable."

The "disappeared" were primarily men. The men ranged in age from their early twenties to their fifties. Many were from Algiers and its outskirts (Tipaza, Blida), or Médéa and Constantine, which were badly afflicted by political violence. The security forces often kidnapped people based on circumstantial evidence of their association with militants—for example, kinship or social or professional connections.

Between 1992 and 1998, Algerian security forces were believed to be responsible for the disappearance of no fewer than 7,000 people, many of whom are still missing. On the other hand, armed groups used this tactic and are believed, according to *Somoud* [steadfastness], a nongovernmental organization created in 1996 by families of missing persons, to have kidnapped no fewer than 10,000 individuals, with more than half still missing. No serious investigations were conducted to locate these people.

Due to local and international criticism, government rhetoric on the "disappeared" has shifted dramatically over the years. Authorities initially dismissed the problem. Then, in 1998, they began downplaying it, claiming to be examining and settling individual complaints. To this end, they established offices across the country to receive complaints from families.

Yet the issue continued to taint Algeria's international image. Former president Bouteflika was the first to break the taboo and acknowledge governmental involvement in "disappearances"; this was during his first campaign. However, Bouteflika's rhetoric on "disappearances" began to shift once he was elected in April 1999 and received a mandate for the reconciliation agenda. On September 15, 1999, during a meeting in Al-Harcha auditorium in Algiers, the newly elected president became exasperated with the families of the disappeared and screamed, "I have no interest in keeping them [the disappeared] in my pocket" (Nefla, 1999).

However, officials in Algeria have recognized the situation as a challenging one that must be handled. In May 2001, Ministry of the Interior Abdelmalek Sellal stated that his office had received 4,880 missing-person complaints from families. However, he did not specify how many of these cases were traceable to state operatives. The narrative remained that the state is responsible but not guilty.

The gendarmerie confirmed receiving a total of 7,046 complaints in 2003 (Algeria-Watch, 2003). Farouk Ksentini, President of the National

Consultative Commission for the Promotion and Protection of Human Rights (CNCPPDH), had announced, in a 2005 report never published and, according to him, submitted to the President of the Republic, having identified 6,146 cases traceable to state operatives. The 2013 annual report of the CNCPPDH specified that it had identified 7,200 missing between 1992 and 1998. Algerian organizations for the protection of human rights and the leading associations of families of the disappeared estimated that the number of disappeared was between 10,000 and 20,000. Human Rights Watch lists 3,600 cases as disappeared by the security forces or their sympathizers (Human Rights Watch, 2003).

The lack of transparency surrounding the question of the disappeared is best illustrated by the mysterious mass graves found in some regions. Since 1998, several mass graves have been discovered in Haouch Hafiz (Meftah), in Ouled Allel (Sidi Moussa), in Haouch Sbihi Mohamed (Larbâa), to cite but a few. In 2001, Mohamed Smaan of the Algerian League for the Defense of Human Rights (LADDH) informed the national media of a mass grave near Sidi Mohamed Benaouda, seventeen kilometers south of Relizane. He claimed that the bodies were those of 20 people who were believed to have been "disappeared" by security forces and the GLD. Smaan informed the press in February 2001 that gendarmes and the leader of the GLD were attempting to exhume and transfer the bodies to conceal the evidence. Smaan was charged with defamation, sentenced to one year in prison, and had to pay a fine of $2,000 (Observatory for the Protection of Human Rights Defenders 2002).

The failure of the authorities to disclose the procedures for preserving evidence and identifying human remains is a common feature of mass grave exhumations. Regardless of who is found to be responsible for the mass graves, the existence of a mass unmarked grave in the context of Algeria's political violence is, according to the Collectif of the Disappeared, "*prima facie* proof of a crime against humanity" (Collectif des Familles de Disparus en Algérie, 2006). However, the government has not managed these sites in a way that protects the available evidence. Moreover, in a country where thousands of families are searching for missing relatives, the government has no political will to build a sound system for integrating these families into the site examination process or alerting them to the exhumation results.

Basically, even though it lifted a taboo and admitted that disappearances took place during the civil war, the Algerian state has done precious little to uncover the fate of the disappeared. Indeed, none of the state institutions that authorities have appointed to address the problem—the judiciary, the Ministry of Interior's missing-person bureau, and the National Human Rights Commissions (ONDH and its successor, the CNCPPDH)—have been able to produce tangible results for the families who have approached them. The ONDH and the CNCPPDH never had the authority to compel anyone to give sworn testimony or hand over official documents or information. Both agencies have a long history of systematically downplaying government crimes, condemning international human rights organizations that released findings critical of the Algeria state's conduct, and offering no relevant information to the families of the "disappeared." Algerian courts proved similarly ineffective in ascertaining the fate of missing people, identifying and prosecuting those responsible for kidnappings, or even establishing the involvement of state agents in the operations.

2001: The "Black Spring"

In more ways than one, the 2001 riots in Kabylia, the Black Spring, were a continuation of the 1980 Berber Spring. The resurgence and the central role of *thajmaath* [traditional village assemblies or councils] in the supervision of communities and protests showed the continuity and prevalence of the ethnic composition of the protests. However, these riots cannot be limited to the "ethnic question" because other demands besides recognizing Tamazight as an official language were made. In this sense, the Black Spring can also be seen as a continuation of the 1988 riots, because socioeconomic grievances were also at the heart of the protests. These grievances included economic marginalization and *El Hogra* from officials, especially members of the security forces who abused their power without consequences. The slogan "you cannot kill us; we are already dead" highlighted the symbolic and physical violence that the people felt. At the time, Tizi-Ouzou and Béjaïa, parts of Kabylia, had the highest suicide rates (Chachoua, 2008).

The feeling of identity denial coupled with social violence characterized by *El Hogra*, bad socioeconomic conditions—lack of housing and unemployment, which stood at 28% (Temlali, 2003), life without leisure, as well as the impossibility of getting through to politicians without resorting to rioting and violence—placed great stress on the population of Kabylia. The identity question was front and center and forced the elite to address the question of the "official" national identity. However, it is reductionist to state that the Black Spring was solely a response to perceived ethnic discrimination. To begin with, on the political level, Kabyle Berbers were not as marginal as some Berber nationalists suggested. On the contrary, they were associated with the various institutions of power since 1962, and there was a large number of them in critical political and military positions (Werenfels, 2007: 50). The Black Spring was more about political representation of the population than about Kabylia's ethnic specificity. It was about a conception of the state and democracy and redefining Algeria's democratic framework. Second, regional imbalances existed throughout the territory at the economic level and were not unique to the Kabyle region. Spatial disparities, a legacy of colonialism that persisted under the independent nation-state, did not affect Kabylia as much as other regions, such as the south. The central government had concentrated its development projects in coastal and northern cities, which Kabylia belongs to, leaving most natural resource-rich areas in remote areas in the south of the country underdeveloped. In this sense, the Black Spring was about improving social justice and economic conditions all over the territory.

The riots erupted following the murder of a 19-year-old, Mohamed Guermah, aka Massinissa Guermah, while he was in the custody of Béni Duala's gendarmerie on April 20, 2001. As soon as the news of Guermah's death spread, Berber activists in the region organized a resistance campaign against government brutality. The gendarmerie forces, whose presence had always been perceived as an unwarranted intrusion into the community, as they were from other regions, were accused of brutality and "attacking the villagers' honor." As a result, strikes, and protests spread throughout Kabylia. In the first three months, the gendarmes fueled and maintained violence using live ammunition, looting, beatings, and nocturnal arrests in four *wilayas* and over 22 localities (Issad, 2003). Between April 22 and 28, the security forces killed no fewer than 51 individuals, mainly youths (Mouhoubi, 2001). At the end of the violence, more than 126 people had died, and 5,000 were injured.

Berbers were angry, and calls by the central authorities and the Cultural Berber Movement (MCB) for peace went unheeded. Young rioters attacked the state's symbols and the office of the FFS and RCD,

184 D. GHANEM

parties perceived as pillars of the regime. The regime lost, momentarily, the possibility of using its networks (parties, civil society organizations, notables, and representatives) to mediate.

The protesters' refusal to engage with the leadership via the traditional mediators showed their lack of influence in a region where the rupture between generations was absolute. Indeed, young people did not recognize themselves in the populism and ideology of the "elders," whoever they were, parents or political leaders. The divorce was total, especially with the RCD and FFS. While the RCD and FFS officials were busy being integrated into political life in Algiers throughout the 1990s, a new elite formed in the Berber hinterland. It was younger, more radical, and its local roots more pronounced (Temlali, 2003).

The new local elite gathered within the Kabylia Coordination of the *Aârush*. The *Aârush*, plural of *aârch* [tribe], were a gathering of tribal confederations and villages committees in Kabylia that were originally absorbed, under the banner of the nation-state, by the FLN within its regional *Kasmas* (sections) (Roberts, 1980). In 2001, the structure was revived in the service of modern grievances, and the *Aârush* brought together representatives of villages and neighborhood committees to organize the protest movement (Amrouche, 2011). From the first week of May, the first *aârch* Council of Larbaa-Nath-Irathen was set up.

The *Aârush* consisted of delegates from Tizi-Ouzou, Béjaïa, Bouira, Boumerdès, Borj Bou Arrerij, Sétif, and Algiers. Many members were FFS and RCD members, as rioters rejected only these parties' leading political figures, such as deputies and national representatives. Lower-level party activists were welcomed into the *Aârush*. They became representatives of their community, village, or district. The *Aârush* refused to replicate traditional politics and had an elected leadership to preserve its autonomy. The fear for the *Aârush's* autonomy was such that several suspect unions, such as Béjaïa's Teacher's Union, were excluded. While the RCD supported the *Aârush* to redeem itself in the population's eyes, the FFS denied it any political recognition, going as far as to accuse it of being on the payroll of Military Security.

On June 14, a peaceful march started in Kabylia to reach Algiers to deliver to President Bouteflika the fifteen demands of "The Kseur Platform." The demonstrators were not received by the president and were stopped by the police. The confrontation was severe, leading to dozens of deaths, hundreds of injuries, and multiple arrests. Prime Minister Ali Benflis tried to open a dialogue with the *Aârush* but without success.

6 THE POLICIES OF VIOLENCE AND REPRESSION   185

Splits appeared in the *Aârush* on whether to negotiate with the government and whether to reduce their demands. While part of the *Aârush* wanted to open lines of dialogue, another part of the movement was more radical and wanted all the demands of the Kseur platform to be met; otherwise, no dialogue or cooperation with state agencies should be entertained. This second faction was less inclined to compromise largely because of a desire on its part to win the hearts of young protesters, who tended to be more radical than organized groups. This faction's call in December 2001 to organize sit-ins in front of gendarmerie brigades in Kabylia is a case in point.

The security forces used unlawful and lethal force during the Black Spring, and the government stated in 2003 that troops or gendarmerie officials found guilty of violating human rights would face disciplinary action. However, impunity remained a source of concern. Data about the number of police, military, or other security force personnel infractions were withheld by the authorities. Since the Black Spring, as part of human rights training, all security forces have received a copy of the code of conduct, which sets behavior norms and punishments for violations. According to human rights attorneys, increased security force training and alternative intelligence collection procedures reduced the prevalence and severity of torture. They claimed, however, that torture was still being used in military cells, particularly against people held for "security reasons" (Home Office, 2006).

The *Aârush* forced the elite to address the question of the country's "official" national identity. In its aftermath, Tamazight, the Berber language spoken by Kabyles, was recognized as a "national language" by constitutional amendment on May 8, 2002. That meant that it could be taught officially in schools in Berber-speaking regions. On February 7, 2016, it was recognized as an "official language" alongside Arabic in a constitutional resolution, meaning that it could be used in official administrative documents. On the other hand, the *Aârush*, by its very existence, helped the regime in the fragmentation of an already weak opposition elite. The *Aârush* weakened the existing Berberophone parties, mainly the FFS and RCD, and to a certain extent, the Movement for the Autonomy of Kabylia (MAK). This last, established by former RCD member, Ferhat M'Henni, was the only political force to openly demand the autonomy of Kabylia. The *Aârush* succeeded in attracting part of MAK's young electorate and constituencies and further dividing the Kabyle community. Yet despite concrete victories (recognition of the Berber language, closure of 14 gendarmerie brigades), the *Aârush* seemed to lack a long-term vision.

At first, the *Aârush* regularly affirmed the national dimension of the protest and stood out from MAK's autonomist discourse. However, its localism quickly came to the fore and engendered a gap between it and forces with a national outlook. The most striking illustration of this localism is to be found in the *Kseur* platform. While it is true that it denounced the "policies of underdevelopment of the Algerian people" and asked for an unemployment benefit of up to 50% of the minimum wage, it is also true that these demands were surpassed by the demand for the departure of the gendarmerie forces from Kabylia. The *Aârush* eventually had no more national perspective than the "rejection of the system as a whole" and the "refusal of any dialogue with the murderous *pouvoir*." Essentially, the *Aârush* lost its cause and momentum when it buried itself in an "ethnic" coffin (Temlali, 2003). For instance, during the 2002 legislative and municipal elections, the *Aârush* called on Kabyles to boycott the ballot, and punished "traitors" who decided to show up at the voting booths or, worse, run for elections, by forcibly preventing them from doing so. This, the *Aârush* achieved by mobilizing rioters hardened by months of street fighting.

Second, the fact that elements of the RCD took over the *Aârush* completely buried the social motivations of what started as the revolt of the marginalized. The *Aârush's* growing isolation from many of the people who were initially taken with it pushed it into the RCD's arms, and more generally, into the "republican camp." Compromised by its support for the regime during the 1990s, the republican camp hoped to find a partner to restore its image. This rapprochement pushed the *Aârush* further away from youths who started the protest movement and on whose behalf it claimed to speak (Temlali, 2003).

Finally, the regime co-opted some of the *Aârush's* most well-known members, who were then integrated into the country's political elite. Taking advantage of the political immaturity of the *Aârush* and the decline in popular mobilization, the authorities sought to divide the movement while showing that they were "open to dialogue." One way the regime did this was by using the people it had detained, whom the *Aârush* wanted released, as a means to pressure the *Aârush* to moderate its positions. Eventually, the political scene reverted to normal. Whereas they had refused elections in 2002, in November 2005, two provinces in the Kabylia area held elections for 131 local councils and 90 members of provincial parliaments.

The loss of the *Aârush's raison d'être* led to its loss of momentum regionally and nationally. Protests declined in most areas, and elsewhere, the regime dealt with protests with ease, using the carrot and the stick. However, above all, the regime relied on its efficient networks (i.e., civil society organizations, notables, parties, etc.) to quell social dissent—this further isolated Kabylia from the rest of the country and the *Aârush* from the population.

Despite all this, the Black Spring was a vital sign of the revival of social movements, which had been paralyzed by the regime's mobilization of people to "fight against terrorism" during the civil war. The revolt in Kabylia had aftershocks in other regions. In a severe form, it exposed the absence of mediation between the leadership and society. However, the regime rebounded from the initial setback and emerged from the instability, which lasted for two years, in a strong position.

The 2019 *Hirak*: Calibrated and Targeted Repression

The contempt of Algerian leaders toward their people and the disgust the regime provoked led hundreds of thousands of people to take to the streets in February 2019, and to continue protesting. This popular movement, called the *Hirak* and sometimes the "revolution of smiles," was born amid widespread refusal of a fifth presidential term for Bouteflika, who had already spent twenty years in office (1999–2019). Hundreds of thousands, and later millions, of people, marched through Algeria's cities and towns chanting *Bouteflika mekech el khamsa* [Bouteflika, there will be no fifth one].

The advent of the *Hirak* led the regime to avoid using widespread repression—at least to begin with. The very nature of the *Hirak*, peaceful and civic, made it difficult for the regime to justify using high-intensity repression. After the first three mass demonstrations (held on February 22, March 1, and 8, all Fridays), the regime oscillated between toleration/attrition and concessions. Tolerating protests can wear protesters down through attrition (Bishara, 2015). After a heavy police presence for the first three Fridays, when the mobilization reached its peak, police presence was noticeably modest. Demonstrators interviewed by this writer at Place Audin, a large square in Algiers, were puzzled by the very reduced presence of the police (author's interviews in Algiers, March 2019). The authorities pursued this strategy of toleration/attrition, week after week, to identify discontented communities/individuals so that they might, at a later stage, crack down on them if co-optation did not work.

The regime also offered concessions. It sacrificed Bouteflika by shunting him aside, jailing his brother and members of Bouteflika's *Issaba* [gang], which is how his coterie was widely referred to, and arrested high-ranking political and military figures associated with the deposed president. The regime also tried to use counter-protests to weaken the *Hirak*. Regime supporters were mobilized extensively in the country's interior from April until June 2019. They were instructed to raise slogans that contradicted those of the *Hirak* (initially, such slogans even included yes to a fifth term for Bouteflika). These regime stalwarts did not dissuade participants in the *Hirak*, but they did succeed in leveraging their presence on social media and television channels (all more or less state-run) to inflate their significance and generate public support.

The COVID-19 pandemic offered the regime the perfect excuse to stifle the movement and silence voices of dissent. Throughout the year-long lockdown that began in March 2020, during which travel to and from Algeria was barred for virtually everyone, the regime used calibrated and targeted repression against opposition figures, activists, bloggers, students, civil society individuals, and journalists. Dozens of people were arrested on charges of "illegally gathering," "harming state security," "endangering the integrity of the national territory," and "distributing documents harming the national interest." This targeted repression was meant to increase the costs of collective action and eliminate opposition steadily without alienating large sectors of society.

The authorities also used the legal system to arrest activists or place them in long-term pretrial imprisonment on false charges. Well-known figures subjected to such treatment included activists Samir Belarbi and Suleiman Hamitouche, and journalist Khaled Drareni. Drareni, who writes for Reporters Without Borders and is a co-founder of the Algerian news website Casbah Tribune, was arrested multiple times before being charged on March 27, 2020, with "undermining national unity." In August 2020, he was found guilty and sentenced to three years in prison, which were reduced to two the following month. He was released in February 2021 after having received a presidential pardon. Similarly, Karim Tabbou, the head of the Democratic and Social Union, which is not recognized by the authorities, was imprisoned several times. In a rushed trial on March 24, 2020, Tabbou was sentenced to a year in prison for "inciting violence."

The regime escalated its use of targeted repression each time co-optation through the legislature took place. Following the presidential election on December 12, 2019, the referendum for the new constitution on November 1, 2020, the legislative elections on June 12, 2021, and the local elections on November 27, 2021, the security forces arrested people while the regime was claiming the empowerment of its citizens' rights with elections and a new constitution. The legislative election of June 12, 2021, is a case in point. Afraid of the mobilizing potential of the *Hirak* (despite a one-year halt) in the face of a legitimacy crisis intensified by an election marred by protests, disruption, and a significant boycott, the regime took a series of measures. First, on February 18, 2021, two days before the *Hirak*'s second anniversary, the dissolution of the lower house of parliament was announced as a way to calm protesters. However, the subterfuge did not work. Second, while tolerating protests for a few weeks, the regime intensified targeted repression and deployed and extended preemptive violence against perceived threatening actors, including women, academics, university professors, and youths, to increase the cost of participation in the protest movement. Third, it actively tried to discredit the *Hirak* to neutralize its mobilizing potential.

For this last measure, the regime declared, in April 2021, that the *Hirak* was infiltrated by *Rashad*, a movement composed of former FIS members, and proceeded a month later to criminalize *Rashad* as a terrorist organization. Activists of the *Hirak* were now arrested on the basis of supposed links with *Rashad*. The Algerian authorities then announced, via the Ministry of Interior, that demonstrations as a whole were illegal because they were detrimental to national security. This criminalization dramatically raised the participation cost in weekly demonstrations. On Friday, May 14, the security services closed all roads leading to the capital as a further precaution. For the first time since 2019, there was no demonstration. People who insisted on making their way to squares in Algiers, where demonstrations usually took place, were tear-gassed and arrested.

This provoked a public outcry on social media, and people wanted to mobilize, but the repression was escalating, and many were exhausted. Still, on the following Friday, May 21, no fewer than 800 people were arrested throughout the country during attempted demonstrations

(AlgérieEco, 2020). Meanwhile, the regime took advantage of the stagnation of the movement post-Covid-19, avoided using full-on repression in favor of a calibrated one meant to avoid a backlash on the part of the protesters, stopped making concessions, and used court injunctions and arrests to end the popular mobilization on Tuesdays and Fridays.

The regime wanted to have a more legitimate channel of repression, and for this, the judiciary was called upon more than before. The Algerian legal system, which is in practice subordinate to the regime, made the judiciary a third-party actor. Also, even before a protester was hauled before the courts, the authorities were careful to marshal the police force to carry out repression in order to avoid dispatching the military to the scene of demonstrations, an act which would have tarnished the Army's reputation anew and possibly provoked an international outcry. The General Directorate for National Security (DGSN), the country's national police force, falls under the control of the Ministry of the Interior and has played an essential role since the advent of Bouteflika to power in 1999. In 2005, Bouteflika launched a drive to professionalize the police, providing better pay, benefits, training, and equipment. Naturally, this led to more recruits. The police force, 100,000-strong in 2005, doubled to 200,000 in three years (Kateb, 2008). As police departments across the country regained their traditional roles and responsibilities after the end of the civil war, during which the military was the main state actor, the regime reaped the benefits. By the time the Arab Spring occurred in 2011 and then the *Hirak*/Revolution of Smiles in 2019, the police did not need much aid when called upon to quell protests.

To further strike the *Hirak*, the regime used disinformation and propaganda. The regime, after all, acts as a gatekeeper that grants and withholds access to the internet. For instance, since the beginning of the *Hirak* in February 2019, the authorities have disrupted or simply cut the internet every Friday during the protests so protesters can no longer communicate or share their experiences in real time. While the regime has blocked content that it deems threatening, it has also used ideological dissemination through pro-regime online outlets and trolls, and especially traditional media (which is state-controlled or state-manipulated) to make it seem as though support for the regime is widespread. For example, regime supporters on social media launched a campaign to return "the streets to the people," arguing that twice-weekly demonstrations (every Tuesday and Friday) were a source of disruption for all those living in the areas where they took place. This affected the image of the *Hirak*

6 THE POLICIES OF VIOLENCE AND REPRESSION   191

by reinforcing the impression that there was public opposition to it and amplified ordinary citizens' grievances related to the *Hirak*'s activities.

Souad. B, a 40-year-old teacher whose parents live in Place Audin, explained it thus:

> When I saw that people were talking about it on Facebook, I felt relieved because I felt the same way. I was for the *Hirak* initially, and was saying until Bouteflika's departure, but then the *Hirak* was useless; it did not achieve anything. My parents live in Place Audin, and I am sorry, but their lives every Friday became a nightmare. What is the point of demonstrating like that? I started saying this on Facebook with some friends who agreed with me. My parents are tired of this noise, and today they do not want it anymore. They want their peace, and it is their right. (Author's interview, September 3, 2021)

The small anti-*Hirak* protests/discourse helped reframe the protests as social polarization between supporters and detractors instead of between the state/regime/system and the people. A *Hirakist*, Yassine, responsible for a local committee that used to deal with security during protests, made the following observation:

> The pro-government protesters were a joke, whether they protested in the streets or online. We all laughed about them, mainly because we knew that the majority were electronic flies....they were ridiculous; even the silent minority who did not join us in the streets knew this about them. But they impacted us morally and also in terms of our image and our narrative. They convinced people that the movement was not unanimous, that many people wanted the system to remain the same and that the fight was over. (Author's interview, September 15, 2021)

Another *Hirakist,* one who was in the streets every Friday, explained:

> In my family, we agreed on the *Hirak* for the first year, but then things changed. Today my brothers and sisters show no support for the *Hirak*. For them, we got what we wanted, meaning the departure of Bouteflika and his *Issaba*. [...] Before, it was the people against the state, and today it is the people against people against the state.

The regime also mined the internet and social media channels for information on protesters that it could use to harass them. Oftentimes, regime agents have published personal information about political opponents and journalists on the internet, hoping to humiliate or discredit them. During the second year of the *Hirak*, the regime used a more targeted online repression of dissent, monitoring social media posts and arresting people based on highly restrictive laws regarding free speech. People went to jail for Facebook posts; such was the case with Soheib Debaghi and Larbi Tahar, who were handed one year and 18-month prison sentences for posts on Facebook.

Although protesters and the movement's figureheads criticized court orders as an abuse of the legal system and as a sign of the non-independence of the judiciary, such measures further eroded the power of the *Hirak*. It continued to mobilize, but essential segments such as women and the middle class started to feature less in the demonstrations. Indeed, the number of women in the protests dwindled seriously in the second year. When women stop protesting in a movement, that is a sign of stagnation in the best case, decay in the worst. As *Hirakist* Nayla. B said:

> There were many women and children in the beginning, and it was like a weekly carnival, but after the Covid-19 confinement, fewer and fewer women were present. They were scared of repression […] My cousin Amina continues protesting every Sunday—but in Paris, in Place de la République. Nobody is going to arrest her for protesting there. […] Arrests and tear gas became more critical here, and the fear grew. I mean, I stopped going because the threats were serious. (Author's interview, September 15, 2021)

Ultimately, the regime's strategy worked: tolerating the protests for a year, halting them through lockdown measures for the second year, and using calibrated repression the third year. Arbitrary and targeted arrests, prolonged pretrial detention, denial of fair and expeditious trials, restrictions on civil liberties, and limitations on freedom of speech, the press, assembly, and association have achieved their aim. The *Hirak*'s capacity to continue challenging the regime has weakened considerably. The cohesion of the elites, which appeared shaky at the start of the *Hirak*, rebounded, and the regime leveraged counter-movements and legal interventions to increase the cost of participation in protests. This enabled the regime to block any serious concessions that could lead to genuine political change. In effect, the *Hirak* knocked down a rotten door, but the house is strong and still standing. Nevertheless, even though COVID-19 and repression put an end to protests in 2021–2022, when these lines were written, the country continues to experience more localized protests, which may balloon and provoke a violent response from the state.

REFERENCES

Abdenour, A. Y. (2007). *La dignité humaine*. INAS éditions.

Aït-Aoudia, M. (1988). Des émeutes à une crise politique: les ressorts de la politisation des mobilisations en Algérie en 1988. *Politix, 4*(112), 59–82. https://www.cairn.info/revue-politix-2015-4-page-59.htm#re58no58. Accessed January 24, 2022.

Al-Ahnaf, M., Botiveau, B., & Fregosi, F. (1991). *L'Algérie par ses Islamistes*. Karthala.

Algeria-Watch. (2003). Réponse de la part de Zerhouni à l'interpellation d'un groupe de députés sur la question des personnes disparues. *Algeria-Watch*. http://www.algeria-watch.org/mrv/mrvdisp/zerhouni_100501.htm. Accessed January 30, 2022.

Algeria-Watch. (2010). Nourredine Belmouhoub: Les ex-internés des camps de concentration attendent toujours une reconnaissance officielle. *Algeria-Watch*. July 25. http://www.algeria-watch.org/fr/mrv/internes/ex_internes/belmouhoub_itv.htm. Accessed January 30, 2022.

AlgérieEco. (2020, May 22). 118e Acte du Hirak: Des Centaines d'arrestations, près de 40 manifestations en garde à vue. *AlgérieEco*. https://www.algerie-eco.com/2021/05/22/118-Acte-Du-Hirak-Des-Centaines-Darrestations-Pres-De-40-Manifestants-En-Garde-A-Vue/. Accessed January 30, 2022.

Alilat, F. (2020, April 21). L'étincelle qui a allumé le Printemps Berbère. *Jeune Afrique*. https://www.jeuneafrique.com/931312/politique/algerie-mouloud-mammeri-letincelle-qui-a-allume-le-printemps-berbere-de-1980/. Accessed January 24, 2022.

Amnesty International. (1993). *Algérie*. Dégradation des droits de l'homme sous l'état d'urgence.

Amrouche, N. (2011). Histoire, mémoire et tribus ou les aarch de 2001 en Kabylie. *Conserveries mémorielles* (9). http://journals.openedition.org/cm/816. Accessed January 30, 2022.

Aouragh, L. (1996). L'économie Algérienne à l'épreuve de la démographie. France: *Centre Français sur la population et le développement*, 97–100.

Arezki, S. (2019). Les camps d'internement du sud en Algérie (1991–1995). Contextualisation et enjeux. *L'Année du Maghreb* (20). https://journals.op(n)edition.org/anneemaghreb/4825#bodyftn44. Accessed January 30, 2022.

Bellin, E. (2012). Reconsidering the Robustness of Authoritarianism in the Middle East: Lessons From the Arab Spring. *Comparative Politics, 44*(2), 127–149.

Benchikh, M. (1992). Les obstacles au processus de démocratisation en Algérie. *Revue des mondes musulmans et de la Méditerranée, 65*, 106–115.

Bennani-Cheraibi, M., & Fillieule, O. (2002). *Résistances et protestations dans les sociétés musulmanes*. Presses de Sciences po.

Benrabah, M. (1998). La langue perdue. In M. Benrabah & A. Jellouli, *Les violences en Algérie*. Odile Jacob.

Bishara, D. (2015). The Politics of Ignoring: Protest Dynamics in Late Mubarak Egypt. *Perspectives on Politics, 13*(4), 958–975.

Blanchet, P. (2006). Le Français dans l'enseignement des langues en Algérie: d'un plurilingue de fait à un plurilinguisme didactisé. *La Lettre de l'AIRDF, 38*, 31–36. https://www.persee.fr/doc/airdf_1776-7784_2006_num_38_1_1691. Accessed January 24, 2022.

Boukra, L. (2002). *Algérie, la terreur sacrée. Avant les 3 500 morts du 11 septembre 2001, 100 000 victimes algériennes de l'islamisme*. Favre.

Carlier, O. (1991). Mémoire, mythe et doxa de l'État en Algérie: l'Etoile Nord-Africaine et la religion du Watan. *Vingtième siècle. Revue d'histoire, 30*, 82–92.

Carlier, O. (1995). *Entre nation et djihad. Histoire sociale des radicalismes algériens*. Presses de sciences Po.

Cesari. J. (1994). Algérie. Chronique intérieure. *Annuaire de l'Afrique du Nord, 31*, 615–683.

Chachoua, K. (2008). Le suicide en Algérie. *Politique et Religion en Méditerranée*. https://www.cairn.info/politique-et-religion-en-mediterra nee--9782356760005-page-387.htm?contenu=article. Accessed January 30, 2022.

Charef, A. (1990). *Algérie 88, Un chahut de gamins ?* Laphomic.

Chikhi, S. (1995). Question ouvrière et rapports sociaux en Algérie. *Review, 18*(3), 487–529.

Christopher, A. (2000). Opportunities, Organizations, and Ideas: Islamists and Workers in Tunisia and Algeria. *International Journal of Middle East Studies, 32*(4), 465–490.

Collectif des Familles de Disparus en Algérie (CFDA). (2006). Les disparitions forcées en Algérie: un crime contre l'humanité (1990–2000). *CFDA*. http://www.algerie-disparus.org/app/uploads/2016/03/CFDA-RAPPORT-digital2.pdf. Accessed January 30, 2022.

Combes, H., & Fillieule, O. (2011). De la répression considérée dans ses rapports à l'activité protestataire. Modèles structuraux et interactions stratégiques. *Revue française de Science Politique, 61*(6).

Comité National Contre La Torture. (1988). *Cahier Noir D'octobre*. Enag.

Cubertafond, B. (1999). *L'Algérie contemporaine*. Presses Universitaires de France.

Dahmani, A. (1999). *L'Algérie à l'épreuve: économie politique des réformes (1980–1997)*. L'harmattan.

6 THE POLICIES OF VIOLENCE AND REPRESSION 195

El Kenz, A. (1992). Algérie: les enjeux d'une crise. *Revue des mondes musulmans et de la Méditerranée, 65,* 21–28.

Fidh. (1998). *Rapport alternatif au deuxième rapport de l'Algérie au Comité des droits de l'Homme de l'ONU.*

Fontaine, J. (1992). Quartiers défavorisés et vote islamiste à Alger. *Revue des mondes musulmans et de la Méditerranée, 65,* 141–164.

Ghanem, D. (2012). S*Sociologie de la violence extrême en Algérie. Le massacre de Bentalha (22–23 septembre 1997)* [Ph.D. thesis. unpublished].

Globe and Mail. (1988, October 13). Algeria Calls for Vote on Political Changes. *Globe And Mail.*

Grandguillaume, G. (1986). Langue arabe et Etat moderne au Maghreb. *Annuaire de l'Afrique du Nord, 23,* 79–88.

Hadj-Ali, B. (1991). *L'arbitraire.* Dar El Ijtihad.

Harbi, M. (1992). *L'Algérie et son destin, Croyants ou citoyens ?* éditions Arcantère.

Harbi, M. (1998). *1954. La Guerre commence en Algérie.* Éditions Complexe.

Haroun, A. (2005). *Algérie 1962: La grande dérive.* L'Harmattan.

Hassen. (1996). *Algérie. Histoire d'un naufrage.* Le Seuil.

Herreman, P. (1967, January 5). M. Mohammed Khider détenait le trésor de guerre du F.L.N. *Le Monde* (archives). https://www.lemonde.fr/archives/article/1967/01/05/m-mohammed-khider-detenait-le-tresor-de-guerre-du-f-i-n_2610869_1819218.html. Accessed January 24, 2022.

Home Office. (2006). Country of origin information report: Algeria. *Home Office.*

Human Rights Watch. (2003, February 26). Time for Reckoning: Enforced Disappearances in Algeria. *Human Rights Watch.* https://www.hrw.org/report/2003/02/26/time-reckoning/enforced-disappearances-algeria. Accessed January 30, 2022.

Issad. (2003). *Rapport préliminaire de la Commission, dirigée par le professeur Issad, mise en place par l'Etat algérien pour enquêter sur les "événements" de Kabylie du Printemps 2001.* Septembre 24.

Junqua, D. (1979). Algérie: Le calme est revenue dans les lycées d'Alger. *Le Monde (archives).* https://www.lemonde.fr/archives/article/1979/12/12/le-calme-est-revenu-dans-les-lycees-d-alger-les-etudiants-arabisants-poursuivent-leur-greve_3054065_1819218.html. Accessed January 24, 2022.

Junqua, D. (1981, July 2). Deux anciens membres du Conseil de la révolution sont suspendus du Comité central. *Le Monde* (archives). https://www.lemonde.fr/archives/article/1981/07/02/deux-anciens-membres-du-conseil-de-la-revolution-sont-suspendus-du-comite-central_2720704_1819218.html. Accessed January 24, 2022.

Kalyvas, S. (1999). Wanton and senseless? The logic of massacres in Algeria. *Rationality and Society, 11*(3), 243–285.

Kalyvas, S. (2006). *The Logic of Violence in Civil War*. Broché.

Kapil, A. (1990). Algeria's elections show islamist strength. *Middle East Report, 166*, 31–36.

Kateb, H. (2008, February 9). 200.000 hommes dans la police. *L'ExpressionDZ*. https://www.lexpressiondz.com/nationale/200000-hommes-dans-la-police-51780. Accessed January 30, 2022.

Kebir, N. (1998). A propos du discours intégriste. *Mots, 57*, 64–71.

Labat, S. (1995). *Les islamistes algériens. Entre les urnes et le maquis*. Le Seuil.

Le Figaro. (2006, June 15). Le Journaliste Algérien Benchicou sort de prison. *Le Figaro*. https://www.lefigaro.fr/international/2006/06/15/01003-200 60615ARTFIG90173-le_journaliste_algerien_benchicou_sort_de_prison.php. Accessed January 24, 2022.

Levitsky, S., & Way, L. (2010). *Competitive Authoritarianism: Hybrid Regimes After the Cold War*. Cambridge University Press.

Mellah, S. (2004). Les droits de l'Homme dans la crise politique algérienne. *Confluences Méditerranée, 4*(51), 11–22.

Mengedoht, U. (1997). La politique d'arabisation de l'Algérie et ses conséquences sur l'islamisme., In Jurt, J. *Algérie, France, Islam*. L'harmattan

Merzouk, M. (1997). Quand les jeunes redoublent de férocité: l'islamisme comme phénomène de génération. *Archives de sciences sociales des religions, 97*, 141–158.

Mortimer, R. (1991). Islam and Multiparty Politics in Algeria. *Middle East Journal, 45*(4).

Mouhoubi, S. (2001, July 30). La commission d'enquête sur les émeutes de Kabylie accable la gendarmerie et le gouvernement algériens. *Le Monde*. https://www.lemonde.fr/archives/article/2001/07/30/la-commission-d-enquete-sur-les-emeutes-de-kabylie-accable-la-gendarmerie-et-le-gouvernem ent-algeriens_211375_1819218.html. Accessed January 30, 2022.

Moussaoui, A. (2000). Algérie, la guerre rejouée. *La Pensée de Midi, 3*, 28–37.

Nair, S (1995). Le peuple exclu. *Les temps modernes, 580*, 34–45.

Nefla, B. (1999, September 16). Il faut oublier. *Le Jeune Indépendant*. http://www.algeriawatch.org/mrv/mrvdisp/disp16999.htm. Accessed January 30, 2022.

OMCT. (2004, December 1). Intervention urgente, Algérie: Libération provisoire de M. Hafnaoui Ghoul. *OMCT*. https://www.omct.org/fr/ressou rces/appels-urgents/algeria-pre-trial-release-of-mr-hafnaoui-ghoul. Accessed January 24, 2022.

Remaoun, H. (1993). En Algérie, l'histoire sous surveillance. In G. Manceron, *D'une rive à l'autre. La guerre d'Algérie de la mémoire à l'histoire*. Syros.

Remaoun, H. (1995). École, Histoire et enjeux institutionnels dans l'Algérie indépendante. *Les temps modernes, 580*, 71–93.

6 THE POLICIES OF VIOLENCE AND REPRESSION 197

Roberts, H. (1980). *Political development in Algeria: the region of Greater Kabylia*. D.Phil., Oxford University.

Rouadjaïa, A. (1993). Le FIS est-il enterré? Al-Azhar au secours de l'État Algérien. *Esprit, 192*(6), 94–106. https://www.jstor.org/stable/24275873. Accessed January 30, 2022.

Rouadjia, A. (1990). L'intégrisme, parti des vainqueurs? In *Les frères et la mosquée. Enquête sur le mouvement islamiste en Algérie*. Karthala.

Skocpol, T. (1979). State and Revolution: Old Regimes and Revolutionary Crises in France, Russia, and China. *Theory and Society, 7*(1), 7–95.

Stora, B. (1995). Deuxième guerre Algérienne? les habits anciens des combattants. *Les Temps Modernes, 580*, 242–261.

Stora, B. (2004). *Imaginaires de guerre. Les images dans les guerres d'Algérie et du Viêt-nam*. La Découverte.

Stora, B. (2006). *Histoire de l'Algérie depuis l'indépendance*. La Découverte.

Temlali, Y. (2003). La révolte de Kabylie ou l'histoire d'un gâchis. *Confluences Méditerranée, 2*(45), 43–57. https://www.cairn.info/revue-confluences-med iterranee-2003-2-page-43.htm. Accessed January 30, 2022.

The Middle East. (1988, November). When Algeria Lost Patience. *The Middle East*.

Thénault, S. (2003). Interner en République: le cas de la France en guerre d'Algérie. *Amnis, 3*. https://journals.openedition.org/amnis/513. Accessed January 29, 2022.

Très Très Urgent. (1995a, January 4). Lettre d'information hebdomadaire sur les questions de défense (76).

Très Très Urgent. (1995b, April 5). Lettre d'information hebdomadaire sur les questions de défense (89).

Werenfels, I. (2007). *Managing Instability in Algeria: Elites and Political Change*. Routledge.

Wieviorka, M. (1988). *Sociétés et terrorisme*. Fayard.

Zerrouky, H. (2002). *La nébuleuse islamiste en France et en Algérie*. Éditions 1.

Zighem, S. (1992, March 13–14). Conférence de presse du ministre de l'Intérieur et des collectivités locales. 6.786 personnes placées dans les centres de sûreté. *El Moudjahid*.

CHAPTER 7

Conclusion: Algeria's Future Prospects—Less Competitive, More Authoritarian

How the Algerian regime has managed to withstand serious internal challenges to its rule—social unrest in the late 1980s, civil war in the 1990s, the Kabylia protests in 2001, the Arab Spring in 2011, the crash of oil prices in 2014–16, and the mass demonstrations of 2019—is instructive. In order to perpetuate itself, the regime has adapted to changing national and regional circumstances. Such flexibility often manifests itself in a lack of institutionalized governing practices, a personalized way of doing politics, as well as political patronage and economic clientelism. This system has produced, renewed, reactivated, and refined strategies to sustain itself. These strategies include the extension of political and (when available) economic resources by creating participatory yet circumscribed political and economic structures. These measures have been accompanied by manipulation, fragmentation, co-optation, clientelism, patronage, and corruption. Some degree of repression is used when need be. The aforementioned measures have successfully appeased the population, mitigated conflicts and opposition, hampered popular mobilization, secured many people's obedience and loyalty, and safeguarded the system's stability and continuity.

Five pillars support the regime. As seen in Chapter 2, the People's National Army (ANP) is the first. As the country's most organized and powerful institution, the army wields tremendous authority through its

© The Author(s), under exclusive license to Springer Nature Switzerland AG 2022
D. Ghanem, *Understanding the Persistence of Competitive Authoritarianism in Algeria*, Middle East Today,
https://doi.org/10.1007/978-3-031-05102-9_7

199

top echelons. The army identifies with the nation, and as such, it is unthinkable that the men in uniform could be relegated to the security sector and shut off from politics. The army decides, and the government, its civilian façade, implements.

The second pillar is the co-optation of opposition parties and political opponents (Chapter 3). Since the end of the single-party system in 1989, the regime has provided some space for political opposition. Today, there is a higher level of political competition than 30 years ago. Nevertheless, competition is tightly regulated to avoid genuine democratization. The new actors adapted to the new implicit norms, which presented them with the choice of de facto allegiance to the regime or marginalization. Political groups and opposition actors have been co-opted to sustain the regime and provide it with a democratic alibi. As such, new parties and associations have outwardly contributed to the pluralistic nature of Algeria's political system even as they have propped up an undemocratic regime. The regime has used the space for pluralism and participation to thwart democratization.

The third pillar is the fragmentation of civil society (Chapter 4). The regime employs various strategies to fragment the civil society sector, restrict its activities, and reduce its impact. These strategies include co-optation, coercion, legalism, scapegoating, and cloning. Civil society organizations are characterized by a lack of financial and material resources, restricted access to foreign funding and a consequent reliance on state money, and a lack of national and regional networking. As a result, they are vulnerable to the government's techniques and unable to challenge them.

The fourth critical pillar of the regime's survival is its reliance on rent distribution and corruption (Chapter 5). Rent is the regime's preferred method of securing political allegiances, defusing protests, and ensuring its survival. The leeway left to political actors is conditioned on their allegiance. They must not turn the political sphere into one of real competition with the regime. Algiers has manipulated democracy by supporting pro-regime incumbents or challengers during elections and assisting them in expanding economic opportunities for their clients and supporters. In essence, corruption in Algeria has a political dimension, as a percentage of ill-gotten wealth is earmarked for patronage networks.

Repression is the fifth pillar (Chapter 6) that enables the regime to keep its grip on power. The regime's repression has a broad reach because the country has a large and effective internal security sector. The latter has formidable intelligence networks, specialized police, and paramilitary groups capable of hounding society throughout the country. The security forces are well-equipped and financed. They have proven their ability to suppress or contain protests all over the national territory, monitor dissent, and penetrate society. Algeria's leadership has a robust, unified, and forceful state machinery that can easily stifle opposition protests. The authorities have alternated between high-intensity and low-intensity coercion. Due to a lack of interest in Algeria's internal affairs among Western nations more concerned with the regime's stability, the repression practiced by the Algerian authorities rarely arouses robust protest. Western countries sacrificed Algeria's democratization process on the altar of security years ago, as they fear that democracy might lead to the advent of a radical Islamist regime, a refugee crisis, and a spillover of terrorism onto their soil.

The regime knows when to lean on one pillar more than another. For example, because patronage networks may be weakened due to the ongoing economic crisis, repressive measures can keep things in check, preserve the system, and rescue the regime when need be. As such, Algiers is likely to continue, and even escalate, its repression of dissent.

The shift toward more authoritarianism by hybrid regimes following the succession of one leader by another is not always predetermined. A hybrid regime under new leadership can go either way. It can attempt reconciliation with the opposition, or at the very least turn toward more consensus-based policies, to reclaim some of its lost legitimacy and reduce conflict. Alternatively, a hybrid regime might endeavor to restrict the opposition to limit the latter's activities and expansion (Corrales & Penfold, 2015). Initially, Abdelmadjid Tebboune showed some interest in the former approach. Tebboune campaigned on a vow to "consolidate democracy," the rule of law, and respect for human rights. He vowed to open dialogue with the protest movement and free political detainees. One month after Tebboune's election in December 2019, the official broadcaster ENTV reported the release of 76 individuals incarcerated for political opposition, including *Hirak*-related activities. Nevertheless, no fewer than 173 persons remained imprisoned. Furthermore, Tebboune increased the repression of the *Hirak* and opposition figures. The trend toward intolerance of the opposition and its repression is worsening under Tebboune, despite his claims of a "new Algeria."

Four factors drive the turn to greater authoritarianism in post-Bouteflika Algeria: strong pro-autocracy state institutions, especially the army and the judiciary; increasing factionalism within an atomized opposition, including civil society organizations; the regime's diminishing capacity to buy social peace due to a challenging fiscal situation; and the regime's increased inability to remain socially and politically relevant.

To begin with, the military, the strongest of the state's institutions that supports autocracy, has not wavered. The military engineered the election of Tebboune and pushed through a referendum on a new constitution. As the true center of power, the military fought and will continue to fight any attempt to move to a more democratic system in which civilians truly rule and are not merely a front. Since Bouteflika's departure, the army has reclaimed its dominance and deployed repression by marshaling other security forces (i.e., the police and the gendarmerie) to silence the last voices of dissent. If the military's calculations lead it to conclude that the costs of tolerating the popular movement and social unrest are higher than the costs of repression, it will resort to even more of the latter.

In addition, the judiciary, with its judges, public prosecutors, and attorneys, lacks independence due to the manipulation of the executive branch. Tebboune's Algeria has even enacted additional legal measures allowing the security forces and the government to carry out and justify repression: laws to restrict the behavior of the opposition, activists, and journalists; the blocking of websites and citizens' access to information; and the criminalization of the publication of reports that contradict the official government line. Courts have been staffed with supporters of the regime who will remain loyal to the system.

The second reason for the rise in repression is its impact and success in increasing factionalism within the opposition so that it does not present a barrier to the expansion of executive power. The regime skillfully used attrition, concessions, limited tolerance, and low-intensity repression to exhaust the recent popular movement and fragment and divide the opposition. Algerian trade unions, human rights organizations, opposition parties, and youth associations, which appeared united in the first months of the *Hirak*, came to have tactical disagreements on the *Hirak's* roadmap, as well as the questions of whether to negotiate with the authorities and participate in elections. Cleavages and a feeling of demoralization grew stronger among the opposition and civil society organizations with the repression that followed the resumption of demonstrations on the second anniversary of the *Hirak* in February 2021.

The third reason for more authoritarianism is the regime's diminishing capacity to buy social peace due to a challenging fiscal situation.

Algeria's leadership has long relied on oil earnings to support a robust social welfare system, subsidies, and rents. This has enabled the regime to buy the allegiance of many segments of the population and has served as a major source of legitimacy. However, the state's fiscal health is deteriorating, hydrocarbons' revenues are rapidly dwindling, and no new sources of economic opportunity are being generated to compensate for these changes. Over the past several years, most Algerians have seen a reduction in essential social services such as education and healthcare. The country was unprepared for the public health emergency created by the Covid-19. Among the problems are insufficient and inconsistent services, a dearth of medical equipment, a drug deficit, and ineffective planning, organizing, and monitoring systems. From the first weeks of the pandemic, the health sector faced a deep crisis, as Algerian hospitals lacked basic products such as protective gear and hand sanitizers.

Unemployment is high, and since the start of the pandemic in 2019, half a million people have lost their jobs (Benali, 2021). However, individuals are not just frustrated by their economic hardships. There is also a simmering, tangible hatred of a social pact that has benefited a tiny group of insiders and allowed its members to act freely in diverting public resources for their private gain. The recent confessions and trials of public officials, state ministers, and other officials for corruption and embezzlement deepened this hatred and animosity among Algerians for their leaders. As socioeconomic tensions intensify, the radicalization of both sides is possible even if the popular movement insists on its peaceful approach. On the other hand, only the stick will remain as the state's carrot contracts.

The fourth reason is the state's inability to remain politically relevant. The FLN long ago lost its credibility, so much so that the state has on occasion sought to elevate (co-opted) parties at its expense. The legislative elections of June 2021, followed by local elections in November 2021, were clearly staged, with ballot boxes stuffed and the entire process turning into a masquerade. The FLN lost many seats in parliament and several localities, and the turnout for both elections was the lowest in Algeria's modern history. To keep its democratic credentials, the state had to allow for the participation of newly licensed political parties with younger actors, for whose campaigns it provided financial support.

Because all other options to remain politically relevant, such as ideological appeal, historical legitimacy, and competent governance, have been exhausted, drifting into more authoritarianism becomes the state's preferred choice. The state's whole FLN-focused system has lost its historical legitimacy, and as a result, it is under growing pressure to emphasize its authoritarian aspects to maintain the system and the regime.

Indeed, as mentioned, the shift toward more authoritarianism seems clear in the post-Bouteflika period. Tebboune's conciliatory phase lasted only a few weeks. By mid-March, with the beginning of confinement measures due to the Covid-19 pandemic, Tebboune had embarked on a path of placing greater restrictions on the opposition and increasing the costs of popular mobilization. Despite the discontinuation of weekly protests due to the pandemic, Tebboune's administration adopted typical full-fledged authoritarian tactics. Arbitrary arrests of opposition figures, students, civil society activists, journalists, and university professors increased, especially during confinement. For the regime, the COVID-19 pandemic allowed for introducing and implementing restrictive measures beyond those needed to contain the pandemic. Indeed, the regime has used the pandemic to stifle voices of dissent, frighten people, and eventually put them off participating in demonstrations once they resumed. The goal was to strangle the *Hirak* and its potential for mobilization.

Dozens of people have been jailed or placed in lengthy pretrial detention on false allegations ranging from "illegal gathering" to "endangering state security," "endangering the integrity of national territory," "undermining the troops' morale," and even "terrorism and conspiracy against the state" (Amrouche, 2021). As of May 2021, the most recent date as of writing for data was available, there were between 175 and 233 political detainees in Algeria, and their detention conditions are inhumane (Ayache, 2021). Also, the authorities have escalated their social media campaign against the opposition and have utilized trolls, closed down Facebook accounts, and publicized the personal information of political opponents and even journalists to embarrass, insult, or discredit them.

The state has even sanctioned state personnel who have been lenient toward demonstrators and detainees. The public prosecutor assigned to the Sidi M'hamed tribunal in Algiers, Mohammed Sid Ahmed Belhadi, was relocated to El Oued, approximately 600 kilometers southeast of the city, in February 2020, after requesting the acquittal of sixteen nonviolent demonstrators. Separately, the deputy prosecutor of the Tiaret court, southwest of Algiers, was detained for allegedly "handing over classified data" to a journalist.

Moreover, the authorities leveraged the health crisis to quell opposition while reverting to their previous practices of opaqueness, concealment, and distortion of information. This aggravates the legitimacy and trust crisis since Algerians see a sustained loss of their fundamental rights. In April 2020, the penal code was modified to criminalize any publication of what is deemed by the authorities "false and misleading information" that would "spread confusion and put the citizen in a condition of fear and panic." Tebboune also ordered the Ministry of Communication to take all necessary steps to prevent the dissemination of coronavirus figures and information that had not been disclosed by the Ministry of Health, Population, and Hospital Reform. The right to independently access and disseminate information on the virus became illegal, and anybody who did so faced arrest. Tebboune's hardline approach reached new heights with the May–April 2021 student protests, which the government repressed despite their peaceful and civic nature. According to independent local media, the police beat up protesters, including women, and 2,000 individuals were arrested.

In short, the Algerian regime may have weathered the *Hirak* storm, however, what has worked for the regime thus far may not continue to function indefinitely. There are signs that Algerian society has reached the end of its tether when it comes to repression. Fear of chaos born of the trauma of the civil war has faded, the rhetoric of fear in the fight against terrorism no longer rallies people around the government as it once did, and the regime's historical legitimacy has withered. As for oil rent, it is diminishing, as are the foreign exchange reserves. And all the while, the political and economic expectations of young Algerians are likely to increase. More educated, connected, and informed than the older generation, they have higher standards for political accountability, participatory governance, and efficacy. In order to survive, or at least to survive without having to battle its people, a regime adept at selling cosmetic change as fundamental may have to face the prospect that it must institute real reforms.

REFERENCES

Amrouche, K. (2021, October 21). En Algérie: la stratégie d'étouffement du Hirak. *Le Monde*. https://www.lemonde.fr/afrique/article/2021/10/21/en-algerie-la-strategie-d-etouffement-du-hirak-se-durcit_6099421_3212.html. Accessed January 24, 2022.

Ayache, S. (2021, December 16). En Algérie: la peur d'être oubliés des détenus du Hirak. *Le Monde*. https://www.lemonde.fr/afrique/article/2021/12/16/en-algerie-la-peur-d-etre-oublies-des-detenus-du-hirak_6106336_3212.html. Accessed January 24, 2022.

Benali, A. (2021, June 21). Impact de la pandémie en Algérie: Plus de 500.000 emplois perdus. *AlgerieEco*. https://www.algerie-eco.com/2021/06/22/impact-de-la-pandemie-en-algerie-plus-de-500-000-emplois-perdus/. Accessed January 24, 2022.

Corrales, J., & Penfold, M. (2015). The Less Competitive, More Authoritarian Regime. In *Dragon in the tropics: The legacy of Hugo Chávez*. Brookings Institution Press. https://www.jstor.org/stable/10.7864/j.ctt7zsw23.12. Accessed January 24, 2022.